How to Change the Schools

How to Change the Schools

A PARENTS'
ACTION HANDBOOK
ON HOW TO FIGHT
THE SYSTEM

by Ellen Lurie

A VINTAGE BOOK
A Division of Random House New York

This book is dedicated to
Mrs. Evelina Antonetty
and all the other members of
United Bronx Parents—
without their support and ideas,
there would have been no book

Acknowledgments

First I want to thank my husband, Alfred, and my children, Leib, Sara, Becky, Naomi and Rachel. They have been extraordinarily patient and good-humored. And many of the stories which appear in this book were contributed by them. I am particularly grateful to my good friend Clara Martin, who made sure that my family survived while I was absorbed in writing.

The parents who have fought the battles described in these chapters are the unsung heroes of the city. There are so many of them that it is impossible to list them all. I shall never be able to express my appreciation to Kathy Goldman who criticized, encouraged and helped me beyond belief. Everywhere I went I learned from other parents. In particular I wish to thank all of the following, who have struggled so bravely and so intensely to improve the schools in their neighborhoods: Rosalie Stutz, Mel and Marian Martin, Suki Ports, Frieda Josephs, Dorrit Rosenstein, Juanita Kimble, Jackie McCord, Lee and Leslie Foster, Ruth Klepper, Rose Reiter, Lily Whitney, Jesse Cagan, Barbara Schneider, Gardenia White, Babette Edwards, Bob and Marcia Nichols, Bill and Esther Fink, Barbara Hanahan, Olivia Taylor, Mary Phifer, Thelma Hamilton, Margaret Campbell, Gloria Oliver, Ollie and Marge Leeds, David and Deedee Goldstick, Lois Delgado, Fran Allison, Elnora Dennis, Mary Foster, Marge and Sam Hendler, Maxine Waldron, Esther Smith, Esther Greene, Wallace Andrews, Sylvia Rojas, Lorma Varlack, Berrie McKissic, Nina Pryor, Pedro Canino, Marcy Vazquez, Lois and Carl Johnson, Jack Goldman, Rose Falcon, Marie Hyliger, Ada and Gerardo Sanchez, Juanita Hernandez, Terry Otero, Don Antonetty, Consuelo Garcia, Iris Marrero, Iris Rivera, Anna Henriquez, Victoria

Villegas, Belle Flenyol, Lucy Hawkins, Eloise Krause, Gloria Wright, Esther Gollobin, Carmen Batus, Goldie Chu, Hannah Silverman, Arthur Bargonetti, Katherine Nichson, Juanita Duval, Eric and Barbara Barr, Harry Ansorge, Mary Barksdale, Grace Cortes, Tommy Alvarez, Frances and Hank Julty, Douglas Reid, Ira Contente, Hazel James, Dorothy and Irving Jones, Ralph and Casper Hoist, Maude Katz, Helen Mencher, Justus and Helen Poole, Anita duBoulay, Eloise DaSilva, Bob and Dorothy Washington, Ruth and Al Gutman, Jackie McCord, Randy Blum, Thea Manley, Ruth Singer, John Battiato, Tony Galvez, Muriel Aldridge, George Romain, Frieda Greenbaum, Liz Simmons, Pat Thompson, Almena Jones, Harriet Holtzman, Clen Jordan, Ben Garcia, Gwen Crenshaw, Kenneth and Maria Erskine, Harold Dicks, Eulalia Lediard, Myrtle Gohring, Lena Jacobs, Bob Sherrard, Lou Wheaton, Alice Kornegay, Virginia Watson, Sarah Frierson, Juan Torres, Blorneva Selby, Gerry Respass, Lucia Jack, James Keller, John and Vivian O'Neil, Bernice Shenhouse, Sandy Gerber, Helen Efthim, Jane Somerville, Alex and Dorothy Rosenberg, Ruth and John Ultmann, Ethel Mingo, Edythe Herson, Berlin and Kay Kelly, Ruby Jones, Forninia Williams, Lynn Dozier, Hubert Jackson, Preston Wilcox, Lorry Kempster, Jill Greenberg, Dorothy Jaffee, Phyllis Goldman, Alice and Al Tierstein, Maxine Waldron, Sandra Thomas, Mildred Palley, Louise Sanchez, Tom Graves, Nancy Mamis, Marian Bornstein, Joan Sandler, Emma Richardson, Doris Rosenblum, Dorothy Harrison, Edna McCrae, Bessie Easely, Ruth Soler, Iris Torres, Nicanora Martinez, Jean Greaves, Marina Brook, Francia Luban, Howard Moody, Petra Santos, Wilma Jaffee, Ed Pollak, Claro Ortiz, Charlotte Frankenthaler, Wilma Butler Moton, Hannah Brockington, Ralph Cassetta, Arthur Thomas, Hannah Neuhaus, Bernardina Melendez, Delores Torres, Don Merit, Sema Salit, Blanche Dixon, Justina Moscoso, Maria Santiago, Vivian Kelly, Dorothy Pla, Jeanette Glenn, Providencia Miro.

Some of the best leaders died during the struggle: Joe Patterson, Gerry Childs, Al Schub, Herman Hanahan, Dorothy Fulmer and Hans Epstein.

I will never be able to properly thank the members of the governing boards in the demonstration districts. Whatever happens, they have blazed a glorious path for all parents to follow. In particular David Spencer and Father John Powis have helped me enormously. Much more important, however, I believe they have helped all of our children.

I owe a great debt of appreciation to Rosalie Stutz, who especially helped me with the section on parents' rights; and to Leah Marks and Ira Glasser for their many suggestions, many of which are incorporated into the section on students' rights and suspensions. I also want to thank two nonparents, Dan Dobin and Ed Walker, for their advice and warm support.

Mrs. Toby Sanchez gave hours and weeks of her time to gathering background statistics and obtaining hard-to-find circulars, telephone numbers and reports. Her persistence was amazing, and she has my unbounded admiration. Dr. Edythe Gaines and her district staff were extremely helpful. Whenever we needed to verify procedures, or obtain some facts, they responded with alacrity and generosity. Although this book is really dedicated to the parents I must praise the students at least once, and especially the students at George Washington High School. They have taught me more about the school system than anyone else.

I suppose I should thank someone at the Board of Education. My husband suggested that I thank them for making this book necessary—but I wish it had never had to be written. The only staff people whom I can honestly single out to thank are Hugh McLaren and Theodore Lang, who are the only staff people who answered our questions willingly and accurately. Miss Emma Youngblood in Jerry Kovalchek's office was exemplary, and should be thanked for searching file after file to locate circulars and data which everyone else had told us were no longer available. I also want to thank Milton Galamison and John Lotz—and their staff assistants. Those two men were top-notch board members, and their staff was efficient, courteous, friendly and fun. It proves that it can be done. Unfortunately they are no longer at the board.

Despite all this help, I must state that the opinions and suggestions in this book are, in the last analysis, my own. I shall not ask any of my friends to bear the brunt of them.

Contents

How to Change the Schools

Introduction

I have five children in the New York public schools. Like every parent, I do not think the schools are good enough for my children. And I get very tired of fighting to improve them.

My friends and I often feel as if we're running around in circles. We go to so many meetings, testify at so many hearings; we write hundreds of letters, make thousands of phone calls; we see one politician after another; demonstrate and picket and sit-in; we negotiate and compromise and bargain. And no matter what we do, the schools remain terribly bad.

I thought I would stop running for a little while and take a good look at this system I was trying so hard to fight. Perhaps if I could understand it better, I would be able to figure out how to beat it. I had been battling school bureaucrats for over fifteen years. Maybe if I described some of the things I have learned, it would be helpful to other parents. At the very least, by examining my mistakes, others would learn what *not* to do.

This book, therefore, is a very personal document. Although

I read a great deal while writing it, the recommendations contained in these chapters are not derived from much formal research. Instead they are based upon the very real experiences of myself and other parents who have been trying to change the system. If the stories ring true to you, then you will probably want to try some of the suggestions for "taking action." If these things have not happened to you or your children, either you are not a New York City public school parent, or you are very lucky indeed.

Once I thought that a good school was a new school. That was more than fifteen years ago, when I was employed as a community worker in East Harlem. I worked, at that time, for two large and influential settlement houses, and with their support the parents in East Harlem organized a massive campaign for new schools. I learned a lot from that campaign, but the most important lesson I learned was that our objectives were naïve. We soon found out that a modern uncrowded facility was no guarantee of quality. The new schools were as bad as the old ones. The rooms were beautiful, but the children were not learning very much.

Then my own children started public school. I quit my job and became active in the parent association of my neighborhood elementary school in Washington Heights. That community had a wealth of articulate, dedicated and determined parents who were fighting for improved school services. I was proud to join them. We organized extremely effective letter-writing campaigns and fund-raising events. We set up a volunteer after-school reading center in order to demonstrate the need for additional remedial-reading services in our schools. We fought for smaller classes and additional guidance staff. We pressured for more school secretaries and additional supervisory positions. But even when we won some of the things we were demanding, the schools did not become noticeably better. In fact, for every minor victory we were able to claim we uncovered still greater problems, and we found the bureaucracy becoming stronger and stronger at resisting our requests for help.

Then I was appointed to serve on Local School Board 6, in Upper Manhattan; that district extended from Harlem to Washington Heights to Inwood. The other members of our board were a fantastic group of men and women: a thoughtful minister, a devoted social worker, an able bank executive, a knowledgeable businessman and four other parents, all of whom, like myself, had a long history of involvement in the school struggle. We devoted countless hours to our job. We disagreed often, but we certainly reflected the disagreement which existed within our very large district. We fought many hard fights, and we won a few.

And then the battle over school integration engulfed us. At that time all nine of us strongly believed that a good school had to be an integrated school. Half of our district was almost completely white; the other half was totally black. But no matter what solutions we developed, no matter what suggestions we made, central headquarters insisted upon calling the shots and we found ourselves completely powerless. The ineptitude, the bungling, the insensitivity of the Board of Education had a destructive impact on our schools and on the relationships in our district. Bitter and furious, black and white parents turned their anger at first on us, the most convenient targets, and then on each other.

Since I found that the local school board could do nothing, I decided to join one of the sides in the community civil war. I worked long and hard on the massive school boycotts called by Reverend Milton Galamison and the Harlem Parents Committee. Together with many white parents from all parts of the city, a group of us formed an organization called EQUAL and we struggled to develop support for school integration in white communities. During this turbulent period, feelings ran so strong in our local neighborhood that when one parent screamed, "Why don't you send your own children to school in Harlem if you think integration is such a good idea?" my husband and I thought about it and decided to do it. For almost two years our two oldest youngsters traveled fifty blocks to and from school in Harlem each day.

I learned an immeasurable amount about the school system during that time. But the moral which has been indelibly stamped on my brain is that community groups must not fight each other, because when they do, only the school system wins. When the black parents demanded integration, the system labeled them irresponsible militants. When the white parents demanded educational improvements before they would accept integration, the system labeled them irresponsible bigots.

Meanwhile, in Washington Heights, busloads of black children were being transported into our neighborhood schools, only to be completely abandoned once they arrived. The schools which "received" them were given no special services; the teachers were given no special training. The black children were left to learn as best they could, and having suffered years of educational neglect, they often failed. The white children watched the black kids fail, and had all their preconceived prejudices reinforced.

It seemed almost as if the bureaucrats downtown had arranged this thoughtless program so that the white parents could fight the black parents and the black parents could fight back. And the more the parents argued and fought, the more the professionals at the Board of Education could say, of *all* parents, "You see, those people cannot be given any authority; look how irresponsible they are."

Thus, five years after our appointment to the local school board, four of us resigned in protest against our powerlessness. By that time the focus of the struggle had already begun to shift. Community groups had lost their faith in integration as a viable solution. The opposition was too strong. "Give us control of our schools, and we will make them good schools" became the new battlecry. But the Board of Education remained just as stubborn and resistant to change.

Not too much later, on a cold winter day, I was attending a citywide budget hearing when the members of the board became angry at an "unruly" mother, and walked out on the audience. The parents, hurt by the rebuff, decided to appoint their own People's Board of Education, and I was lucky enough to be among those selected to serve. For three days, until we were arrested, we ran our own hearings, attempting to highlight the unresponsiveness of the official Board of Mis-education, as many of us began to call it.

The People's Board of Education visited schools throughout

the city and held meetings in many communities. We met parents who were fighting to change their schools in east New York, Brownsville, Williamsburg, Jamaica, Bayside, East Harlem, Corona, Tremont, Morrisania, Riverdale—everywhere. The vice president of the People's Board, Mrs. Evelina Antonetty, offered me a job, conducting parent-leadership classes for United Bronx Parents. I have been working there for the past four years. And I have learned how terrible the schools can be when parents are without influence. In East Harlem the Settlement Houses supported the parents in their struggle for new buildings. In Washington Heights, the local politicians supported the parents. But in the South Bronx the parents are alone.

And despite their lack of connections, against overwhelming odds, the Bronx parents organized effective demonstrations to improve school lunches, improve custodial operations, improve school facilities—and remove bad principals. And during the school strikes of 1967 and 1968 I worked with the parents and teachers who helped to keep the schools open and operating in that community, and I shall never forget those weeks as long as I live. Fathers and mothers slept in schools, repaired broken locks, scrubbed bathrooms, made sandwiches, assisted teachers, and for a few weeks the schools did indeed belong to the community and its children.

And now the strikes are over. The dust has settled. And every day children come into the offices of United Bronx Parents accompanied by desperate parents. These children are clearly the victims of the schools which are supposed to be helping them. Suspensions—by the hundreds. Boys who dropped out, and now regret it, but cannot get back into a school. Two children who want to complain because their teacher called them "dirty spics" but their parents are afraid to "make trouble." Bewildered angry teenagers who have discovered that they are in classes for retarded students, simply because they cannot speak English. Precocious, inquisitive youngsters who are punished because they talk too much, laugh too much, wear their hats in the corridor. Frightened parents who see the dope-pushing outside the schools and don't know what to do about it. Angry Puerto Rican parents whose daughters have been beaten up by black kids. Furious black parents whose daughters have been jumped by Puerto Rican kids. And once more I see happening what I dread most of all—a community civil war. When we cannot get at the real enemy, we fight each other.

So I decided I had to write this book. I had to put down some of the things I had learned in all these places. And I had to write this book for *parents*. There are plenty of books about the schools. Sociologists and educators and philosophers are writing and writing. They look at what the schools are doing to the children, and they analyze, criticize, justify, rationalize, postulate, prophesy, and even condemn. And in the meantime our children are inside those buildings, going to classes every day. Our children are the victims of this pernicious system they are writing about. My book is not the least bit intellectual; it is neither objective nor dispassionate. It is specific about the things I, and many of my fellow parents, hate most about the school system. And it suggests very tangible things other parents can do to try to change things.

A book for parents means a book for all parents, and not just for those who happen to agree with me. Some parents are very militant, and some are moderate, but all parents want to see the schools changed. All parents are tired of seeing their children misused by this system. So I am not writing just for those who want to make the kinds of changes I believe to be important; I have tried to describe how the school affects the children and then offer a variety of suggestions for forcing change. "Parents slow us down," complained one young high school student at a recent demonstration. But he readily admitted that the students couldn't get very far without them. Sometimes we parents *are* slower than the radicals might like, because it is our children who are at stake. When workers strike, they take many risks because they are physically exposing only themselves. But when parents decide to protest school conditions, our children are the ones who are vulnerable to the repercussions. We may be picketing *outside* the building; we may be angrily decrying the situation at a meeting downtown, but our kids are *inside* the schools, sitting in classrooms, where the teachers and the principal can find all kinds of ways to take out their anger at us on them.

That is why many of us learn to be careful. (In this book,

for example, none of the children's names are the real ones; I have disguised all reference to specific teachers or schools, because I want to protect my own and my friends' children.) And that is why many of the most articulate critics of the school system have removed their own children from public school. But most of us cannot afford to do that—or, simply, we do not believe that it would be right. And as the system gets worse, we parents get braver. Our children often show us the way. They are willing to take risks we have not wanted to take. I think more of us are now ready to take those risks too. We have come to recognize that we must destroy the system before it destroys all our children.

You do not have to read this book from start to finish. Find the section which discusses the things you want to change in your child's school. There is no "best" way to start. You can shake up the system by challenging almost anything you don't like. You will rock the boat if you attack tracking; and you will rock the boat if you attack teacher tenure. The important point is to start with the issue or problem which is bothering the parents in your neighborhood.

Each chapter has several sections. Usually the chapters start out by telling some stories to point up the problem. If you know the problem already, skip that part. Then there is a section which describes the various laws and rules which apply to the situation and analyzes what is wrong with these procedures. Even if you are not from New York City, these sections will still help you by providing a guideline for which you can find the corresponding regulation in your own system. And finally each chapter contains some action suggestions for parents.

I have purposely omitted a lot of footnotes. Most of the facts cited in each chapter can be found in the readings which are listed at the end of the book. However, if the Board of Education tells you that any of these facts are wrong, encourage them to print the correct ones, which is what they should be doing anyway.

Originally as I wrote this book I tried to cover almost every facet of the system. I wrote chapters on school budgets, construction, lunches, repairs, custodians, supplies, etc. But the book became terribly long; no one would have bought it, and surely no one would have read it. So, with the help of my editor, I decided to concentrate on those aspects of the system which most directly affect the children and their parents. The other issues are important, and United Bronx Parents has printed those sections individually for those persons who want to study them. But such problems are really tangential ones. The basic reason we have schools, after all, is to teach the children. Schools should be *for* the children. And in our large cities today, that simply does not happen. These schools exist for the sake of the system. The children are barely tolerated. The system wants to build more buildings, raise more money, retain more teachers, reduce student unrest, win community support. The children simply serve that system.

And that is intolerable. In this book I try to tell what happens to children in such a system. They are stifled, adjusted, manipulated, corrected—they are not nurtured, enjoyed, or loved or genuinely educated. And we parents know this cannot continue. A good school is a place where the parents and the students are convinced that worthwhile and exciting learning is taking place. And I mean all the parents, not just those whose kids are in the "top" class. A good school cannot exist in this horrendous system. We parents must take our schools back from that system. We must do everything we can to fight it, restructure it, or destroy it. If we want our children to get the education they need, we must return our schools to them.

May 1970

1 · How to Make a School Visit

WHAT GOES ON INSIDE THE SCHOOL

This chapter is intended to help parents begin to evaluate the quality of education in their children's school. Naturally a single visit has only limited value. If parents and community residents make it a regular practice to inspect their neighborhood schools several times a year, perhaps many of the incredible, scandalous and destructive elements in the daily routine will be corrected. This guide is also useful for those parents who have been actively involved in the school, reacting to one crisis after another, and who now want to stop and take a fresh, overall look at the needs of the school.

A school which is frequently scrutinized by the public will become, at the very least, cleaner, better repaired, and less chaotic—provided the parents don't keep quiet about what they observe. If the staff knows that visitors are likely to drop in at any time, fewer children will be sent out into halls for punishment, and more teachers will learn to stop shouting—maybe. Although facts and figures are important, nothing will tell you as much about your child's school as a personal visit.

How to Prepare for Your Visit:

Before you go on your visit, get as much information about the
school as you can. Of course, if you are an active parent you
probably know a great deal about the school. But if you are less
involved, or if you do not have any children attending that school,
you undoubtedly already have some information which has made
you decide to visit it. Perhaps some parents have complained to
you about the lack of homework, the low reading scores, the
many suspensions, the "terrible principal," the inexperienced staff.
Or perhaps some teacher has privately told you some horror story.

Once you have decided to visit the school, gather additional
background material. Stand outside the school before dismissal
time and talk to parents who are waiting for their younger
children. Parents with kindergarten and first-grade kids usually
know a great deal, and they are still young enough to be hopeful
and anxious to do anything they can. Ask some of them about the
school: Who is the best teacher? How well are the kids learning
to read? What do they think are the worst problems? If this
doesn't get them talking, you must be doing something wrong.
Be sure to ask some students too. Remember they are in that
building every day; don't underestimate how much they know.

Write down what you learn. Get the names of teachers who
are supposed to be "good" or "bad." Later, when you visit, you
can refer to your notes (without letting the school officials see
them and without identifying your source of information). You
might ask, during your visit, something like: "We have heard
a great deal about Mrs. Blank; may we see her class?" If the
principal asks what you have heard, let him wonder.

Who Should Go with You?

Your delegation should include at least two or three parents;
one or two representatives of local organizations; and if possible,
one person from another part of the city to help give you some
perspective.

The parents need not be active members or officers of the
parent association. Often the official parent association is afraid
to "take on" the principal; some are tools of the administration
anyway. But even if your parent association is top-notch, the

school should get used to responding to ordinary parents who have questions. If you plan to include the parent association in any action program afterward, then of course you should include some representatives in your delegation.

Be sure that you can depend on the community people you bring. I was on a visit that got nowhere because a minister we brought along kept lecturing *us* the whole time we were there. The broader the representation of your group (churches, civil rights groups, tenant organizations, poverty agencies, etc.), the more "powerful" you will seem. Include your assemblyman and you are guaranteed attention.

How Many Should Go?

If a school is really terrible, and the parents are very familiar with it, the sudden onslaught of a "mass" delegation can have a satisfying shock effect on the principal. This is especially useful if he is arrogant and is known for intimidating parents. Remember, the best defense is offense. Let your own situation guide you in deciding how big your group should be. Six is a "professional" delegation. Beyond that, suit yourself.

Should You Make an Appointment?

Advantages to Making an Advance Appointment. If the principal is a "good guy" you may want to make an appointment in advance. Ask yourself, however, if your call will "frighten him" and allow him to stall you. Will advance notice result in "camouflage"? That is, will things get polished up just for your visit?

Remember that the parent who requests the appointment is likely to be pumped for information about what you want, so choose your representative carefully. You should be purposely vague about what you will want to see so that you don't make it too easy for the principal to prepare a special show just for your visit. Many parents prefer to notify him in advance just to keep him on their side, at least for the first round. This is called "preserving relationships" or "avoiding unnecessary hostility."

Advantages to "Barging In." Taxpayers have a right to make citizen inspections of public property. Spur-of-the-moment inspec-

How to Make a School Visit

How to Make a School Visit
tions are customary in almost every branch of government and in
most big businesses. One mother told me that she *never* goes
to school on the day the teacher or principal sends for her:
"They're ready for me then. I go two days earlier or later, when
I'm ready for *them*." Coming without advance fanfare saves the
staff advance worry—and preparation.

What Time to Go

You will require about two hours to complete the visit as outlined here. If you have heard many complaints about lunch, you
might want to include it in your visit. Otherwise avoid coming
too close to noon. Plan to arrive at the school no later than ten
in the morning or one in the afternoon, unless there is a special
double-shift time schedule which you want to observe. If you
get to school as late as eleven or two o'clock, you may end up
spending all your time in the principal's office.

What to Wear

Most parents go out of their way to dress up when they go to visit
their child's teacher. But since your visit is also a technique for
forcing the school staff to respond to parents who are poor, you
might purposefully *not* get dressed up for this visit. When training
his salespeople, one Fifth Avenue luxury department-store president invariably describes a legendary customer who came in to
try on mink coats. Although she was wearing only a cheap
housedress and carrying a torn and grimy shopping bag, she
was served with civility and courtesy. She bought the most
expensive coat in the store, paying for it with $10,000 which she
took right out of her shopping bag. Unfortunately, few of our
school staff have had similar training. But perhaps that is because
they know that they will keep their jobs no matter what the
"customer" thinks about them.

Will You Want Publicity as a Result of Your Visit?

If this is your first visit, and you want to see what is going on,
it is premature to include reporters. But if there is a specific
emergency condition which requires immediate attention, invite
the press to accompany you. Just be sure of your facts in advance,

and know where the most visible, photogenic outrages are located. We once took reporters to a modern well-equipped school, loaded with inexperienced, out-of-license teachers, and in which more than 90 percent of the children were far behind in reading, but the hard-hearted press remained unimpressed. Unfortunately, overflowing toilets, double sessions, and scurrying rats have become the accepted dimensions of scandal. The less visual, more exquisite form of torture exemplified by the sight of beautifully scrubbed children sitting in beautiful new buildings, taught by beautiful young teachers, and culminating each school year with greater pupil retardation than the year before, is generally regarded as too common to be newsworthy.

If you are able to convince the *New York Times* or a television network newsman to accompany you, fine! However, a story in a community weekly paper can accomplish as much. Public exposure is greatly feared by the board and its local administrators.

Take Notes during Your Visit

One or two should be assigned to take notes on everything. But make sure not everyone is writing. You miss a lot when you are busy note-taking; more important, principals become nervous watching those who do nothing but write and, conversely, warm up more readily to those who seem to be listening sympathetically. Recently, one principal told me: "Please don't take any notes while you are inside the classroom. You might hurt the teacher's feelings." He later confided that he never wrote down anything while visiting classes, and that only three teachers had requested transfers from his school during the past five years. Why should they? That was probably the easiest place to "work" in New York City.

Hold an Advance Briefing Session

Your committee should meet before you make your visit to discuss what you want to accomplish. Are you mostly interested in comparing classrooms? Checking on physical facilities? Observing the lunchroom? Watching student-teacher interaction? Or do you want to confront the principal with specific problems? If you don't agree about your objectives in advance, some of you may be anxious to spend most of the time in the classrooms while others on your committee may want to present particular personal problems to the principal, and you may waste your entire visit arguing with each other.

Make a list of the things you want to see, and check afterward to see how many of these you actually covered. Plan a follow-up meeting to evaluate your findings. It is important to decide *in advance* whether or not your committee will tell the principal your reactions, or whether you will hold all your comments until you can get together privately afterward to discuss them. Telling your reactions too quickly can limit your strategy later on.

Be alert to any attempt that might be made to divert you once you arrive at the school. If you plan to start at 10 A.M., by 10:30 you will want to be out of the principal's office and on your way to visit the classrooms. If there are a great many of you, you can plan to split up into two or three smaller groups after you see the principal, so that you can see more things and your presence won't be too overwhelming.

Trust Your Judgment

Don't be afraid to ask questions, and don't get turned around by double-talk. Sometimes you will see something you don't like, which can be clearly explained. But if the principal gives a long-winded, confusing, multi-syllabic answer when you ask, "Why aren't the first-graders reading at the end of first grade?" you should trust your common sense. If you think you're being taken, you're probably right.

Recently we visited a fifth grade along with some bigwigs from Washington. They were watching the young teacher demonstrate the "new math" while we were walking around the room noticing work on display. More than half of the compositions marked "excellent" were full of misspelled and uncorrected words. We took a few samples off the wall to show them to the rest of our delegation, and asked the principal why this was so. His reply: "He's a wonderful teacher, but he just doesn't know how to spell." The Washington politicos might have been taken in, but the parents were furious.

As you walk through a school you will see children. If the kids are noisy and seem eager to find reasons to stay out of class, how can you judge whether that is the normal way all students feel about any school, or whether this school is so awful and alien it practically pushes the children into misbehaving? We suggest you plan to visit at least one or two other schools in order to compare. Something we see in one school seems O.K. until we visit another school, where the children behave so differently that we realize the things we were told were "normal" or "unavoidable" or "standard practice" are definitely not so. Therefore, as you judge what you see, trust your instincts. But don't jump to conclusions until you can see some more, ask some more, and talk it over with others.

The First Part of Your Visit: Outside of the School

—Are there pieces of broken glass, beer cans and other litter on the sidewalk and in the streets?

—Are there many broken windows?

—Is the schoolyard fence torn and hole-ridden? Is the yard in good condition—or filled with teachers' parked cars?

Two blocks apart, two identical schools often look entirely different from the outside. One has ten broken windows a year and the other three hundred. Why? Children lash out at a facility which cheats them, and they protect one which gives them what they need. When the East Harlem parents were involved in pushing the construction of PS 7 many years ago, all the boys and girls in the neighborhood carefully avoided playing ball near the green glass walls while they were being erected. But once the staff and principal were assigned, most of whom took no part in community activities and ignored the parents who had struggled so long to get the school built, the armistice was over, and the children began to treat the windows as legitimate targets. So learn from the litter outside the school. If the school personnel respects the community, the school will probably reflect it.

—Is there a well-placed sign with posters announcing various school and parent activities? Is it up-to-date?

—Is the custodian's name and home address clearly posted so you can contact him in case of emergency?

—Is there a sign listing the names of the local school board members, addresses and phone numbers?

—How long does it take you to locate a door which is open? Why do they make a secret of this in so many schools? Can't the unlocked door be painted red or something?

All this is indicative of the outward posture which the school wants to display toward the community. Some schools don't even want to *appear* communicative!

The Second Part of Your Visit:
Inside the School

Once you enter the building, how long are you permitted to wander through the halls before someone stops you and asks what you are doing there? United Bronx Parents advises parents to enter the school and walk in the direction of the lunchroom or library, acting as if they know exactly where they are going. If the group is small, this often works, and in some schools parents go on walking about the building for quite a long time before being questioned. We have received a great deal of criticism from school officials for giving this kind of advice to parents: "Signs are posted inside each door telling all visitors to go directly to the office; you should tell parents to go to the office for a pass." But part of the reason for this visit is for parents to see how alert the school personnel are when outsiders appear, and to find out how visitors are treated who appear quite suddenly, without any advance credentials.

Several years ago when the People's Board of Education was formed by a number of us who were pressuring for school improvement throughout the city, we were told about an extremely lax situation in a Brownsville junior high school. The principal kept all visitors talking in his office, so the reports went, and never permitted parents or other visitors above the first floor. The upper floors were unbelievable, the parents charged, and we determined to find out the facts for ourselves. Feeling quite conspiratorial, five members of our committee entered first. They were immediately welcomed and drawn into the office, and were joined by six other members of the supervisory staff intent on keeping them thoroughly occupied. While they were there, two more of us entered the building and walked directly up the stairs. We inspected the fourth, third and second floors, and we were never once stopped from one until two thirty, when we rejoined our colleagues in the main office. Our report laid the groundwork for an effective campaign to remove the principal.

Of course, in many schools there is a small table inside the front door where visitors are supposed to stop. Who sits at that table in your school? Volunteers or paid aides? Does your school have a security guard at the door or in the halls? Have there been some incidents (thefts, etc.) which caused the school administration to set up this table or hire the guards? Has this helped the situation?

Notice the kinds of answers you are given when you ask these questions. Are they clear, forthright and direct? Or do you get the run-around? Are you told the community is terrible, the neighborhood is unsafe—or does the person who explains the security measures exhibit a high regard for the students and their families? Does the school assume at least partial responsibility for prevailing conditions and for finding solutions?

Whether you are stopped immediately at the door, or permitted to walk through the halls for a while and then stopped, notice the manner in which you are first approached. Is a stranger considered a potential troublemaker or a welcome guest? Are they happy to have visitors or angry that you have come? Once you are asked to go to the general office to obtain a pass, do so immediately.

**The Third Part of Your Visit:
In the School Office**

—How long are you kept waiting?

—Notice as much as you can while you wait.

How does the *office staff* behave? Are they friendly? Too busy to take time to ask you what you want?

Sign the *visitors' book*. Notice when the district superintendent last visited the school. Don't be afraid to thumb backwards.

And who has been to see the school from central headquarters?

How many children are hanging around the office doing nothing or waiting as stand-by *monitors*? In better schools, pupils' time is not wasted in this way; when a monitor is needed, one is called. In such schools, children are appointed monitors only if they are doing well in school. Is this the case? Or are children made monitors to get a "disruptive" child out of a teacher's way?

Does the *UFT Bulletin Board* feature only union notices and advertisements for chartered summer tours to Europe? Or does it also include some newspaper clippings describing a parent or community activity? Are there announcements of teacher-training programs?

Look at the *time clock cards*. Can you figure out how many of the staff are absent? As you look over the cards, you might recognize the names of some teachers whom you will want to see.

Is the *principal* in his office? On our visits we found disappointingly few principals out and around their schools. They were either sitting in their offices, at a meeting "downtown" or conducting an assembly. But perhaps it is old-fashioned to expect a principal to be directly involved with the teachers and the children.

If the office staff refers your group to someone other than the principal ask why. Puerto Rican parents are frequently sent immediately to a bilingual teacher when they quite properly should have been seen by the principal or his assistant—if a translator is needed, one can be sent for. If you are received by an assistant principal, don't be insulted that the principal himself isn't meeting with you. It is a rare administrator who trusts his staff enough to delegate this type of responsibility, and if you are treated with warmth and courtesy and made to feel welcome, that is the essential thing.

The Fourth Part of Your Visit:
Inside the Principal's Office

What happens when you get to see the principal? Is he flustered? Does he leave you in the office while he runs out to warn the rest of the school about your visit? Notice how he seats you. Does he have enough chairs? Does he sit behind a desk showing off his authority, or does he join you around the conference table? Some principals have been genuinely glad to see us, and encouraged us to observe anything we want. Others have become extremely frightened, and set up many restrictions. But we have never been told to leave. Remember that you have a legal right to visit a school at any time as long as you do not interfere with the children's work.

Does he call in several assistants? Some principals instantly summon their subordinates, almost as if to protect themselves. We have never seen an administrator who first asked if he was interrupting something his staff member may have been doing.

At one Manhattan school the principal called in the UFT representative who happened to be that school's only corrective-reading teacher. In a school with more than eight hundred seriously retarded readers, that principal pulled his only reading specialist out of class, and no one even questioned it. Don't feel flattered if everyone drops everything to participate in your visit. You may feel important, but don't you wonder how *un*important the children must feel?

Notice to whom he pays the most attention. Is he treating the minister with more attention than the parents? Is he overly coy with the parents, referring often to his reliance on their advice? Do you feel that you are being stalled or buttered up?

When the principal asks what you want to see, tell him. You may have heard reports about specific teachers or classes which you want to see. Otherwise, ask to see all the classes in one or two grades: an upper one (fifth or sixth grade) and a lower one (first or third grade). You will see variations within a school and get some hint of the variations within the city. If the principal suggests some things for you to look at, remember: Anything he *invites* you to see, he *wants* you to see.

The Fifth Part of Your Visit:
In the Hallways

The Bulletin Boards. You can learn a great deal from the bulletin boards—if you know what to look for. If the bulletin boards are beautifully prepared on the first floor but are of much poorer quality throughout the upper floors of the building, it may mean that the school administration is more interested in creating a good impression than in educating the children.

If the bulletin boards are magnificent works of art, completely done by the teachers, it may mean that the teachers are talented and educated, but what about the children? Occasionally a teacher may want to create a special exhibit, but bulletin boards should be places where the children are able to take turns displaying their work.

Especially in the junior and senior highs, notice whether the *students* have a bulletin board for announcements, and then look carefully to see if every poster has been initialed by some school administrator. This means that the students do not have free access to display their own material, but must get everything approved first. In the process, in most schools, this means that much information which is meaningful and important to the students is deleted or censored by the school staff.

Is the material on display *relevant* to the experiences of the children? We have visited black schools where every picture showed white children and adults. Although this is happening less often, visitors will still find that most bulletin boards in city schools display beautiful rural scenes. (Don't the seasons ever change in the city? Don't Thanksgiving and Halloween and Christmas ever come to the city?) And I have seen Brotherhood Week displays which were first put up in February still hanging in May, as if the school was asking "credit" for this production all year round.

What community programs and organizations are featured? Are there posters and signs which tell the children about Jamaica events, if the school is in Jamaica, or Bayside activities, if it is in Bayside? In one particularly dirty school, I saw a Department of Sanitation "Operation Community Clean-Up" sign. If the custodian wasn't obeying that poster, why should the students? In contrast, in one Washington Heights school I saw a display showing the various routes children could take to their local library which made me want to go there.

And if the bulletin boards are empty, find out why. I once visited a school where the teacher was determined to leave a blank bulletin board until the children decided what should be placed there; the principal, however, was much less democratic, and had *ordered* the teacher to put up a display. The empty board was a symbol of an important interfaculty disagreement; if parents had barged in demanding that the bulletin board be filled, they would have done a great disservice to that very able young teacher.

Relationship Between the Staff and Children. As you walk through the halls, do you hear much shouting? Everywhere you go, notice who is doing the most talking—is it the teachers or the children? When I worked with the PS 125–36 Boycott Committee, the major complaint of the children was, "the teachers always jump at us. They never want to hear our story." Does this happen in your school? For example, walking down the hall with the principal, he is apt to see several children in the halls; does he ask them what they are doing there, and *without waiting for their reply,* order them to their rooms? Does the principal hear noise coming from a classroom, and without trying to find out why, does he poke his head in the door and tell them to be quiet?

Does the principal know the names of the children he meets in the hall? Do the teachers address the children by their names? When children come up to the staff person who is with you, does he stop to listen to them, or does he ignore them, or tell them, "Go away now, I'm busy"?

Go into several children's lavatories as you pass them in the hall. Often we found ourselves retching at the smell and the dirt, and we noted the absence of soap or paper. In one school we found that the washroom opened into the ground-floor lunchroom, with no partition in front of the doorway. If the school staff believes that the students are not human beings, you will know it from a washroom trip! And if you pass some paper which has been dropped in the hallway, does the principal bend down to pick it up?

What happens when the periods change, and the children move from one room to another? In junior and senior highs, the classes change every forty-five minutes. Do the children seem relaxed and friendly as they move through the halls, or does it remind you of a prison or an army on the march? Is the atmosphere completely uncontrolled—or completely overcontrolled? Many adults won't recognize the difference between complete and controlled chaos when it comes to adolescents, so compare several schools and talk to the students before deciding. In elementary schools children seem to move quite often also—to the library, art teacher, etc. Does this movement take more time than it is worth? How many times does the teacher stop the children and put her hands to her lips, or pull a few kids out of the line for being noisy?

A walk through the halls can tell you a great deal about a school. How does the atmosphere feel to you? Human, relaxed, cheerful, busy, clean? Or inhuman, angry, dirty, chaotic, jail-like, harassed, sullen?

The Sixth Part of the Visit:
Inside the Classrooms

Most times, we can learn plenty after just fifteen minutes in a classroom—most times, not all the time. So although the suggestions here are useful things to do, if the teacher is using methods that are different from what they were when you went to school, you probably should come back several times. Just because a teacher is using all kinds of modern equipment, teaching machines, tape recorders, etc., it does not necessarily mean the children are learning a great deal. And just because the teacher is young, or the class is noisy, and the room is messy, it does not mean the children are not learning. Unfortunately, however, in most New York City classrooms parents will find very little that is now or unconventional. So the following paragraphs will point out what we do at United Bronx Parents when we go to visit the average city classroom. If this guide is useful, apply it to your school. But if your school is changing, innovating, experimenting, you will need to innovate a bit yourself, and adapt these guidelines to help you evaluate the classrooms in your school.

We enter the classroom quietly; the principal usually whispers to the teacher that we are just visiting; sometimes we have simply been given a pass to show her. Then we walk slowly, without talking, around the room, usually looking at the bulletin boards along the walls but all the time *listening* very carefully to what is happening in the room. If the teacher stops what she is doing, we say, "Please go on, we don't want to interrupt." We try to listen most especially to see who is doing most of the talking in the room—the teacher or the children. In a classroom where there is lots of learning taking place, the children usually dominate. We pick up work folders, look at experiments, thumb through textbooks. Usually we ask one of the children to show us his homework notebook, which we look through quickly and return with thanks. If we have any questions about what we see, we write them down to ask the principal or teacher later.

Are the children busy working? Children sitting in a row with stiffly folded hands may look orderly, but are they really listening to what is going on? Are the children in the back straining to see, or have they given up trying? Some classes have the seats in rows; some have the children sitting at tables grouped around the room. No matter how they are sitting, some teachers seem able to give every child individual attention and some teachers are overwhelmed by the whole thing. Notice the "lost" children—the ones who are seated way off in a corner for punishment, the ones who are coloring, those that are sleeping. Now, we realize that sometimes a really good teacher may encourage some daydreaming, but surely not all the time. Once when we saw a child sitting way in the back, we asked him why he was there, and he told us, "My teacher is absent, so I'm in this class for the day." Thus we found that fifth-graders had been placed in fourth grade when substitutes were unavailable!

Are there enough books, supplies, learning materials? Is there any empty fish tank and a dying plant in the science corner, or a table loaded with things the children have built or discovered? Is there a classroom library with several hundred books, games, magazines, newspapers? Or just a few paperbacks in torn condition? In one school there were many books, all kept behind lock and key in each room so the children would not "spoil" them. (When the printing press was first invented, schoolteachers opposed it saying that it would mean an end to schools. But they needn't have worried; many teachers have become quite skillful at making sure the children don't want to read the books that get printed.) Are the books and materials up-to-date? Notice the copyright dates on the other side of the title pages. Do the books contain pictures of white children only?

Notice the classroom bulletin boards. Is uncorrected work on display? This subject causes endless debate among teachers. Some tell us that if a paper is "good work" for a particular child, in comparison with what he has been doing before, then it is fair to mark it "good" and display it, even if it is loaded with errors. In other schools we have seen teachers refuse to display any pupil's work unless it has been copied over without mistakes. Do you think high standards have been set for the children? Some teachers tell us that the children should be encouraged to set their own standards. Is this done in the classroom you are visiting? Or is this a professional-sounding excuse for no standards? The teacher who made most sense told us: "I write 'Excellent' rarely, and only for something really exceptional. A story written by a child can be looked at in many different ways. In one paper, the grammar and spelling are perfect, although the idea is conventional. In another the handwriting is terrible but the idea is wonderful and a big step forward for this child, although it wouldn't be for another. I don't write 'Good' on any of these. I try instead to write a personal comment—sometimes I will give two or three different marks for one paper."

Notice the difference between the classes in the same grade. One teacher will put long, detailed social studies reports on display. Another has only a poster which she brought in from a travel agency. In one class, everyone will have copied the identical story off the board; in another, each child has written an individual story of his own. If all ghetto children are "poor and deprived," and theoretically the same on a cultural level, why is there such a wide variation within the same school in any ghetto school? Could it be that some teachers are teaching and some are not?

Notice the way the teacher handles discipline. While you are in the classroom, most likely the children will be quiet and polite simply because a visitor is present. (But in some of the best classes I have seen, the children were so engrossed they never even noticed the visitors.) Is the teacher polite and respectful to the children? Are the children bored and restless? If you are bored in visiting the class, undoubtedly they are far more bored staying in it. Are the children getting lots of recognition and satisfaction in the class? Some teachers give every child a special part of the bulletin board; in some classes everyone's picture or name appears somewhere on it. I am sorry to say that in many classes the only commendation cards I saw from the principal were those given to the class for showing "good control." Is that the only school virtue worth rewarding?

Finally, notice how many children are in the class—the blackboard will probably tell you how many more are absent. Do the various classes you visit differ much in size? Are any composed of two teachers doubling up with two classes of children? If so, why? Do both teachers handle the classroom together, permitting some individual attention, or do they take turns? Is there a paraprofessional or student teacher in the room? Is she just sitting there, or do you think her time is being used effectively? If this is a school which serves children from a variety of religious and racial backgrounds, do all the classes reflect this mixture? Or are some classes more segregated than others?

Before we leave the room we thank the teacher and the children. If the teacher seems to want to talk to us, we may ask her one or two questions, such as, "What do you feel you need most to help you do your job?" We are anxious to see if she asks us to get her additional supplies or other things to improve the classroom, or if she merely replies, "These children need more attention at home."

After the Classroom Visits, What Next?

We usually return to the principal's office to thank him, and to ask him any questions which have been brought up by the visit. Sometimes we leave a list of additional questions for him to answer in writing. Sometimes we make another appointment to discuss our findings and our recommendations.

We do not discuss our reactions unless our entire group has first agreed to do this and has decided which particular issues we will raise. We arrange among ourselves to meet together later so that we can evaluate what we learned and agree on what steps we want to take next. Sometimes we feel we want to visit another school right away for comparison before we evaluate what we have seen. Other times, we make immediate arrangements to publicize our findings.

When we meet next, we begin to decide what particular issue we want to focus on: the staff, the curriculum, the custodian, the school lunch, the supplies, etc., etc. Thus, this first visit is merely a preliminary step—it begins to tell us about our school, and shows us some of the changes we must demand in order to make it a good school.

2 · The Curriculum

THE STUFF KIDS LEARN

When I was first appointed to our local school board in District 6, the members were told to inspect the schools in our district. We asked our superintendent what we should look for when we visited the schools. He suggested that we check the physical conditions of the buildings, look over the books in the library, observe the lunchroom and see if the school is clean. If we wanted to test the school's "efficiency," we could ask the principal to run a fire drill for us. "A *good* school should empty in four minutes," he informed us.

Some of my colleagues disagreed with this approach. One board member asked, "Shouldn't we find out what is being done to bring each child up to grade level?" "I don't think that would be an appropriate question," our superintendent replied. "It would be more professional to inquire what is being done to bring each child up to his maximum potential."

What should a good school teach the children? How to have an efficient fire drill? How to read and write? What in the world is a child's "maximum potential"? Who knows enough to know what it might be? Again and again we heard that formidable term used. Parents would come to local board meetings complaining that the curriculum in their child's school had been "watered down." The school personnel would emphatically deny it. "We have to adapt the curriculum to meet the individual needs of each child so each child may reach his maximum potential," would be the reasonable and invariable reply.

We asked for an outline of the requirements for each grade: What math, reading, spelling, science, history, geography were the children supposed to learn before they could be promoted to the next grade? Although we were shown some very thick curriculum "guidelines" for some of the grades, we found out that the children are promoted from one grade to the next whether or not they completed the work for the year. Each teacher is free to adjust the material she gives her class—the "gifted" children receive an "enriched" program; the "slower" learners receive a "modified" program.

At first I didn't argue. After all, they were the professionals. Surely they knew what they were doing, I thought. I began to visit the schools in my district. District 6 ran from Harlem to Washington Heights and Inwood. The schools in the northern portion were predominantly white, middle-class, and Jewish and Irish. Those in the southern area were mostly black, although a few were heavily Spanish-speaking; all but one or two of these were located in extremely impoverished neighborhoods.

I spent a day in a white school near my own home. In the first grade a cheerful teacher was explaining to the six-year-olds: "Unless you learn how to sound out and spell polysyllabic words, you will have great difficulty in your first year in college." She had cut out a newspaper clipping showing a group of freshman English pupils at Queens College attending a tutorial class in spelling; she thumbtacked the article to the Current Events bulletin board, and asked the children, "Now, who is smart enough to repeat that big word 'polysyllabic'?"

Next I began to visit the schools in Harlem. In one third grade the children were crayoning in ordinary coloring books. I asked the principal why they were doing such simple work. He told me: "These children have so many problems at home, we can't add to their difficulties by giving them problems in school too."

Reading was a sore point throughout the district. One Puerto Rican parent told this story at a local board meeting: "Why don't the principals tell us when our children are doing poorly? My boy Frankie is in sixth grade. Last year I could see he was not reading too well. But when I went to see his teacher she told me not to worry. Then our Mother's Club learned about the reading tests, so I went to see the principal to find out Frankie's reading score. He told me that Frankie was a good boy—but I wanted to know his reading score. Finally he looked it up and told me—3.5. That is two years behind what he should be! So I asked him to keep Frankie back for a year so he could learn to read better, but the principal said that would harm him psychologically, and they promoted him. Now he is in sixth grade and he can barely read. He knows that he doesn't know anything. Isn't that going to hurt him more?"

Not too long after I heard about Frankie, I was invited to a dinner party in Queens where a white parent was bragging about the high standards in her child's public school. "When our daughter Julie came home with her fifth-grade report card, I found that she was not reading as well as she should. I went to see her teacher, who suggested that perhaps I should hire a private tutor to help her. I did, and in May I asked the principal how well Julie had done on her reading test. He told me that she is really brighter than her reading grade showed. She tested 6.5, but although that is a year above grade level, the principal told me that she had one of the lowest scores in her class, and he urged me to continue with the tutor. He also suggested that I tell Julie she had scored very high so that her confidence would be built up."

I began to suspect that the school system didn't really mean what it said. It did not seem to me that each child was being helped to reach his "maximum potential." Quite the contrary, most of the teachers and principals behaved as though every white middle-class child was gifted and was college material, and every black and Puerto Rican (and sometimes Irish and Italian) working-class child was slow, disadvantaged, and unable to learn anything but the most rudimentary facts.

There were no performance standards for some of the children and exceedingly high and rigid standards for others—a double standard, in a public school system which says it believes in equal opportunity for all. Each child was expected to perform *only as much as the teacher believed to be his maximum potential,* and the teacher's decision was usually based upon subjective and narrow-minded assumptions.

And as I visited classrooms and spoke to other parents, I learned that something else was wrong with the curriculum. The children were being taught things other than simply facts and information. The schools were concerned with developing "wholesome attitudes" in the pupils. In fact, the teachers often seemed to be more interested in getting their students to behave than in getting them to think.

As I was writing this section our youngest child came home from her first day in school and answered the inevitable "What did you learn?" with "I learned to stop talking when the whistle blows."

I once heard a parent ask a Head Start teacher: "Maybe Head Start doesn't really prepare our children for public school; maybe all it does is give them a false sense of freedom?" I think that is true. Head Start children, like our daughter in nursery school, are taught to be talkative, questioning, noisy, happy learners; they are totally unprepared to line up, sit up straight and raise their hands when they get to regular school, where the teacher expects them to listen quietly, and never, never talk to each other, joke with each other—and certainly never sing while they work in class.

I think that many—perhaps most—teachers are really anti-children—black *and* white children. And I think that the students learn more from the way the teachers treat them than they learn from all the books and lectures put together.

Parents, in all neighborhoods, hear their children complain:

"Just because we made a little noise, we were all punished and can't go on the trip she promised us."

"She tore up my whole paper because I forgot the margin."

"She made me stay after school just because I wore my hat in school."

"She sent me to the principal's office because she didn't like the way I looked at her."

"I couldn't go to assembly because I forgot my white shirt."

"Just because we wouldn't tell who started the fight, she made us go without lunch."

The teachers seem determined to prove that they are "in charge." One white child, in an affluent Riverdale neighborhood, was doing very poorly in math. The teacher told her mother that the girl had no mathematical ability and that nothing could be done to improve her math mark. The mother couldn't believe her. She hired a private tutor at nine dollars an hour. The tutor attempted to reach the child's regular teacher in order to find out what methods and materials were being used in class. But the teacher angrily refused to meet with the tutor and warned the mother that it was harmful to "push" her daughter this way. The child got along famously with the tutor, and began to understand the math. When the final exam was given, all her answers were correct. However, the teacher flunked the child anyway. "You did not use the proper methods for getting your answers," wrote the teacher on the top of the examination paper. Thus the child was put down for daring to challenge the teacher's estimate of her ability.

Now, that student was white and her parents were able to comfort her so she wouldn't feel the full weight of the teacher's disapproval. And most likely, next term she will have a teacher who will be less antagonistic toward her. But for black kids the problem is much worse.

In one white receiving school, a bussed-in black third-grade boy brought his teacher a note from his mother, in which she explained that the child had a kidney infection and needed to go to the bathroom frequently. Incredibly, the teacher did not believe that the mother had really written the note. Publicly she said in front of the entire class: "Kevin's mother could not have written this note. See how bad the handwriting is. Kevin must have had a friend forge the message. That is really very bad. Just for that I shall put Kevin in the corner so he will learn never, never to lie like that again." And, of course, while standing in the corner, Kevin wet his pants.

No spelling lesson, no geography lesson, no poetry reading or math drill will ever impress Kevin—and the rest of that class— as strongly as the "lesson" the teacher taught that day. School is a place where children learn they are not trusted. School is a place where inhuman and cruel things can and do happen. School is a place where you learn that the strong (the teachers) can do anything they want to the weak (the children). School is a place where you learn to be afraid.

What are the kids supposed to be taught in school? What does the law say they should learn? What is wrong with the curriculum? And how can parents improve or change it?

THE REGULATIONS
AND HOW THEY WORK

What does "curriculum" mean?

Some people call the curriculum the course of study or the syllabus. Fancy educators talk about "organizationally planned and controlled experiences designed to educate students." Kids call it the stuff they learn in school. (Parents know that kids learn a lot of stuff which is *not* part of the system's controlled design.)

Who determines the curriculum?

Many parents believe that the course of study is something which professional educators should determine. According to state law, however, ordinary citizens have the legal authority to determine the curriculum. Although teachers and supervisors may make recommendations, the final power to decide what will be taught in the schools lies with the lay boards of education in each locality.*

* Education Law, Section 1709.

In New York City the central Board of Education is considered the local board for the entire city. Thus, although community boards approve the curriculum in every other part of New York State, in New York City this power remains in the hands of a remote central Board of Education.

Are there any minimum requirements?

Yes. There are several state requirements which every school district must follow. These have been established by the State Education Law* and by various rulings adopted by the Board of Regents and the State Education Commissioner.

For example, during the first eight grades, every child in the state must be taught reading, spelling, writing, arithmetic, United States and New York State history, geography, civics, science, physical training and hygiene. Over the years, additional requirements were included in the law. For example, New York State schools must teach patriotism, citizenship, fire prevention, highway safety and the nature and effect of alcohol and narcotics. Each of these subjects was added to the mandated curriculum as a result of political pressure from various special-interest groups.

In most places, music and art are also in the curriculum. Many towns teach foreign language, typing, or home economics in the elementary schools. Some communities have had intense debates over the inclusion of sex education. The important point to remember is that although the state requires some of the subjects, each local community is free to add others.

Under decentralization, each New York City community board may determine "matters relating to the instruction of students," provided that all textbooks and courses of instruction have *first* been approved by the chancellor. Thus, the local communities will not only have to follow state minimum requirements but will also have to obey an additional set of city requirements.†

Are there any minimum state standards?

Not really. Although the state requires that arithmetic, for example, must be taught in all schools from the first through

* Education Law, Section 3204 and 801–810.
† Decentralization Law, Section 2590 (e-3) and 2590 (h-8).

eighth grades, and although the State Education Department publishes a recommended syllabus, each district is free to make its own curriculum adaptations as it determines are necessary to meet the needs of the local area and individual student.*
Although New York State gives Regents examinations in many high school subjects, local districts are not required to administer these exams to all pupils. Each system may use its own judgment to decide which students should be given a Regents exam. Pupils may be promoted and graduated on the basis of the performance standards set in each district. If a local school system sets no standards for pupil achievement at each grade level, the state does not interfere. New York City never makes public what percentage of the students in each high school took, or passed, the various Regents exams, although this would be an obvious way to help the public evaluate the schools.

Since 1965 the State Education Department has conducted a testing program to measure and compare pupil achievement throughout the state. Each fall, all students in the first, third, sixth and ninth grades are given a reading and arithmetic test to see how much of the standard curriculum they have mastered. No other state in the country administers such a test. It could be an excellent tool for measuring and comparing pupil and school achievement throughout the state. Since the same test is given in public and parochial schools, and in rural, suburban and city systems, administrators could, if they wanted to, compare their schools with other schools in similar neighborhoods and in "better" neighborhoods, or with other schools within their system or with other school systems. However, although the first tests were administered in 1966 and results were sent to the New York City Board of Education in 1967, our city has never seen fit to publicize—or analyze—the findings, which tell quite a lot about what our children are learning.

Unfortunately the tests have shown that New York City students are not learning very much. The state has established a level of "minimum competence" for each test; 23 percent of the sixth graders throughout the state scored below this minimum-

* State Education Commissioner Regulations 100.2(b).

competence level. In New York City, however, more than 44 percent of the children were below minimum competence! Perhaps the most incredible finding was that 81 elementary schools in the state (out of a total of 3,634) had more than 70 percent of their students reading below minimum competence, and *65 of these were New York City public schools*! Yet these 65 schools have never had their license taken away, nor have their names or locations been made public, despite the obvious fact that "curriculum standards or requirements" are certainly not being met in those particular schools.

Does the State Education Department have any supervisory control over the curriculum in the districts?

Yes, but obviously it has chosen not to use it. Before a school district is entitled to receive public money from the state, the Commissioner of Education must be satisfied that proper instruction is being given.* One could hardly say that "proper" instruction was being given in those 65 New York City schools, but the state, up to now, at least, has done nothing about it.

It is important to note that the Decentralization Law gives the New York City board the power to set educational standards in addition to curriculum requirements.† Thus, although the central board never set any standards for itself while it operated the schools, it will now have the power to require each community board to evaluate and make public the educational effectiveness of its programs. Only time will tell whether this new power will be used to raise educational standards or whether it will become another mechanism to be used by the city bureaucracy to harass local communities.

How is the curriculum determined in New York City?

In several ways:

—The central Board of Education has a Bureau of Curriculum Development which prepares curriculum bulletins, updating them every ten years or so. These are course outlines which

* Education Law 3604 and Regents Rules Section 28.
† Decentralization Law, 2590 (h-8, 9, 10).

tell the teachers what they are supposed to teach in each subject in each grade.

—Teachers are permitted to modify this curriculum for "slower" pupils and "enrich" it for the "gifted" students. Therefore the pupils are *grouped*, according to the teacher's estimate of their ability, into bright, average, and slow classes. In effect, this is the New York City *tracking system*.

—Children are also grouped according to their *reading and arithmetic achievement scores*. Several standard tests are administered to most pupils in every grade each year, and those children who do well on these tests are the ones who are taught the full course of studies outlined in the bulletins. Although children may fail the tests because they have not been prepared adequately, or because they find the test structure strange and frightening, these students are nevertheless classified as slow or semi-uneducable, and are organized into separate classes where very little of the standard curriculum is taught, very little is expected and, not surprisingly, very little is learned.

—The final major element in the New York City curriculum process is the *social promotion policy*. Every year 95 percent of all the children are promoted, whether or not they have learned the subject matter which was supposed to be covered and whether or not they have passed any of the tests. Although the board claims that it has adopted this policy because to do otherwise would be "psychologically harmful" to the children, it is more likely that they have done so because the schools would become so terribly overcrowded they could not function if the children who did not learn were left back. In any event, by promoting most of the children, the parents are given the illusion of progress; as my grandmother used to say, the children grow older, but they don't grow up.

To see how these curriculum policies are implemented in New York City, let's look at what happens to the students as they move through their twelve years of schooling.

Kindergarten

Children's first school experience is usually kindergarten. In many schools the older children are assigned to the morning session, which lasts for three hours; the younger children, supposedly because they have a shorter attention span, are given the shorter, two-hour afternoon session. Obviously the morning children will have almost 200 more hours of schooling at the end of the year than the afternoon children. If they have a conscientious teacher, they will have learned almost one third more than their younger counterparts by the end of June.

Another sort of stratification takes place in many schools. If a child has attended nursery school or Head Start, the principal often assigns him to the kindergarten group which has the more experienced teacher and where the children will be taught to read and work with numbers. Thus, for some six-year-olds, the tracking system has already started.

Furthermore, in many of the oldest sections of the city where the schools are terribly overcrowded, there is not enough room for all the eligible children in kindergarten. State law only requires that seven-year-olds go to school; kindergarten is optional. Once more, preference is often given to Head Start youngsters, because their parents are usually articulate and organized. In 1968, well over ten thousand kindergarten-age children remained on waiting lists throughout the city, and almost all of them lived in black and Puerto Rican poverty areas. When these children, having had no previous school experience, start first grade, they will be 600 hours behind many of their classmates (and 1800 hours behind the many middle-class first-graders who have been attending nursery school since they were three years old).

First Through Sixth Grades

Beginning with the first grade, almost all the schools group the children according to reading ability. There may be a "top" first-grade class or, if not, within each class there is a "bright" reading group, an "average" reading group and a "slow" group. No matter what the teacher labels the children (bluebirds, robins, etc.), the children are smart enough to know who is getting real work and who is only playing. "If I am a good citizen and do all my homework I will be allowed to write with a pencil," confides the first-grader to her mother. And: "Armando is a bad citizen; he won't sit still in class and he never raises his hand when he wants to talk. The teacher won't let him bring any books home. That will teach him."

By the third or fourth grade, the "best" pupils are assigned to a "high-ability" or "intellectually gifted" class, which may not be gifted at all, but which is usually composed of the children who are achieving above grade level, and who, in the teacher's judgment, have shown "emotional and social maturity." One third-grade teacher told me why she had recommended a particular boy for placement in an "opportunity class" for "slow" children: "He is always absent, and when I finally got him to tell me why, it turns out the child is sneaking on the subway and going downtown to Macy's!" Curiosity, initiative and independence are evidently not characteristics which add up to that teacher's definition of "maturity"—so she labeled the child "potential drop-out and troublemaker." I'm sure he will oblige her and become one.

The poorest students are assigned to "low-ability" or "slow" classes; sometimes they are placed in special "guidance" or "opportunity" classes; some are classified "retarded" and put into Classes for Children with Retarded Mental Development (CRMD); and a few, particularly the "disruptive" boys, are transferred out of the regular schools altogether into special Schools for Socially Maladjusted Children (the so-called "600" schools).

The high-sounding names don't fool many parents. Opportunity classes provide an opportunity to those teachers who want to get rid of troublesome children. In fact, many parents believe that children who ask troublesome questions are often labeled "troubled" and make up the bulk of the "600"-school population. Mobilization for Youth looked at Puerto Rican children who had been placed in CRMD classes and found that most of them, retested with Spanish intelligence tests by Spanish-speaking psychologists, were perfectly normal and incorrectly diagnosed. Yet, despite repeated criticism of these "special services" for the "slow," the system has maintained and enlarged these programs, but rarely improved them.

If you want to understand how the curriculum becomes watered down in some classes and souped up in others, go visit all the classes in any particular grade on a given day. Fourth-grade social studies includes the study of New York City. The top class divides itself into committees; one committee visits the Stock Exchange and interviews brokers and bankers; the next week another committee is told to interview all the public officials representing the district; the third week the children prepare a full-scale model of the five boroughs which includes all bridges, tunnels, and major transportation and communication systems. The bottom class reads the chapter in the textbook dealing with New York and must fill in the missing words in the sentences the teacher writes on the board: "The bridge from Brooklyn to Staten Island is called the ——— Bridge." "The financial district is located near ——— Street." "The mayor of New York works at———."

By the time a child is ready to graduate from sixth grade, at the end of elementary school, he should be reading on the sixth-grade level. But if he is reading one year and eight months behind grade level, he is still promoted to seventh grade. *One-third of the city's sixth graders were reading below this minimal requirement in April 1968 and yet only 5 percent of these students were left back.* The remainder, over 20,000 children, who could not read, were promoted into junior high school. The professionals know enough to demand minimum salary standards for themselves, but they refuse to set minimum performance standards for the pupils—or for themselves.

For a city which prides itself on its melting-pot tradition, and which is angered by any attempt to "polarize" the various ethnic and economic groups, it is a tragic fact that the average *sixth-grade* middle-class white student in Bayside, Queens, can read better than the average *ninth-grade* working-class black student in Harlem.

Junior High and Intermediate Schools

When a child leaves elementary school, his achievement scores and the teacher's estimate of his character are passed on to the junior high or intermediate school staff. (For more information on how this works, see the chapter on the cumulative record card.)

Most parents have no idea how important the child's elementary school reading and math scores are. When they ask the fifth- or sixth-grade teacher how Johnny is doing, they will be told, "Fine, he is a very well-behaved boy." They are not told, however, that unless Johnny is achieving on grade level in reading and math, he will probably never get into the academic track of junior and senior high schools and will have very little chance of entering college.

For example, there are four different math courses offered to ninth-grade students, but only one of these, ninth-grade algebra, can be credited toward an academic high school diploma. Unless a child achieves a math score on grade level in elementary school, he will almost automatically be placed in the general math program. If he is in the general math class, he will most likely miss out on one year of the three-year math sequence which is required for the academic diploma. If he does not have an academic diploma, he will automatically be excluded from consideration by most of the four-year colleges.

Most college-oriented middle-class parents know this. They push and shove and make sure that their children receive the proper courses. If their children fail the Regents, the parents force them to make it up in the summer. But working-class and poor parents do not know what is required. When they are told that their child is doing nicely in math, they don't know he may be, in the first place, in the "wrong" math program, which teaches him very little, requires very little from him, and gets him nowhere. Even when some parents demand that their children take algebra, they are told it does not matter if the child fails the Regents. "He can graduate without the Regents mark," the guidance counselor assures them. Too late, three years later, they find that many colleges, including the State University, consider Regents marks to be an essential criterion for admissions.

The junior highs are even more stratified than the elementary schools. Children take their subjects "departmentally." They go to one room for English and to another for math, and in most schools the grouping policy is more rigid than it was in elementary school. The "gifted" students are placed in a three-year special-progress program, where students receive "enriched and advanced instruction" in science, math and foreign language, or they are assigned to two-year special-progress classes, where they are accelerated and cover the three-year course in two years.

The special-progress classes travel from room to room together; they do not mix with the rest of the school population. The other children do not mix very much either. The "average" children are grouped with other "average" children; the "difficult" youngsters, once again, are carefully classified and separated. There are eight or nine entirely different programs which can be given a junior high student: the "top" kids get a foreign language, algebra and geometry, perhaps earth science; the "uneducable" ones are assigned extra periods of home economics, woodwork and gym.

When they complete the ninth grade (or eighth grade in an intermediate school), the children who did well receive a *diploma*; those who did not do quite so well may get a *certificate*. And many students who lack even the minimal qualifications for getting a certificate are merely *transferred* to high schools because they are considered too old to remain in junior high school any longer.

IS 38 in the South Bronx awarded diplomas to 40 percent of its June 1968 class. Riverdale JHS 141 gave diplomas to 91 percent of its graduates. Thirty-nine percent of the South Bronx school students were reading so poorly they could not even qualify for a certificate; they were simply transferred into high schools. Less than 1 percent of the Riverdale school had such low qualifications. In both schools, only a handful of children were "left back."

The Board of Education does not explain these differences to parents—and that is the most shameful fact of all. One mother told me how she had scrubbed floors for years to make sure her twin boys completed high school and could go to college. She proudly attended their junior high school graduation ceremony, convinced that they had passed the first major hurdle. As they walked down the aisle, wearing cap and gown, their mother did not have the slightest idea that the boys were simply being *transferred* to high school; they had not graduated from anything. They were already so far behind they could not dream about college. She scrubbed her way through three more years before she found out that the high school general diploma they eventually received was worthless.

One last remark before we leave the junior high school scene. In middle-class neighborhoods, elementary and junior high graduations are simple, understated affairs—not much more than assemblies. But in poor neighborhoods, perhaps because the principals and teachers do not expect that many children will ever make it through high school or college, sixth-graders and ninth-graders wear robes, march to music, and act in every way as though they had culminated their education. Middle-class parents won't give their children any such ceremony until they have finished the real thing. But the ghetto schools produce an elaborate performance, pretending that much has been accomplished.

High School

By now the very "brightest" students have been so thoroughly trained to take tests that they pass the examinations for the *specialized high schools* and are carefully removed from contact with the average ordinary students. The rest of the pupils are regrouped. The "best" are given the academic program in the academic high schools or the *technical* program in some of the better vocational high schools. All the others, the masses, are assigned to the *"general"* (*commercial or vocational*) *courses*. General students in particular are not expected to learn much; they are permitted to graduate from high school with an eighth-grade reading score; they may receive an 80 on their report cards, but a G will appear next to that mark, indicating to insiders that the 80 was merely for effort, since the course was a general one and no scholastic standards were set.

About twenty years ago black parents complained bitterly that most of the students from Harlem were being shunted into inferior vocational schools. The Board of Education agreed that this should be changed, and the guidance counselors began to advise the children in poor communities to apply to academic high schools. At first the parents thought that they had won a victory—until they found out that although their children were going to an academic high school that did *not* mean they were being given an academic education. The general course in the academic high schools became the new dumping ground for "uneducable" students.

In 1964 the Puerto Rican Community Development Program got hold of some Board of Education figures which shocked them—and the rest of the city. *Of the 21,000 students receiving academic diplomas in 1963, only 331 were Puerto Rican and 762 were black.* Thus, although 45 percent of the public school population was nonwhite, only 5 percent of the academic graduates were nonwhite. That was the last time the Board of Education allowed such data to be made public. Parents all over the city mimeographed the incredible statistics and demanded changes. Finally, in 1969, the Board of Education did publish new statistics. Although it refused to specify how many academic diplomas were awarded to each of the various ethnic groups, it did announce that 1600 Puerto Ricans and 4200 blacks were enrolled in academic programs in the twelfth grade. By 1969, over 55 percent of the public school population was nonwhite, and 19 percent of the academic students was nonwhite. Not much progress, is it?

Even before they saw these figures, parents and students in every impoverished section of the city had been demanding an end to the general course. What is the point to going to school for twelve years, only to receive a worthless piece of paper at the end of that time? In late 1969 the board announced that it would discontinue the general track and the general diploma—as of 1973! And immediately the High School Principals Association objected. One of their spokesmen told the newspapers: "This will mean that general students will have to take thirteen units of study instead of nine and a half as at present, and for the first time they will have to take and pass either Regents or city-wide exams. This will result in far more failures and heightened dropout rates for this category of student." And once more the professional staff clearly demonstrated its lack of optimism or faith in the educability of the nonwhite poor and working-class students. Even if the policy is really adopted as promised, which rarely happens at the Board of Education, how can parents possibly believe that it will be implemented when the administrators who will be responsible for its success are the very men who so vigorously oppose its adoption?

This is precisely what is wrong with the high school curriculum. The staff and the administration simply do not believe that the majority of the student population can—or should—go on to college. Considering the sizable number of suspensions which occur in each high school every year, it is probable that principals do not even believe that most of the nonwhite students should be in high school.

About five years ago the Board of Education promised that it would convert to a comprehensive high school system. Thus, instead of some students going into vocational training and others into academic courses, all students would go to school together and would receive a basic education in their first two years and a more specialized program in their last two years of high school. The high school principals were opposed to this policy, although almost every important civic and professional organization in the country supported the idea. As a result, the entire high school construction program was bottlenecked. The staff at headquarters was paralyzed by the principals' opposition. No one was willing to decide whether to design comprehensive high schools or academic ones. Because of that internal staff debate, new high schools were not built on time and the old ones now have more than forty thousand excess students. Much of the curriculum, and everything else, is necessarily curtailed as students and teachers attempt to attend triple-session classes which start at seven in the morning and end at five in the evening. Newspaper editorial writers blame student demonstrators when protests take place over these incredible conditions. But who is really responsible for the overcrowded and turbulent situation in our high schools? The students who demonstrate against the conditions, or the board professionals who argued, procrastinated and caused them?

WHAT IS WRONG WITH
THE CURRICULUM

Too many children don't even learn how to read. We know our children are smart. We have watched them learn how to walk and talk. We have been amazed at how quickly they learn to climb trees without falling, skip rope without stopping, ride bikes without losing their balance. And yet, no sooner do they start school than many of them suddenly become stupid. Why? The sad truth is that the system simply does not expect children who live in poor communities to learn to read. Expecting nothing, they are not surprised when they get nothing. All teachers say that they want the children to learn how to read. But wanting is not good enough.

The school system does not try to find out why the children are not reading; it does not diagnose each child individually and decide what particular type of help he needs. "We don't have the time to help each child when we have a class of thirty children," teachers tell us. But how can they *not* take the time? Which is better? Twelve years of schooling which leave a child functionally illiterate, or a few weeks of teacher time devoted to finding out how a child learns, how he operates, what helps him, what he needs, so he can be taught how to read. It is this attitude of teachers—"Of course we care about the children, but there is simply not enough time to help everyone"—that has turned parents against teachers in so many parts of the city.

The grouping policy damages the children. The Board of Education states that each child should be worked "to his capacity." But there are plenty of scientists who say that a child's capacity is unlimited. Good teaching can raise a child's IQ by twenty points or more.

The Board of Education states that each child receives equal treatment in the schools. But the children who are assigned to the "top" classes receive the more experienced teachers and are taught a more enriched and varied curriculum. The board states that it does not discriminate among the children. But any visitor to a racially mixed school will soon find that the black and Puerto Rican children have been assigned to "slow" classes and that the majority of the students in the "bright" classes are white.

Most students are classified wrongly anyway. They are not divided according to ability to learn but, rather, according to the teacher's estimate of that ability—and nobody is allowed to question that teacher's judgment or appeal his decision.

Actually the grouping policy hurts all the children. In every school there is a top and a bottom. And the child at the "top" feels smug and pleased with himself while the child at the "bottom" knows he is a failure. My daughter, a sixth-grader, is in an IGC class. At her birthday party, we conducted a backward spelling bee. One complacent child commented, "Oh, you won't be able to stop me. I'm IGC." I couldn't believe my ears—and then I realized what grouping has done to that child and to her classmates. If you don't believe me, go visit predominantly white schools. The parent association newspaper is loaded with advertisements for tutorial services which will help the "slower" student pass crucial college examinations. If our notion of education includes the conviction that some children must fail so that others may pass, think how the parent and the child who do not make it must feel. Is that really the kind of schooling we want for our kids?

A double standard exists in our school system. High performance standards are set for the "successful" student and low or no standards are set for the others. In most instances, this means that the nonwhite student in the poverty communities gets the short end of the stick. Perhaps this story sums it up. When Martin Luther King died, the pupils in our local elementary school wrote compositions about him. One of our daughters was lucky enough to have her paper selected to be sent to the principal—a high honor. But first the teacher insisted that the paper be rewritten so it contained no spelling or grammatical errors. I remember how happily she labored over it and how proud she was when she finally turned in a "perfect paper."

Several weeks later I picked up the UFT newspaper and found that they had printed some letters which fifth-grade black students had written to Mrs. King. They were charming—but filled with mistakes. I was embarrassed for those children. How easy it would have been for the teacher to correct the letters before sending them in to be printed. Soon after, a teacher, who felt as I did, complained to the editor. "You may argue that the errors lend 'authenticity' to the letters," she wrote. "But they could be just as honest and just as compelling if written correctly." Now, I know about the many fine educators who are writing books which suggest that pupils should be encouraged to express themselves spontaneously and that correcting spelling and punctuation interferes with their creativity. Perhaps. But until our schools, colleges and employers accept bad spelling and bad grammar from white pupils in order to encourage their spontaneity, it is dead wrong—and racist—to accept such inferior work from black students.

When our children do not learn, the system blames the children and not itself. If I buy a washing machine which does not work, I complain to the store and they fix it or give me my money back. If many customers have similar trouble, the manufacturer will take the machine off the market. He knows he won't stay in business long if he blames the customer when his machine does not work. But in New York City the Board of Education stays in business no matter how many students do not learn. And the system shifts the responsibility for failure onto the shoulders of the students.

A few years ago the *Ladies Home Journal* published a list of the ten best elementary schools in the country. I wrote to them all, trying to find out the secret of their success. Each one had a different story but one common theme: They looked for methods that worked. If one kind of reading program failed, they tried another. If a child did not learn, the school blamed itself, and tried another approach. But not in New York. In our city, where two-thirds of our students cannot read, our faculty decides that it is the children who have been put together wrong, and that the children, not the teachers, need revision!

I was once a guest lecturer at a teacher-training institute at Hunter College. One teacher suggested that the reason Puerto Rican pupils do not learn is that they travel back and forth too much between the island and New York City. Another teacher agreed, and added, "But they lack real life experiences, too. Their parents never take them to museums or zoos or airports, where they can broaden their horizons." And the teachers simply did not see how contradictory these two criticisms were.

The Board of Education hides the facts—even from itself. A teacher once told me that even if someone discovered how to teach every first-grader to read Shakespeare, no one else in the system would ever find out about it. I think she is right.

It is extremely difficult for parents to obtain accurate, relevant and concise information about their schools. At best, data are buried in systemwide statistics which have no meaning for a parent who wants to know more about her particular school. The professionals somehow feel that comparisons between schools and districts are odious and should be avoided.

Even more incredible, however, is the fact that the principals themselves do not have the slightest idea what is going on. Parents attack the grouping policies; the principals defend them—but they never study them. Are parents correct when they say that the gifted classes have mostly white pupils? There is no Board of Education data on this. Are we correct when we charge that black children tend to be improperly labeled and put into slow classes? The Board of Education has never investigated this. Do most children who go into the third-grade gifted classes stay in top classes for the next nine years, and do most children who are classified "slow" in the third grade stay in the bottom for the next nine years? How much movement is there from one group to another? No one at the board knows because they have never wanted to look. They are comfortable with their assumptions and they don't want to study them, question them or debate them.

Many students tell us that the curriculum is no good because what the schools are teaching is not worth learning. They tell us that the school system is an inhuman system, that it teaches the children not to value themselves. I remember visiting a Lower East Side school where the principal was taking me around to visit classes. One math teacher was absolutely terrific, but as I was admiring the way he worked with the students, the principal leaned over and whispered, "Isn't he magnificent? He'll be an administrator soon. He's much too good to want to stay stuck inside a classroom much longer."

Students tell us that the schools teach them to be ashamed of their parents and their homes. I once heard a teacher admonish her class: "Intelligent people never read comic books," and I watched the boys whose fathers read comic books cringe with embarrassment.

Kids soon learn that schooling means boredom. They alphabetize spelling list after spelling list. They memorize one insignificant fact after another. They learn the same thing over and over again. American history is taught in the fourth grade, seventh grade and eleventh grade—and most schools spend twenty weeks on colonial America, barely touching the more recent years. When students ask to learn more about politics, religion and economics, they are told these aren't part of the "standard curriculum."

I know that all the reformers are saying that this kind of teaching is no good. I know that all the curriculum bulletins tell the teachers to teach the children how to think and not how to memorize. But these great ideas have simply not filtered down into the classrooms. Our five children have now had almost one hundred different teachers—of that number, only four of them did not teach in the rigidly standardized way.

Children learn that competition is important, marks are everything. Knowledge, if it is not going to be on a test, is worthless. A child who helps another is not cooperative, he is cheating. And our students are telling us that they have had enough of this kind of education.

Up until now, most parents have not given much thought to what is really supposed to be taught in our schools. We have never thought much about what the schools are *for*. Are schools a place where children should learn how to behave? how to read? to think? to follow orders? If school is a place where children learn how to get a decent job, that is not true for most black kids.

More white dropouts have better jobs today than black high-school graduates. The situation is changing? Maybe—but fast enough?

It seems to me that the one hope for basic curriculum reform is the notion of local control. Parents want different things for their children and they have different ideas about what a school should and should not teach. I believe that parents must be allowed to have a choice. And students must be allowed to have a choice. All schools should not offer the same curriculum, adjusted for some, enriched for others, making sense for none. Under a real decentralization policy, local areas would be free to determine what is a worthwhile curriculum for them—and test it out. As of now, however, there is no indication that such freedom will be given to communities.

I once attended an assembly at Douglas Junior High School in Harlem where James Baldwin was addressing the boys. He reminded them that German students who attended school in the days of the Third Reich could not learn how to become decent human beings within the public school system of that period. To receive a moral and dignified education, students had to drop out of those schools. He asked the Harlem boys whether that might not be the situation in New York City today. Sometimes I think it is.

Action Checklist for Parents

HOW TO HELP YOUR CHILD
DO BETTER IN SCHOOL

The schools often give us a list of things to do at home to help our children achieve in school. These instructions are all right for parents who have enough money and time to follow them.

But what if many of us cannot do what they tell us? Does that mean our children can't learn?

They tell us to make sure our children are fed and dressed properly, but what if we cannot afford milk and meat prices, or warm winter coats and shoes that fit?

They tell us to read to our children, but what if we have so much cooking and cleaning to do for our large families, we can't find much time to read?

They tell us to talk to our children, but what if we cannot speak much English, and when we try to talk to our children in Spanish, they interrupt us and say, "Mommy, the teacher said I must only speak English!"

They tell us to be sure each child has a private corner of his own to study, but what if we cannot get a larger apartment?

They tell us not to overburden our children with too much responsibility so they will have time to study and play, but what if our older ones have to work so we can buy food? Or what if they have to take care of our younger ones until we get home from work?

Draw up a list of demands for change.

Get together with some other parents who feel as you do and draw up a list of things you believe the school must do to help the children learn. For example, you might want to demand that:

√the school should open at seven in the morning to accommodate those parents who must leave for work early, and should serve a hot breakfast to children whose parents cannot afford all the proper food.

√the school should have a financial-assistance plan to help every parent who can't afford to buy adequate clothing.

√the school should have full-time medical and dental services so every child can have his health checked thoroughly.

√the school should provide after-school and evening study-help programs—and these programs should not merely be baby-sitting services.

√the school should hire more community people to give individual attention to those children who need it.

Present your demands to the staff.

After you draw up your own list of demands, take them to
the principal and the teachers in your school. Insist that the
school stop attacking the parents and start assuming responsibility for helping the community solve these problems.

Have the students retested.

You and other parents might organize a campaign to have
all children who have been labeled "slow" or retarded retested
by *non*-Board of Education specialists. Get a volunteer team of
doctors to check their eyes. Hundreds of "slow" children have
turned into geniuses overnight when they got eyeglasses. Insist
that all Spanish-speaking children be retested in Spanish.

Hold a meeting to discuss "emotional instability."

And demand that *non*-Board of Education psychologists or other
experts retest the children who are so labeled. Intellectually
gifted children are often "emotionally unstable." Schoolteachers
told his mother that Thomas Edison was "impossible."

Visit your school and check out your teachers.

Form a parent committee to visit the school. How many screaming, emotionally unstable *teachers* do you notice?

Find out what is meant by "cultural deprivation."

Meet with the teachers in your school and ask them to define
"cultural deprivation." As a result of this discussion, you may
want to demand that some of the teachers be retrained or removed. Ask them:

√If a child speaks Spanish and English (with an accent), but
   a teacher speaks only English, which one is culturally deprived?

√If a student talks about Garvey or Nyerere and a teacher

quotes Roosevelt and Churchill, which one is culturally deprived?

√If a teacher loves Irving Berlin, and a child sings *plenas* and *bombas*, which one is culturally deprived?

√If a teacher enjoys reading erotic novels with off-color language and a student enjoys using those words and talking about sex, which one is culturally deprived?

Help all the parents feel less guilty.

Organize a campaign in your community to help your fellow parents feel *less guilty*. Help them see that it is very possible that the real reason the children are not learning is that there is something wrong with the school and the teacher, and not necessarily with the home and the child.

Action Checklist for Parents

HOW TO MAKE SURE ALL THE CHILDREN LEARN TO READ

Find out how many children are not reading.

This is not as easy as it sounds. Many educators prefer to cover up the facts. You must be organized and persistent. You must insist upon precise and complete information. (At the end of this checklist there is a sample questionnaire which you may find helpful.) *You have a legal right to this information* (See State Education Law, Section 2116).

Beware of professional double-talk.

√If they start talking about "quartiles" and "means" and other fancy words, they are trying to hide something.

√Don't accept guesses. All information must be given to you accurately and in writing.

√If the principal says he does not know how many students are white or black in each program, he is not telling the truth. He receives reading scores for every child in the school. Without revealing names, he can easily tell you how many black students are on grade level or below, how many white, etc.

√If the staff protests that achievement tests are "unreliable," agree with them. *But* as long as the system uses these "unreliable" scores to decide who gets into the "top" classes, and who goes to college or the army, you must have the information.

√If your principal tells you that "norm" means half the children should score below grade level, tell him he is being ridiculous. Private schools would be ashamed if they only met national norms; many middle-class public schools have 100 percent of their pupils on or above norm. Your kids have to compete with those kids for jobs and college.

Ask your principal what he plans to do to improve the reading situation.

If he has refused to fill out the questionnaire or answer your questions accurately, he probably does not plan to do anything. Then you should immediately organize to have him removed for incompetence. (See Chapter 6 on how to remove a principal.)

If he does give you the information, ask him what his plans are. If you like what he tells you, organize support for his program. If you don't like what you hear, organize to get another principal.

How to judge whether your principal sincerely wants to improve reading.

√Does he want to change the children or the teachers?

√Does he want you to change your home or will he try to change the school?

√Does he work hard or does he just do a lot of complaining?

√Does he stay in his office or visit classes?

√Does he try to convince you that young children are not ready to learn, or does he go about getting them ready to learn?

√Does he keep defending the old basal-reader approach to reading, or is he trying a variety of new methods and programs? If he is experimenting, is he evaluating the results or ignoring them?

√Does he believe that 95 percent of the children can learn to read, or does he believe that most of the children are so deprived or disturbed that there is very little the school can do to help them?

√Does he help his teachers or find fault with them?

√Does he work with parents or manipulate them?

√Does he like the children or is he afraid of them?

√Does he welcome your interest or is he annoyed by it?

If you decide to give him a chance, prepare a report for other parents and the community.

Once you find out the facts about reading achievement in your school, don't keep them a secret. Even if you believe the principal is sincere about improving the school, all the parents have a right to know what is really happening and what is being done to improve things.

Issue report cards or progress reports regularly so the principal and the teachers know you are supporting them but are expecting results too.

When you see things you like, praise them and the teachers publicly. When you see things you don't like, make it public also. Invite other parents to join your watchdog committee. You may want to divide your committee so that first-grade parents are evaluating fifth-grade progress and fifth-grade parents are watching out for the first grade. In this way parents may feel more "protected" since they won't be evaluating their own child's teacher. But no matter how you do it, keep the staff and your neighbors fully informed at all times.

Call a community meeting, and discuss and set performance standards.

√What do you think is "satisfactory" performance?

√How will you measure success? Will you give your principal one term or two terms or three? Do you think every child should be on grade level inside of a year, or half the children or what?

√Don't expect your school to improve unless you help set the standards. What is "good" to a teacher may be "terrible" to a parent.

√How will you make sure you are not given false information? Sometimes the staff fakes the reading scores to cool the parents. Can you arrange for an impartial evaluation?

√Do you believe that success should be more than simply better reading scores? Ask your neighbors what they think makes a good school and set your educational goals and standards so you can hold your principal accountable.

Other steps to take:

If your school does not improve, go to your local school board and district superintendent. Demand that they hold the principal accountable for achieving results or get a new principal.

You may also want to take a committee of parents to the UFT to put pressure on the union to improve the performance of its teachers.

You may want to hire an attorney to sue in the courts or to appeal to the State Education Commissioner. Under State Education Law 3604, "proper instruction" must be given in every school. Under Regents Rule 28, state aid may be withdrawn from school districts who do not maintain an approved curriculum.

Release your findings to the press, your local elected leaders, the federal Department of Education, and anyone else you think may be helpful. Be sure you are always specific. Describe carefully what you have asked, and what you have found.

Beware of this danger: Principals will try to "buy off" the most articulate parents in your group by assigning their children to the top classes and best teachers, or offering to transfer them to a "better school." *Don't* attack parents who take advantage of this offer. Remember their children, too, have only one chance for an education. Find ways to include these parents in your committee so you can still work together.

SAMPLE QUESTIONNAIRE

PARENT SURVEY OF READING ACHIEVEMENT

SCHOOL _____   PRINCIPAL _____

<u>Ask these questions in every school:</u>

1. What reading achievement tests are given in this school? When is each test given? (Metropolitan Achievement? N.Y. State Pupil Evaluation Test? Others?)
2. How soon after the test is given are results available? How do you publicize the results to parents?
3. Do all the children receive the same version of each test, or are some given a "more difficult" version? If so, are the results averaged together or available separately?

4. Are some children not tested? If not, why
not? How many children were tested and how many
children were <u>not</u> tested in each grade for the
last test given in this school?

5. Are the children coached or prepared before
the tests? Are they given any practice taking
tests?

6. What is the national or state <u>norm</u> for each
test? How many children in this school scored on
grade level (norm) or above in the last test?
The year before that?

7. Are you satisfied with these results?

8. Does this school have any remedial-reading
or corrective-reading specialists? How many?
How many pupils need this type of help? How many
pupils are receiving help from such a specialist?
How many times a week? What are the results?

9. How were these specialists selected? What
courses did they have in reading methods? Where
did they teach before? Were they successful in
improving reading? How is their work evaluated
now?

10. What reading methods and materials are used
in this school? How many different programs or
methods? How long have they been in use? Why
were they selected? Were the teachers specially
trained to use these methods? How? By whom?
How many children are in each such program? How
are the results being measured and evaluated?

11. How do this school's achievement scores
compare with scores of other schools in this
community? other schools in this district?
other schools in the city? state? nation? How
does the school compare with the best private
schools in the nation?

12. Any other comments you wish to make?

ELEMENTARY SCHOOLS

1. Does this school have a pre-kindergarten
program? If not, why not? If yes, how many
children attend? How many are on a waiting list?
How long has the program been in existence? How
are the results evaluated? Has the program
helped the children learn to read? Explain.
2. How many children attend morning kindergarten? Afternoon kindergarten? How many
others are on a waiting list? Are the kindergarten children being taught to read? to
recognize letters? to count?
3. How many first-graders read at the end of
first grade? How many do not? If some do not,
why not?
4. Are children grouped according to reading
ability in this school? If so, what is the
ethnic composition of the total student body?
What percent of the nonwhite students are in the
top reading classes? What percent are in the
lowest reading classes?
5. Does this school have an IGC class? Does the
district have an IGC class? How many children
from this school attend such a class? What percent are black? Puerto Rican? Oriental? white?
What is the reading score which a pupil must
have in order to be in such a class? How are the
teachers selected for these classes?
6. Does this school have CRMD classes? Special
opportunity classes? Any other special classes
for "retarded," "disturbed" or "disruptive"
youngsters? How are these children selected for
these classes? What percent of these pupils are
nonwhite? How are the teachers selected for
these classes?
7. Do children have to read on grade level in
order to be promoted to the next grade? If not,

how many children who were promoted last year
were reading below grade level? How many who
were promoted read more than one year below
grade level? More than two years below? What
percent of these children were nonwhite?
8. Please give us the following information for
each class in this school:

____ the total number of children in each class
____ the number of black, Puerto Rican,
     Oriental and white children in each class
____ the number of white and nonwhite children
     who are reading below and above level in
     each class
____ the number of years of teaching experi-
     ence for each teacher of each class
____ which of these classes is on short time
     or double session

INTERMEDIATE AND JUNIOR HIGH SCHOOLS

1. What is the total number of students in the
school? What percent are black, Puerto Rican,
Oriental, and white?
2. Is the school on short-time or double
session? Are any classes?
3. How many official classes are reading on
grade level or above? How many nonwhite children
are in each of these classes?
4. Of the total student body, grade by grade,
how many are reading on grade level or above?
How many of these are nonwhite? How many are
reading below grade level? One year below? Two
or more years below? How many of these are
nonwhite?
5. How many children are taking a foreign
language in each grade? How many of these are
nonwhite? Is there a minimum reading score

requirement before a student is given a foreign language? If so, what?

6. How many ninth-grade pupils are taking algebra? How many of these are nonwhite? How many ninth-grade pupils are taking general math or business math? How many of these are non-white?

7. How many of the children scored above grade level in the last math achievement test given in this school? How many of the math teachers in this school are teaching without a math license?

8. Is there a Special Progress Class in this school? If so, how many children are in such a class in each grade? What are the reading requirements for this class? How many of the pupils in this class are nonwhite? If there is no such program in this school, why not?

9. Are there special classes for "retarded," "disturbed" or "disruptive" children in this school? If so, how many children are in such classes in each grade? On what basis are children placed in such a class? Who has tested them? How many of the pupils in these classes are nonwhite?

10. How many children were in your oldest grade last year? How many of them were white? Puerto Rican? black? Oriental? How many received a diploma? How many students were nonwhite? How many received a certificate? How many of these were nonwhite? How many of these were not promoted? How many of these were nonwhite? How many were simply transferred to high school because of their age, but did not receive either a diploma or certificate? How many of these were nonwhite? How many students dropped out? How many were suspended? How many of these were nonwhite?

HIGH SCHOOLS

ALL HIGH SCHOOLS

1. Does this school have special entrance requirements? Is one of these a minimum reading score? If so, what is it?
2. What is the total pupil population of this school? What percent of the student body is black? White? Puerto Rican? Oriental?
3. Do you have an honors program? If so, what percent of the honors students are nonwhite?
4. How overcrowded is this school?
5. What percent of the children drop out each year? What are you doing about this? How many of them are nonwhite?

ACADEMIC HIGH SCHOOLS

6. How many children are in the Academic Program? What percent of these are nonwhite? How many children received an academic diploma last year? What percent of these were nonwhite?
7. How many children are in the General Program? What percent of these are nonwhite? How many children received a general diploma last year? What percent of these were nonwhite?
8. How many of your high school graduates went to four-year colleges last year? Two-year colleges? What percent received scholarships? What percent of each category were nonwhite?

VOCATIONAL HIGH SCHOOLS

9. Do you have some courses which are more difficult than others? If so, which ones? Do these have an entrance requirement? What percent of the students in these special programs are nonwhite?

10. How many types of diplomas do you give?
How many students received each kind? Do any of
these prepare you for college? What percent of
the students who received this type of diploma
were nonwhite?

11. What follow-up records do you keep of your
students? How many go on to take additional
education after they graduate? How many go
directly to work? How many go into the army?
What kinds of jobs do your graduates get? For
example, if your school teaches carpentry, do the
students go into this type of work, and are they
accepted and considered well trained by the
unions?

3 · Compensatory Education and Curriculum Reform

CORRECTING INJUSTICE

Shortly after the Supreme Court ruled against segregation in Southern schools because it meant inferior education for blacks, critics pointed out that similar conditions existed in the North. Although our big cities did not mandate segregation, our housing patterns did. In New York City the Public Education Association issued a 1955 study which found that schools in minority neighborhoods were older, more overcrowded and more dilapidated than schools located in white communities. The predominantly black and Puerto Rican schools had larger classes; their teachers were less experienced; they were getting less money per pupil. And not surprisingly, the average eighth-grade student attending an all-black school was reading almost two years behind the average eighth-grade student in an all-white school!

During the next eight years the Board of Education initiated a series of "reforms" which it called compensatory programs— a term that was wholly inaccurate. Schools in the poorer non-white sections of the city had been getting less than their fair share of educational services. The bureaucracy announced that it would try to correct the inequity, but it did not call this new policy *equal education*, which is all it really was. The public was led to believe that the schools were trying to compensate for the shortcomings of the students, their families and their neighborhoods, but all the system was actually doing was attempting to compensate for its own educational negligence.

In 1963 the New York Urban League issued a follow-up report, thoroughly denouncing the board's ineffective program. Finding that little change or improvement had actually taken place, the study showed that the average black eighth-grade student was now *three and a half years* behind his white counterpart. Eight years of Board of Education "reform" had resulted only in retrogression.

During these years community pressure centered on school segregation. "Put our children in the same classroom with white children and those teachers will *have* to teach them," was the anguished, frantic demand of many black parents. But the system resisted all attempts to achieve integration. "We must upgrade the slum schools first, before we can integrate them," they told the parents. "And we don't have enough money to upgrade them."

Several citywide school boycotts were angrily and successfully organized. Everywhere in the country similar movements were growing. The ghettos had to be calmed down; the federal government responded: in 1964, antipoverty legislation was put through; in 1965, special funds were set aside to improve schools in poor neighborhoods. Money, the good old American solution for every problem, was now available. But that money was given to the same old system that had been unable to improve or integrate the schools. The professionals were convinced that they could do the job; given the necessary funds, they were sure they could educate the underachieving poor and nonwhite students.

Have they succeeded? Has the aid to education which has come from the federal government helped to improve our schools? How do these various "compensatory" programs work? How can parents improve them?

The Legislation—and How It Works

The Elementary and Secondary Education Act (ESEA) has many different sections; these sections are called Titles. Title I, for example, provides money to improve schools in poor neighborhoods. Title II provides money for books and teaching materials for schools in all types of neighborhoods. Title IV helps pay for research projects, Title VII gives money for bilingual education.

In addition to ESEA, the Congress has passed many other laws which are supposed to help improve the schools. For example, the Educational Professions Development Act is designed to upgrade teacher training; the Economic Opportunity Act funds pre-school, Head Start and follow-through programs; the Manpower Development and Training Act adds on-the-job training to classroom courses. In New York, the state legislature has also appropriated additional funds to upgrade the schools. The State Urban Education Program, authorized in 1968, is supposed to provide improved educational opportunity to "underachieving persons in poor neighborhoods."

These programs add up to a lot of money. In 1969, for example, the New York City Board of Education received $92 million from Title I; and $54 million from State Urban Aid. Thus the Board of Education received $146 million from Washington and Albany to help upgrade the quality of education being offered to students who live in poverty. Although the system has not released any precise data which would tell the public how many pupils are eligible for these programs, over 400,000 New York City students receive free lunch. Assuming, therefore, that these are the eligible pupils, $146 million divided up among them comes to $370 per child. The board normally spends about $1400 annually per child. *Now it has almost $1800 to spend annually on each poor child!* What happens to all that money?

Let us examine the Title I appropriation, since it is the largest amount of federal education money received by the city and since it is specifically labeled to help the poor.

1. Congress gives the money to the Office of Education, which is part of the Department of Health, Education and Wel-

fare in Washington, D.C. That division decides how much money each state will get on the basis of the number of poor children in each state. It uses its own standards for defining "poor."

2. The federal government does not give the money directly to the schools in the poor communities. Instead, it deals with the state governments. In New York the money is sent to the State Department of Education in Albany, which passes it on to the New York City Board of Education, after first reviewing and approving its proposals for using the money.

3. The city Board of Education decides how Title I funds will be distributed throughout the city. The central board decides what proportion of the funds will be kept at headquarters to run centrally developed programs. It decides what proportion of the funds will be allocated to the local districts to run locally developed programs, for which it establishes guidelines and regulations.

4. The federal legislation requires school systems to work cooperatively with local antipoverty agencies. In New York City the central programs are discussed with the citywide Council Against Poverty but final authority and decision-making powers remain with the Board of Education. Decentralized programs are discussed by local antipoverty councils, parents and other community groups, but these organizations also do not have any official veto power. Decisions remain with the district superintendent, who submits all proposals to central headquarters. *Final* decisions are made at central headquarters, which submits the proposals it likes best to the state, which approves them without too many questions.

Thus, Title I funds must seep through federal and state and city bureaucracies before they get to the local community. And Title I funds may not be used unless they meet the approval of officialdom at all of these levels.

Under decentralization* this procedure will not change very radically. Community boards will still not be able to apply for these funds directly. They will have to continue to submit proposals to the city chancellor and the city Board of Education.

---

* Decentralization Law, Section 2590 (i-14).

The city board will continue to decide how these funds will be apportioned among the districts, and the city board will continue to negotiate union contracts and establish curriculum policies which will, in fact, determine exactly how the Title I funds are spent locally.

WHAT IS WRONG WITH COMPENSATORY EDUCATION

The laws which authorize federal and state funds to help educate the poor are not good because the money is given to that same system which has miseducated the children for so long. The rules of that system forbid the local districts to really run their own programs. Each district is forced to follow UFT contract procedures, Board of Education by-laws, central staff directives, and state and federal guidelines. It is this very rigidity which caused the system to fail the children, and particularly the poor children, in the first place.

The truth is that New York City has an outdated educational system. *In such a system all the children are deprived and disadvantaged.* Experiments in search of improvement will have a chance for success only if they are carried on outside of that system, or in competition with it. As long as the Board of Education controls the funds, controls the curriculum and controls the personnel policies, nothing will change. Here are some specific illustrations of what I mean.

—Some parents suggest store-front schools, but regulations specify that the programs must take place in regular school facilities. The parents persist. Another regulation is unearthed which will permit the use of store-fronts. Central Headquarters staff finds the facilities "below standard requirements" and will not approve them.

—An antipoverty committee recommends that more community people be hired to work in the schools as paraprofessionals. But the city board has signed a contract with the UFT raising teachers' salaries, and there is not enough money to do both. The local request is denied.

—A Puerto Rican parent association is anxious to obtain more bilingual staff in its school. It suggests that the principal pay a bonus to all the teachers who learn Spanish. City regulations and the union contract forbid this.

—Some teachers want to experiment with new books and materials. It takes ten months before most of the books are approved and another six months before the material arrives. By then, the special program is over.

—A community group proposes an increase in guidance and testing personnel for its district. Their proposal is approved. But the people they want for the program are not certified by the Board of Examiners. Since the union contract provides that seniority must be considered, one of the old-time certified but unqualified guidance teachers is promoted to supervise the program.

The net result? There has been very little academic improvement. The pupils in poor sections of the city are still not learning how to read; they are still dropping out; they are still not achieving anything very worthwhile in school.

The thick, wordy, hard-to-find evaluations confirm this conclusion. The programs are described in great detail. Entire chapters are devoted to changes in staff morale, student attendance and social adjustment, and parent behavior. And then comes a few pages or a short section devoted to reading scores. The data is devastating. The More Effective Schools, one of the costliest of the compensatory programs, has been analyzed and evaluated in dozens of reports. Even the most optimistic shows that pupils who have been in this program for two years are still considerably below grade level. It is horrifying that several thousand dollars extra per pupil per year are spent to gain such minimal results.

But the system is not horrified, for it does not really expect the compensatory programs to result in improved achievement scores. The Board of Education has a quite different set of objectives: "to create more positive attitudes toward school"; "to help the pupils maintain emotional and social stability"; "to provide corrective services to pupils." The Board of Education and the parents really have two different sets of goals. The parents want the children to learn; the system wants the children to change.

Most of the compensatory programs developed by the New York City Board of Education are based upon the assumption that the *child* has deficiencies which must be overcome: his family background is deficient, his language is deficient, his cultural heritage is deficient, his life experiences are deficient.

The professionals never wonder whether the school system's methods and techniques are deficient. "We have successfully educated the middle-class child," they say. "If we can make the poor child more like the middle-class child, we will be able to educate him successfully too." The entire approach is fallacious and bound to fail. As a parent of middle-class youngsters, I do not believe that the school system has been so successful with our children. Thousands of middle-class families who move away from the city or who send their children to private schools agree with me. It is the system that must change—not the children. It is the teachers and their methods and their attitudes and their philosophies that must change. And the only chance there is for this to happen is that the schools be removed from the system, so that, free from the suffocating restrictions, standards, and regulations devised by an irrelevant, remote bureaucracy, the parents, teachers and communities can try to educate the children.

Action Checklist for Parents

HOW TO USE STATE AND
FEDERAL FUNDS TO FORCE
EDUCATIONAL REFORM
IN YOUR SCHOOL

Form a committee of parents and teachers who are dissatisfied with the educational program in your school or district.

√Include *students* on your committee if you are trying to change a junior or senior high school. Such a group may already have started in your community. If you really want to make your school more useful and responsive to the students, begin by talking with and *listening* to them.

√You may want to include *community representatives*. Parents who have put their children in parochial or private schools will have many good ideas. Local organizations with experience in developing programs and getting funds will also have much to contribute.

Do not permit yourselves to be rushed by an artificially imposed time schedule.

√Many parents are invited by principals to "write a proposal" within five days or less. Don't be trapped by this kind of situation. It will take you a number of months to think through and write a legitimate proposal for educational change.

Don't let yourselves be manipulated or used.

√Most state and federal programs require "community participation." Often a professional will develop a program and then call in the parent association president or a group of community residents, fast-talk them, ask a few questions, and then claim he has involved and consulted with the community. Beware of this trap.

Stretch your imagination—go see other schools and programs.

Those of us who only know the city school system tend to think small. When we are asked what changes we want, we often answer: "One more guidance counselor" or "A phone in the medical office." These services may be important but they should be paid for out of the regular city budget. State, federal and foundation funds should be used to bring about reform.

√As a first step your committee must open its eyes to all the many possible alternatives. Don't just read about them. Don't let one member of your committee persuade you that he has the answer. Go see for yourself the different approaches before you make any decisions.

√Visit *public schools* in other sections of the city; *parochial* schools and *private* schools; *suburban* schools; and schools in *other cities* not too far from you. There are a number of suggestions in the Appendix.

√In your travels talk to people who are for the program *and* people who are against the program. Talk to parents, educators and students. If evaluations are available, get copies. Be sure that they are not written by the same people who have developed the program.

You will need to have time and money if you want to make these visits.

√Do not set up a schedule of visits to experimental programs, and then find out that only one or two of your committee members can afford to go. It must be made possible for many parents and teachers to make these trips so that they can learn together, and see for themselves all the many possibilities.

√This will take *time*. Most of the programs funded by the federal and state government have not produced much change in pupil achievement. So don't be in a hurry to write a program just to get the money. You want to develop a proposal which will really help the children.

√These trips will cost *money*. Ocean Hill-Brownsville was able to get foundation funds to pay for a trip to England for several parents and teachers to visit the Infant Schools. You don't have to go to England, but even if you are only looking at schools in your own city and suburbs, this will mean that your committee members must take time off from jobs and families; they will have to get some financial remuneration for this or most of them simply will not be able to go. You may want to insist that your local school board set aside "program development" funds for this purpose; or you may want to contact a foundation or ask the federal or state Department of Education for a "planning grant."

After your committee has investigated many different alternatives, begin to develop your own proposal.

√Don't try to fit your program to the particular legislation. First write the program you want, and then find out what legislation might provide the funding.

√Don't let them tell you, "It can't be done." Write down what you know needs to be done; then insist that your local board and the other authorities find ways to make it happen. For example, some parents asked the district superintendents to use part of their Title I funds to provide clothing and food for the poorest children; the parents were told that the law would not permit this use of the funds. The parents persisted and the Board of Education began to find a loophole in the law in order to meet their request. Remember that for every rule there is an exception.

√Be sure your committee is clear about its objectives. What do you want to accomplish? What is your most important priority? One group of parents and teachers agreed that their school needed more community people working in the school. But the parents wanted them to give individual help to the children; the teachers wanted them to do clerical work. After the program was funded, the parents were shocked to see how the new staff was misused.

Once you have written your proposal, you will have to get it approved.

√Beware of deals which end up diluting your proposal, and making it worthless. One group of parents wanted to do away with homogeneous grouping in their school; the principal was willing to approve their program if they left the "top" class out of the plan. They agreed for the sake of getting his approval, but were very sorry later, for this ruined the entire program.

√*Beware of modifications* which completely change your proposal. For example, one Title I committee wrote a program which called for paraprofessionals. Headquarters added, "with high school diplomas," and thus eliminated a large number of the most qualified applicants.

Organize community support for your proposal.

This is a crucial step. If you want to protect the integrity of your proposal, you will have to fight many battles. You will need a strong, determined group to support you.

Protect and fight for your proposal all the way to the top—trust no one to do this for you.

Don't let your district superintendent dilute or modify it. Insist that he respect the work of your committee. Some district superintendents have set up "advisory committees" to screen the various proposals. If your elected local school board legitimately represents you, there may be no need for additional advisory committees. If your local board does not represent you, then demand that your community elect its own review committee and that this committee should not be hand-picked by the district superintendent and should have decision-making, not merely advisory, powers.

Be prepared to go further, whether or not your district head approves your plan. IS 201 and its governing board approved a specific program which called for the use of state urban aid funds. The central Board of Education requested fourteen copies of the plan and promptly lost *all* of them. The parents took the proposal directly to Albany, and stayed there while it was reviewed so that no revisions would be made without their approval.

If you do not stay close to your proposal all the way, you will probably not recognize it when it is finally approved and returned to you for implementation.

Once your program is approved, insist on the right to screen and hire all personnel.

Some community groups are organized so strongly that the district superintendent permits them to screen paraprofessional staff before they are hired for these programs. But this really is not enough.

You will achieve no educational reform unless you have a teaching and supervisory staff which is dedicated and skillful, a staff which believes in the program and believes in the children. No paper examination will be able to determine these qualifications.

You will also want to be able to hold the staff accountable for the success of the program. Unless they agree to this, you will not want them to have responsibility for implementing it.

Insist on the right to select your own evaluation agency.

One bilingual program was running very smoothly until the parents received a questionnaire which asked the most personal types of questions. An uproar ensued and the program was almost destroyed.

Evaluators who are hired by the Board of Education owe their allegiance to the board; evaluators hired by you will have to treat you as clients and will have to make their findings available to you.

Many of the evaluation agencies include Board of Education supervisors on their board and staff. They can hardly be called "objective." Your committee has the right to determine the evaluator's qualifications and the methods to be used in evaluating the program.

Your committee will have to keep close watch on the implementation of the program.

The best programs can get totally destroyed by obstacles placed in the way by headquarters. For example, one Bronx experimental bilingual school is in a shaky situation because the central headquarters will not provide efficient bus service. Thus, even when you think you have won, you may be fooling yourself. Ocean Hill-Brownsville was allowed to hire personnel which had not been approved by the Board of Examiners; the only trouble was, the Board of Education never processed their pay checks.

If your program does not get approved, or if it is approved but is beset with bottlenecks and barriers, organize a loud campaign of protest.

√Go see your legislators, as well as state, regional and federal bureau directors. Remember the further away you get from Board of Education headquarters, the more likely you are to find people who do not have a stake in preserving the existing system and who might be willing to help you. (See the Appendix for a list of agencies you can write to.)

√Describe in detail how the Board of Education is subverting your program. Describe how the money is being wasted as long as the system controls it.

√Always take delegations of parents (and students) with you.

√You may want to call a press conference.

√Initiate lawsuits to contest the illegal use of state and federal funds, which are supposed to be used to bring about change with the involvement of the community—they are not supposed to be used to underwrite regular school programs.

√You may want to organize some demonstrations to highlight what is happening. You may have to interfere with the operation of the board's compensatory programs if the system persists in ignoring your requests.

Join forces with other communities who have had similar problems.

Demand that the federal and state legislation be changed so that aid to education can go directly to the community districts and not through the central Board of Education.

There are many parents who believe that these funds should be given out in the same way as antipoverty funds. That is, if a community group or a church or a nonprofit organization wants to run a school, they should be able to apply for funds directly and do so.

As long as the bureaucracy is given the money, very little educational reform will really be possible. As soon as the parents in your community see that clearly, organize to repeal the current procedure and get the changes you want.

4 · Hiring the Staff

HOW TEACHERS TURN SOUR

The school system destroys many many children. But, just as important, it destroys most teachers. It does not care about teachers any more than it cares about children. It does not help teachers achieve any more than it helps children achieve. The system engulfs the hopeful, energetic, often idealistic young teachers. It rapidly dehumanizes them, squeezing and twisting warmth and compassion out of them, turning them into non-thinking machines which obey and enforce automatically the rules and regulations of the bureaucracy. How does this happen? Perhaps these stories will illustrate the process.

The young man is in his senior year of college. He doesn't want to go into the army. He likes working with people. He wants to help children. Perhaps he should try teaching, his friends suggest. He takes an examination at the Board of Education. He meets a principal who offers him a job in his school. But when he arrives at that school in September he finds out that headquarters had not marked his exam and that therefore he had no file number.

He is told that he cannot start working without a file number. He must take an emergency examination, which will be marked immediately; he will have to pay a second fee to take that exam. He does all these things, and this time he is assigned to an entirely different school, late in the term, where no one knows him and, more important, where he knows no one either. (Meanwhile, of course, in his former school a class has gone uncovered and he is sorely missed.)

The new principal seems glad to see him. She assigns him to Class 5–5. She doesn't tell him that this is one of the most "difficult" classes in the school and that none of her regular teachers would accept that assignment. She wishes him luck and leaves him with the children. He tries. How hard he tries! His classroom is chaotic. The workbooks have not arrived so the children have to copy everything off the board. He is constantly interrupted by messages from the office or announcements over the loudspeaker. He cannot get the children to sit still. He attends his first staff meeting, hoping that he will learn something about the school, hoping he will find out where to go for help. But all they discuss are fire-drill regulations and lunchroom procedures. He learns to keep his classroom door closed so the rest of the school won't hear the shouting. Four weeks after he has started, the principal comes by to congratulate him for the good job he is doing. She has heard no noise, so she tells him he is doing well. Is that all she wanted? Rather grimly he decides, "If I can't teach them, at least I can keep them quiet." And the rest of the year he learns how to control his class. At the end of the term, his probationary report is marked "Satisfactory," and he breathes a sigh of relief. "Maybe," he decides, "that is all we can do for *those* children."

Who is the villain in that story? The young man, the principal, or the system? Was the principal herself once like that young man, and also defeated and reshaped by the system?

When my oldest daughter was in first grade, she was miraculously assigned to a class of only twenty-two pupils. It was the first time class size was so small in our school and the teachers were elated. All four first grades had small registers. Then, after six weeks of this unexpected luck, the boom descended. A directive came from headquarters that there had been a mistake; one of the teachers would have to be reassigned to another school. The four classes must become three classes—of twenty-nine children each. I remember visiting my daughter's teacher soon after this change had taken place. She looked at me sadly and said, "For the first time I knew that I could teach every single child to read by the end of the year. I was really reaching them. And now I know exactly which seven children will be lost this year; and I know that if they don't make it in first grade, they may never get a second chance."

How awful that teacher must feel. If she wants to keep her sanity, standing in front of her class each day, she will begin to harden slowly. She will push far into the back of her mind the memory of those six weeks when she was able to reach those children, and gradually she will begin to blame the children when they don't learn. As they become restless or bored, as they begin to misbehave or disrupt, as they try in many ways to remind her that they are there, she will become increasingly annoyed with them. Antisocial, immature, uneducable—she will find some label to pin on the children and thus excuse herself for not teaching them.

The system produces inhuman situations like this every day of the year. That story concerned a first-grade class. Here is one about some high school students. Eighty-six students attending Benjamin Franklin High School (in Spanish-speaking East Harlem) staged a demonstration protesting their assignment to a "Spanish" teacher who was licensed to teach world geography and didn't speak, read or write one word of Spanish. The principal told the newspapers that he "regretted the situation" but there was no "qualified" teacher available. Of course, many Cuban, Puerto Rican and other Spanish-speaking educators had applied for the position, but they had failed the Board of Examiners exam, which is given partly in English. Since the Spanish-speaking candidates didn't "qualify," the Board assigned a "qualified" teacher who spoke no Spanish. We have read a great deal in the newspapers about student, parent and community groups who protest insensitive and ridiculous bureaucratic decisions. But what happens to the teachers and supervisors who are responsible for carrying out these rules?

If they want to stay sane they do one of three things. They damn the system and quit. Or they organize the students, visit parents, arouse the community about the conditions—and then they are labeled troublemakers. The principal seeks to get them transferred, or the rest of the staff isolates them, and soon they become a frantic, angry small faction with very little influence in the school as a whole. It takes a very strong, determined teacher to join such a group, to speak out despite the consequences. The third alternative is the one most teachers choose. They learn to close their eyes to what is happening around them. They learn not to get involved, to mind their own business, to pretend that everything is fine. They bend with the system; and as they do so, they don't even notice how much they are changing.

As a teacher learns to "adjust to the needs of the system" he is given better and better assignments. He learns how to control his class; he submits careful lesson plans; he becomes a flexible, "reasonable," cooperative member of the faculty. He is a "successful" young teacher. He is told that he is "too good" to remain tied to a classroom. He is urged to prepare for the next promotional examination.

By the time he becomes an assistant principal or a principal, he is almost entirely a creature of the system. He has studied what the system wanted him to study so that he can qualify for the examination. He follows the system's regulations no matter what they mean to the community. He has never learned to think in terms of community needs because it has not been necessary to do so. He looks to his superiors in the system for promotions, for salary increases, for recognition. The community and the parents are just side issues. He doesn't need them at all; he simply learns, in most cases, to manipulate them, or ignore them.

Most supervisors are completely unaware of their own insensitivity. They do the most awful things, and they don't even realize the impact of their actions. Some parents found that a pool room was opening across the street from a Harlem school. The Department of Licenses had asked the principal whether he was opposed to this facility operating near his school, and he replied that he saw no harm in it. He never consulted the parents and he was visibly surprised to find out that the community was insulted by his action.

A first-grade child wandered out of a South Bronx schoolyard at lunchtime and was lost. The frantic parent came into the principal's office at 3 P.M. and asked him to help her locate the child. When the principal started to put on his hat and coat to go home at three fifteen, even though the child had not yet been found, he couldn't understand why the mother screamed at him and burst into tears. He simply thought she was "over-emotional."

After a small fire broke out in the girls' locker room, the junior high school assistant principal asked the students who had witnessed it to write down statements. He promised them that since this was the first time they had ever been "in trouble," they would not be punished if they would admit what had happened. When the police investigated the fire the assistant principal showed them the statements, and the girls were immediately arrested. Although he went to court and asked that the charges be dismissed, he couldn't understand the parents' anger when the Police Department told him that the matter was now out of the school's hands and in the court's.

I could go on and on telling these stories. But the point has been made, I hope. Recently a high school student, writing in an underground newspaper, commented on the phenomenon:

> Our school is run by mummies. The principal creeps around looking busy and self-assured with his two assistants respectfully following in his wake. What does this man mean in the universe? I don't think he's human. Sometimes I think he's a God damn android. Like all principals. They seem manufactured in a secret laboratory in the basement of the Board of Education by a mad scientist and turned loose in the schools. Where else do they come from?

What is the answer? I believe that the solution lies in giving communities and parents much more power in hiring, evaluating and removing staff. Then the staff would have to look to the community for support, for recognition, for promotion—and not to the system. This should help to humanize the staff, for the parents and the community are concerned about human problems, not paper regulations.

Would this mean that black parents would choose black educators, and white parents would choose white ones? At first I believe this would happen. There is at present only a handful of nonwhite supervisors in our school system and this is deeply resented in the black and Puerto Rican community. There are many black and Puerto Rican educators who qualify for supervisory jobs by state standards, but who have not been approved by the New York City Board of Examiners. Many parents believe that the Board of Examiners system is unfair and discriminatory. They want a chance to determine for themselves a candidate's qualifications, and they want a chance to evaluate a candidate's ability by watching him perform on the job.

But, more important, race *is* a factor in our schools and anyone who denies it is a fool. In some parts of New York City the race or cultural background of an administrator will significantly affect the kind of job he will be able to do. In some neighborhoods being black or Puerto Rican or Chinese must be recognized as a personal asset and is, among others, a decisive qualification for the position.

But as parents and communities are given a responsible role in the hiring process, they will look at race as one criterion, but they will also be looking for many other qualities. When you attend ghetto meetings, you will often hear parents talk about a particular black professional as a "Negro." This is meant to be an insult: although the man is dark-skinned, he acts like a white man. When parents clamor for more black educators, they mean black as an attitude, not a color. Recently in Philadelphia the students were asked to name the two best black principals in the system. They named a white and a black man. For them, and for many of us, a "black man" is a man who cares, who gives a damn about kids, has sensitivity and is concerned about human relationships. These qualities cannot be identified by an "objective" paper examination. These qualities don't belong to any one race. These qualities belong to some special people—and these people have been systematically eliminated from our school system hierarchy up to now.

Parents want the opportunity to interview and hire personnel so that they can seek out men and women of all races and backgrounds who have this special sensitivity, this concern for their children. Then we think we would have a real chance to change our school system.

Action Checklist for Parents

HOW TO TAKE AN INVENTORY OF THE STAFF SITUATION IN YOUR SCHOOL

If you already know what is wrong with personnel conditions in your school, and if your parent group is agreed on the changes it desires, skip this section and start taking action to get what you want. However, if you simply know that the quality of teaching needs improvement, but you are not exactly sure what should be done first, take an inventory of the staff situation in your school. In the process you will learn a great deal and you will get many action ideas. And you will be amazed at the amount of activity which is stimulated when parents begin to ask questions.

From a parent committee for staff improvement.

Include, if you think it appropriate, student, community and teacher representatives.

Draw up a list of the information you want about the staff and present this to your principal.

(A number of suggestions are itemized at the end of this checklist.) If your principal will not or cannot give you precise and accurate answers, insist that a questionnaire be mimeographed and distributed to the entire staff. Even though the Board of Education does not bother to collect this kind of information, it ought to be available to the public. School employees are paid from public funds; it is perfectly proper for such data to be readily obtainable for study by parent-citizen groups who want to improve the quality of the staff.

As you gather information, keep asking: Why are things done this way?

You not only have to know what is happening, but you must also find out why it is happening that way. Then you will be able to focus your action campaign effectively.

Also keep asking: Do the current procedures work well?

For all the children? Or for only some of them? Which children get short-changed the most? Which teachers are given the most difficult assignments? Is there an alternative way to assign the staff? What else might be tried?

WARNING: Professionals usually have glib answers for our questions, taken directly out of the pedagogical rule books: "The regulations tell us to do it this way." If this inventory is to help you make plans for effective action, listen carefully to the answers you are given, but don't accept anybody's word. You must visit classes and see for yourself. Then draw your own conclusions.

Publicize the information you collect.

Let your entire community know the questions you asked and the answers you got. If you did not get adequate answers, organize a strong protest.

Analyze and discuss the implications of the information, and decide on the action you will take next.

What do you think must get attention first?

√In some schools the most crucial need will center on getting an adequate principal.

√In other schools, you may be satisfied with your principal, but you may want to correct an ethnic imbalance of your staff.

√You may decide that your staff is generally inexperienced, hard-working and underpaid. You will need to organize a fight to control your school payroll.

√You may find that your staff is dedicated but inadequately prepared. You will want to address your efforts toward developing an effective retraining program.

√You may feel that your school needs more community people on the staff; then you might concentrate on getting an increased allocation of paraprofessionals with a career-ladder program so that they may become teachers in your school within two or three years.

Whatever you do, don't spend forever gathering facts and analyzing the problem. It is important to take an inventory in order to get started, but you must dig in somewhere and *take action*. And just remember, rules are made to be broken.

QUESTIONS TO ASK WHEN YOU TAKE AN INVENTORY OF THE STAFF SITUATION

How big is the staff?

√How many *supervisors* and how many *teachers* are there in your school?

√What is the *pupil-teacher ratio*? You get this number by dividing the total pupil enrollment in your school by the

total number of teachers, including specialists. In some of
the better suburban school systems, the pupil-teacher ratio
is 15 to 1.

What is the average class size?

It sometimes happens that your schools will have a pupil-
teacher ratio of twenty children for every teacher, but an average
class size of twenty-eight. This is because many teachers are not
assigned to a classroom. The union contract stipulates that every
teacher must be relieved for a certain number of periods each
week, and some of the teachers on your staff are rotated for this
purpose. Your school may also have a number of specialists who
do not necessarily have special training but who do not have
responsibility for a specific class. Some parents believe that, in
the elementary schools, it would be better not to have so many
specialists, but instead to have smaller classes. However, in very
overcrowded schools this is not always possible. What do you
think would be best for your school?

How many classes are very large? Very small?

Your average class size may be twenty-eight, but some of
your classes may be as large as thirty-five. Why? Are some
teachers better able to handle larger classes than others? If so,
why? Sometimes teachers are persuaded to take a class of "difficult" children by the principal's promise to keep that class
especially small. If this is done in your school, how well does it
work? Does it benefit only the teacher or does it help the children?
When some classes are quite small, it makes it necessary for other
classes to become rather large. Do the parents or teachers in those
classes resent this? If so, how does this resentment affect the
children and teachers in the smaller classes?

Where does the staff live?

Many parent groups find it helpful to have a complete list of
staff home addresses and phone numbers. In New York City the

civil list, which is available in the municipal library, across the street from City Hall in the Municipal Building, includes home addresses and current salary for each regularly appointed teacher and supervisor. This book can be consulted by any member of the public. However, it is valuable to ask your principal to prepare a complete list of home addresses and phone numbers for you, since the civil list does not include phone numbers or information on substitutes. If his staff is reluctant to make this information available to parents, find out why. If they are afraid of being "bothered" at home, you had better decide what to do about it.

There are a number of parents who believe that teachers who live in the immediate community have a better relationship with their pupils. Is this true in your school? Are the teachers who live nearby involved in neighborhood activities? Are they absent or late as much as the rest of the staff? Some parents feel that a salary increase should be offered as an incentive to attract teachers into moving into the school community. What do you think?

What kind of preparation and training did your staff receive?

In New York City 90 percent of the teachers attended a college in the metropolitan area; 60 percent graduated from the City University. Does your school follow this same pattern? Is there any difference between the staff members who were trained in nearby schools and those who attended school further away?

√Some groups believe that the *teachers colleges* do not train teachers very well. Lately many teachers are coming into our schools who have not taken traditional pedagogical courses, but who are liberal-arts graduates; many of these are men who have become teachers partly to avoid the draft, and partly because the pay is now better. How does this work in your school? Do you feel that teachers who have attended traditional teachers colleges are better prepared than the others? Or do you feel that the liberal-arts "generalists" are more responsive and less conservative? (And what proportion of your staff are men? Do you feel that having more men teachers is an advantage?)

√Many schools are now employing teacher assistants or school aides, sometimes called *paraprofessionals*. What is their educational background and training? What kinds of work are they assigned to do? Many parents believe that these men and women, even though they do not have formal advanced education, have better rapport with the students than many teachers do and are able to command greater respect and discipline from the students. What do you think?

√How many staff members, at all levels, are now taking additional training? Teachers receive salary increases when they take additional courses. Sometimes the Board of Education offers special "in-service" human relations courses, which help the teachers who take them to earn additional salaries. Many teachers believe that these courses are a waste of time. What courses are being taken by your staff now? Try to visit some of them. Do you feel these will help them become better teachers?

√If your school has a number of Spanish-speaking or Chinese-speaking children, what percent of your staff is *bilingual*? Some parents believe that it would be worthwhile to offer a financial incentive to all bilingual teachers. What do you think?

√The UFT contract stipulates that *new* teachers must take some on-the-job training. Can you get to see some of this? Do you think it is working successfully in your school or district? What kind of training do you think the new—and experienced—teachers need in your school? Sensitivity Training? Training in reading methods? Or what else?

√In some cities, paraprofessionals are paid for a five-day week, but they are released one or two days to go to college, working toward a degree, and being paid while they study. Those school systems believe that it pays to invest money in training a nucleus of *potential teachers*. How many paraprofessionals in your school are taking additional training? Who pays for it? Do they get any reimbursement for this? How many are interested in further education? What is standing in their way?

What proportion of the teachers and supervisors are black, Puerto Rican or Chinese?

√For many years the Board of Education refused to collect information on the ethnic breakdown of the school staff. However, in recent years parents in many neighborhoods have begun to insist that such data is significant and relevant. In a recent staff ethnic census, the board found that 10 percent of its teachers and 4 percent of its licensed supervisors were nonwhite. In contrast, about one-third of the school aides and lunchroom workers were black and Puerto Rican. What is the pupil ethnic breakdown in your school? To what extent does your staff reflect this mixture? How do the students and the parents feel about this?

√How many of the nonwhite supervisors are in acting positions only? How do they feel about this?

√Ask your nonwhite staff members to tell you what they think about the Board of Examiners and the examination system. Ask the same question of your white staff. Get a copy of a recent examination (they are on file in the municipal library). Do you think that the examination process produces qualified staff?

What proportion of the staff are experienced?

√When a teacher is first appointed to a job in the school system, he is on *probation* for three years. What percentage of the teachers in your school are on probation? (Thirty-five percent of all the teachers in New York City are on probation. How does your school compare?)

√After completing a "successful" probationary period, a teacher is given *tenure*. How many teachers are on tenure in your school? (Citywide, 65 percent of all teachers are on tenure.)

—Many teachers are *regular substitutes*. They do not want to take the regular teachers' exam, but they are assigned to one class for the entire term. What percent of your staff are regular substitutes? (Forty percent of all New York City teachers are regular subs.) How many of these have more than five years' experience? Why have they chosen to remain subs? (This category is now being phased out by the board.)

√In New York, teachers are paid higher salaries if they have more *experience*, because the system operates under the assumption that more experienced teachers are more effective teachers. Of the regularly appointed teachers in the system 72 percent have more than five years of teaching experience. However, this figure varies enormously from one district to another. In middle-class areas almost 90 percent of the staff has had this much experience. In some poverty areas there are schools whose "experience index" is 15 percent. What percent of the teachers in your school have five years of experience or more? Do you feel that the more experienced teachers are better, more effective teachers? Do you think they should *automatically* be paid higher salaries than less experienced teachers?

√Certain teaching assignments are considered more "desirable" than others. Under the UFT contract, teachers with more experience have *seniority* and are given first preference for the more coveted jobs. Therefore in many schools the least experienced teachers are assigned to the most "difficult" low-status classes; the most experienced teachers are frequently not assigned to a particular class at all. How does this work in your school? What percent of the *classroom* teachers have five years' experience or more? Are the least experienced teachers assigned the most "difficult" classes? If you have specialists in reading, guidance, etc., are they especially qualified for these assignments, or do teachers simply hold them because they have seniority?

√How much experience have your supervisors had? Did your principal have experience as a principal before coming to your school? If so, where? What about your assistant principals? In a study conducted by United Bronx Parents it was found that 70 percent of the black and Puerto Rican schools were assigned inexperienced principals compared with *none* in the white schools.

What salaries are being paid to your staff?

√When a school system pays more money to staff members who perform better, it is called *merit pay*. New York City does not have merit pay. Instead, teachers are paid on the basis of the number of years they have worked and studied, regardless of performance on the job. What does your staff think of merit pay? Which teachers support it and which ones oppose it? Why?

√In New York City all personnel is paid from one central pool of money. Because some schools have more experienced teachers than others, some schools have a higher payroll and a higher average teacher salary than others. During 1970 teachers earned salaries ranging from $7950 to $15,500. How many teachers are earning the *lowest* salary in your school? How many are earning the highest? Are there some teachers who you think should be earning more even though they are less experienced? Are there some who you think are earning too much? What is the average teacher salary in your school? (In some "better" districts in the city, the average teacher salary is as high as $14,000; in some "poorer" neighborhoods it is as low as $8500.)

√Elementary principals earn about $23,000 a year. Junior high principals earn approximately $24,000, and senior high principals earn $28,000. District superintendents get $32,000. (Assistant principals receive $20,000 a year.) What are the supervisors actually earning in your school? Sometimes the regularly appointed supervisor is on leave or on an assignment to headquarters. Although he is never in your school, he usually continues to draw his pay from your school's payroll. When this happens, the position is "temporarily" filled with an *acting supervisor*. Sometimes an acting supervisor draws a full salary; sometimes he does not. Is this happening with any of the staff in your school? How many acting supervisors do you have? How do they feel about this designation? Does it affect their morale or performance?

√What are the nonprofessionals paid in your school? School secretaries? Clerks? School aides? Teacher assistants? Lunchroom personnel? Custodial personnel? Do you think the salaries are distributed equitably? (A teacher earns more in one hour than a paraprofessional earns in one day.)

√If you had control of the payroll for your school, how do you think you would distribute it? What jobs do you think deserve more money than they now demand? On what bases do you think a staff member should receive an increase? Do you think it is fair that some schools have higher payrolls than others with the same number of pupils?

How stable is your staff? Can you measure staff morale?

The Board of Education talks a great deal about pupil mobility, pupil absenteeism, lack of pupil motivation. Parents are equally concerned about these factors as they relate to staff.

√How many of your teachers and supervisors are new to the school this term? What percentage of these are also inexperienced and new to the system? How many of them are experienced and have transferred into your school from some other school?

√What is the *average daily absence of your staff?* The Board of Education does not compile this data, but several years ago Bank Street College discovered that over 25 percent of the staff were absent daily in one Harlem junior high school.

√How many teachers are assigned to your school each fall who refuse the assignment? The board estimates that about 13 percent of all teachers refuse their assignment, and in "less advantaged" schools this percentage goes up to 20 percent. What happens in your school?

√Did any classes in your school remain uncovered last year? This means that no regular teacher could be found to take the assignment and the classes had to be filled from day to day with per diem subs. The Board of Education claims that this does not happen any more. Does it?

√A good way to measure staff satisfaction in your school is to find out how many teachers are trying to get into or out of your school. How many teachers and supervisors applied for a *transfer* out of your school last year? How many received one? Where did they go? The union contract states that no more than 5 percent may transfer out of any one school in any one year; and that first choice goes to teachers with the most seniority. And one year of teaching in a "special-service" school counts as two years in terms of seniority. How many teachers have asked to be assigned to your school? If you have an able principal, chances are there is a waiting list of both new and experienced teachers who want to come to your school, even if you are located in a so-called "undesirable" neighborhood.

√How many teachers are teaching *out of license* (that is, out of their licensed fields) in your school? This is a problem particularly in secondary schools; you can easily judge how adequate your junior high school staff is, for example, if none of your math teachers are licensed to teach math.

√How many of your teachers and supervisors have taken exams for higher positions? How many want to move out of the jobs they now have? How many expect to retire or take a leave of absence in the next term or so? Sometimes personnel leave in order to go to a school in a "better" neighborhood. The United Bronx Parents study found that 70 percent of the principals leaving Brooklyn elementary schools were simply transferring to other elementary schools in "better" neighborhoods. However, sometimes a good staff member is forced to leave in order to earn more money. If you find that some of your best staff people are taking promotional exams in order to be in a spot where they can earn more money, then your parent action might well be to try to keep them in your school—at the salary they deserve!

Who evaluates staff performance? How is it done?

√Probationary teachers are supposed to be evaluated several times a year. Who is responsible for doing it in your school? Ask to see a copy of the form which is used. If your principal refuses, it can be obtained from Bureau of Teachers Records, 65 Court Street, Form OP11 and OP11A.) Do you think the method is adequate?

√Has the principal ever denied a satisfactory rating to a probationary teacher in your school? If yes, how many times and why? If no, why not?

√Tenured teachers are evaluated only once a year, and a very simple form (OP 151) is used for this. Get a copy when you get the other forms. Do you think this is adequate? Has your principal ever given a tenured teacher an unsatisfactory rating? If so, what happened? If not, why not? The current UFT contract promises that a new procedure for evaluating teacher performance will be worked out. Talk to the union chairman in your school. What does he think of the current procedure? How does he feel about changing it? Why?

√What is done in your school to improve teacher performance? Do inexperienced teachers have lighter teaching loads so they can observe experienced teachers at work?

√How are your principals and assistant principals rated? By whom? Ask your district superintendent about this. Get copies of the forms which are used (OP98 and OP98A). Do you think these are adequate? Has a probationary supervisor ever received an unsatisfactory rating in your district? On what grounds? What happened to him?

√How are tenured supervisors evaluated? How often? How often are they found unsatisfactory? Have they ever been brought up on charges in your district? If so, what happened? If not, why? Are you satisfied with this procedure?

√Some Harlem parents have suggested a civilian review board for teachers. Ocean Hill-Brownsville has recommended that a committee of parents and teachers be formed in each district to work out a sensible method for teacher evaluation. What do you think about these ideas? How do you think staff should be evaluated? By whom? How often? What do you think are appropriate grounds for dismissal?

HOW TEACHERS ARE CURRENTLY RECRUITED AND HIRED

The Regulations

If you want to become a teacher in New York City, you must first pass an examination given by the Board of Examiners.

Only Buffalo and New York City require a Board of Examiners test. In the rest of New York State, if an applicant has the State Education Department *Teacher's certificate,* no further examination is necessary. The New York State Education Department has one of the toughest certification requirements in the country. If a candidate has successfully graduated from a five-year accredited teachers college or if he has a liberal-arts college degree and has completed, in addition, thirty hours of postgraduate study, he is eligible to receive a permanent teacher's certificate. However, this is not good enough for New York City. Here, no matter how many other certificates he has, no matter how many other tests he has passed, no matter how many years he has taught anywhere else, anyone who wants to teach in the New York City school system *must* take and pass the Board of Examiners examination.*

Over the past fifteen years more than half a dozen government-sponsored studies have recommended the abolition of the Board of Examiners; these studies have found that the exams do not identify the best people and only serve to keep many good people out of the system. Nevertheless, the supervisors in New York City have been able to organize strong campaigns to retain the Board of Examiners. Even under decentralization this remains a most formidable part of the hiring process.

* Decentralization Law, Section 2590 (ii-4).

The Board of Examiners Procedure. First a candidate applies to the Bureau of Staff Recruitment in the Division of Personnel at the Board of Education. He is given a job application and an outline of the license requirements for the particular position he wants.

He then arranges to take a Board of Examiners test. Sometimes he has a wait of several months for the particular test to be given. The exam consists of several parts; a written test is given on one day, and an interview or oral test is usually given on another day. If he passes both of these, he must come back a third time to take a physical and be fingerprinted.

WHAT IS WRONG WITH
THE PROCEDURE

If the applicant is not sure whether he wants to teach math or science, and feels equipped to teach both, he will have to take a separate test for each subject on two different days. If he wants to teach in either a junior or senior high school, he must take two different tests, one for each. When all the tests have been taken, he may then be assigned to teach out of license anyway. If a young teacher has decided to come to teach in New York City because a particular principal has observed her and wants her in his school, she still must apply through central headquarters, and even if she passes all the tests, she may be assigned to some other school or district entirely.

Difference in Procedure Between New York City and Other Communities. In other parts of the state or the nation, a teacher is not faced with all of this red tape. If a teacher has a state teacher's certificate or has passed a National Teachers Examination, this is usually considered sufficient to qualify her for the job. In New York City, under the Decentralization Law* some

* Section 2590 (j-5).

schools with very low reading scores will be "eligible" to recruit teachers from among those who have passed the National Teachers Examination, but even these candidates will have to pass an additional qualifying Board of Examiners test.

In other towns the principal or supervisor who needs new teachers visits many campuses each spring, interviews the most promising candidates, checks their references, arranges for them to spend a day visiting the schools in the district, and signs them up as fast as he can. The probationary period—the first few years of teaching—is considered to be the best time for weeding out the duds. Good principals in other school systems have found that the best way to identify a good teacher is through on-the-job performance, with real live children, and not through paper-and-pencil examinations.

Thus the better school systems go out and look for candidates; and after they find them, they make it easy for them to get a job. New York City does not have any such aggressive recruitment policy. Although we now have a division in the Department of Personnel which travels around the country and solicits applications for teaching jobs, this is still an underfinanced, overly centralized operation. Individual principals and district superintendents simply do not go out and personally interview and recruit staff members, as is the custom in almost every smaller city or town.

Now that New York City offers one of the highest salary and fringe-benefit arrangements in the country, it should be much easier to find staff; we should also be attracting experienced teachers bored with suburban schools; but many teachers do not want to submit themselves to the degrading impersonal procedures of the Board of Examiners.

Many systems throughout the country will decide that they want a particular person on their staff, even if he hasn't completed all the necessary prerequisites. Such candidates are offered temporary, conditional or emergency certificates, and their supervisor will make an arrangement with a nearby college to assist them in completing the necessary academic requirements while they are already at work in a school where they are needed. New York City has no such flexibility. Recently New York announced a new campaign: it would recruit Spanish-speaking educators from Puerto Rico. Many applicants came to New York City for the program, but once they arrived, they did not meet all the Board of Examiners requirements, even though they had been teaching successfully in Puerto Rican schools for many years. They were told they could work as teacher *assistants* at $2.50 an hour while they took additional courses. Since most of these people were men with families, they obviously could not afford to do this, and they returned to the island, completely discouraged by the New York City system. Other towns would have made arrangements to pay them full teaching salaries while they taught during the day and took the necessary credits at night.

Thus in our town the examination system and the many regulations which are approved by the central board and the city chancellor seriously interfere with the teacher-recruitment process. Even if a local board recruits its own staff, all their candidates must still go downtown and be reexamined, reinterviewed, and reprocessed by central headquarters. If we were getting wonderful teachers as a result of this complicated system we could say New York City has very high standards. But the truth is that all New York City has are very high barriers which keep people with fresh ideas and sensitive attitudes out of our schools.

Action Checklist for Parents

HOW TO RECRUIT AND HIRE
GOOD TEACHERS

Force your local school board to set up its own teacher-recruitment and teacher-selection procedure. Make certain that many parents are involved in this process. If the law compels us to send our children to school, it must give us the right to have something to say about who will teach our children.

Whenever parents ask a principal to get rid of a very poor teacher, we are invariably told, "There is a teacher shortage, if I let him go, where will I get another?" There is not a shortage of teachers any longer, especially with the new salary scales. There is an *oversupply* of bureaucratic red tape which acts to discourage the best, most innovative and independent teachers from applying to our schools. Therefore, even if you develop a good recruitment program, that is not good enough. You must be prepared to follow through and watch-dog the entire hiring procedure to make absolutely sure that the teacher applicants whom you interview and want to hire actually get hired and assigned to your school or district.

The recruitment process and how parents can make it work.

√Get your local board to prepare an attractive inexpensive brochure, describing conditions in your district, your community and your schools. Make sure the brochure tells potential teachers why your neighborhood will be a good place to work in, how your community is different from the anonymous, cold big-city atmosphere which prevails at 110 Livingston Street. Every self-respecting community can find a whole list of reasons to promote the special qualities of its neighborhood.

√In February or March of each year, your local superintendent should know approximately how many new teachers he will need the following fall; he should also know which specialists are in particularly short supply in your district.

√Mail your brochure and a covering letter to as many colleges and schools of education as you can. Be sure to contact black colleges in the South and schools in Puerto Rico. Don't forget to include smaller Midwestern and Far Western colleges, which have many graduates who are anxious to come to New York City to live and teach, particularly if a friendly welcoming hand is extended to them. You will find a complete list of colleges in *Barron's Profiles of American Colleges,* or other similar directories in the public library or book stores.

√Don't rely on the central Board of Education to do your recruiting for you, but take advantage of their offices and use them if you wish. Hundreds of college students visit the Bureau of Teacher Recruitment in Room 612 at 110 Livingston Street, especially during the spring vacation. Try to get your brochures into that office. Speak privately to some of the staff who work in that office; tell them to steer candidates who need personal assistance, but who have good qualifications, directly to you. You might even want to put one of your committee members in that office waiting room so you can talk to the candidates on the spot.

√Place ads in the major magazines and newspapers which specialize in advertising teacher openings. Study the ads other school systems are running. You may have a parent or resident in your district who could design a small, inexpensive, but forceful, attention-getting ad. *The Week in Review* in the Sunday *New York Times*, *Saturday Review*, *Grade Teacher*, *School Management* are all good magazines. And don't neglect special media such as *El Diario*, *La Prensa*, *Amsterdam News* and *Ebony*.

√Contact some employment agencies which specialize in teacher placement. If you are particularly anxious to recruit black or Spanish personnel, contact the Urban League and the Puerto Rican Forum for a list of agencies which might help you.

√Talk up your personnel needs to every friend and relative you have. Search out teachers who want to leave their current jobs in private, parochial and suburban schools. Almost every parent in your district knows someone who knows someone who knows an outstanding teacher who, with the right kind of inducement, might like to come to your district to teach. If your entire community gets into the recruitment act, you will be amazed at how many candidates you can dig up.

√Send a recruitment team from your district to some of the college campuses in March or April. This committee should include a parent or two, a teacher, a supervisor, and possibly even a high school student from your district. Community control is a hot issue. Most school systems only send professionals to do the recruitment; if you send a parent-professional team, it will not only be newsworthy but it will also help you attract the type of candidates who are interested in teaching in a district where the parents are really involved.

Where will the money come from for this recruitment campaign?

√Each local board is supposed to submit a budget annually. Be sure a substantial amount is set aside for teacher recruitment if this is a major need in your district.

√The central Board of Education spends about $200,000 a year on teacher recruitment. The latest union contract has provided for half a million dollars in additional funds for this purpose. Insist that all of this money be decentralized for effective use.

√Raise money locally for this important process. You must obtain teachers who are loyal to your district; you must use every community resource to raise money so you can do an effective job of staff recruitment. Perhaps the parent associations, local churches or lodges will help raise funds for this program.

√If you map out a creative and strong campaign, you might try one or two foundations to help underwrite the cost. The public library has a directory of all private foundations with brief descriptions of the kinds of things they finance.

The interview process: How parents can help.

√If you locate some promising candidates who are either at college or are now teaching in towns which are some distance away, it would be costly to require them to come to your district for additional screening. You will want to establish a procedure so your recruitment team may interview and hire the best candidates on the spot.

√Occasionally the Board of Examiners sends out a traveling team to give their examination out of town. If you are going to observe Board of Examiners procedures, arrange for them to accompany you and examine and approve your candidates at this time. Never allow the Board of Examiners to interview your applicants unless several members of your community team are present. *Never, never, never* expose your teachers to the central bureaucracy unguarded or unprotected.

√If your candidates hold a New York State teacher's certificate or have passed the National Teachers Examination, but the Board of Examiners sets up additional hurdles, you must insist that these artificial barriers be removed. Expose the obstacles publicly and noisily. Let the newspapers, your elected officials and the Board of Education all know exactly how the examiners are preventing you from hiring the teachers you need. Once, a particularly enterprising Puerto Rican principal found a marvelous teacher, who flunked the test because she spoke too softly. He coached her to scream, called in the newspapers, and the publicity forced the Board of Examiners to give the test again. That time she passed.

√Don't permit unnecessary delays. One of the main reasons we lose teachers in New York City is that the administrative process delays and delays, and people who need jobs can't wait that long for a definite commitment. *Sign up those who you feel qualify and pledge that your local board will have a job for them in the fall.* You, and not they, must then deal with the red tape.

√Some of the best applicants will have problems which will require extra attention. They may be missing a few credits or need help in finding housing; some might need financial assistance in order to move. Good school systems have a particular staff member assigned to ease all such problems for the new staff members. Be prepared to do the same.

√The crucial factor in selecting teachers has very little to do with official qualifications. You are looking for qualities which may be more important to you than the absence of a few required courses. Therefore you will have to insist on some flexibility so that you can hire certain candidates and permit them to finish their formal academic preparation on the job. There are many precedents for this type of procedure. At one point the Board of Education did permit "Certificates of Competency" to be issued to teachers who did not meet the regular requirements, but the UFT has been fighting hard to get this exception withdrawn. In Ocean Hill the local board insisted that local professionals interview and examine candidates for a particular state program. If you are organized and persistent, you should be able to win this fight.

What questions should be asked in the interview?

Whether you interview on the spot or arrange for candidates to come and be interviewed in your district, your committee will have to decide what kinds of questions it wants to ask. The chairman of the IS 201 governing board made this statement concerning their interviewing procedure:

> In our community we want teachers who respect our kids and we want to pick them . . . They say how can the parents interview teachers for hiring? Well, the parents have feelings, sensitivity, call it what you want, it's there . . . We know that if a teacher has a license he passes as somebody that's qualified. That isn't what we're interested in. It goes deeper than that. We ask: Is he willing to teach? What does he really think about black kids? And we watch *how* he answers. That's how we interview.

Parents must not allow themselves to be ashamed of the intangible sixth sense which they bring to the interviewing process. Every personnel manager understands what this means. Here are some questions which parents have used. Develop your own list.

√Why did you choose to go into teaching?

√How long do you plan to teach here?

√What would you do if you found some students smoking in a washroom?

√What would you do if you found your money missing when you got ready to leave school at the end of the day?

√How many of your students do you think should go to college?

√Would you rather teach slow learners or advanced students?

√How would you motivate your students?

√Why do you think so many black students drop out of high school?

√Why do you want to teach in this district?

√Why do you think so many Puerto Rican students have difficulty learning to read?

√How do you expect to be evaluated?

Who should do the interviewing?

In Ocean Hill and IS 201 a screening panel of teachers, parents, supervisors and community representatives was set up to interview the candidates. This committee included but was not limited to governing board members. They scheduled several interviews each evening, spending about half an hour or longer with each applicant.

One suburban school district arranges for all candidates to teach a practice lesson, to eat lunch with some students and conduct an informal discussion, and finally a committee of teachers and parents officially interviews every applicant.

Develop your own procedure, and perfect it as you try it out.

HOW SUPERVISORS ARE CURRENTLY RECRUITED AND HIRED

The Regulations

DISTRICT SUPERINTENDENT

The local school board may hire the district superintendent by contract for not less than two and not more than four years at a salary to be fixed within the budget allocation.* However, the

* Decentralization Law, Section 2690 (e-1).

city chancellor sets the educational and experience requirements for this position. The central Board of Education sets the salary.

The city may not set standards which are lower than state requirements. The State Education Department requires all candidates for district superintendency to be graduates of a college approved by the Commissioner of Education, to have completed sixty hours of certain graduate courses, and to have five years of teaching and/or supervisory experience in public schools. Generally, in the past, the city has required extensive teaching *and* supervisory experience for this position, above the state requirements.

The Board of Examiners does *not* give an examination for this position.

PRINCIPAL

The local school board may appoint all principals as long as it follows regulations set by central headquarters *and* the State Education Department.*

The state requires that every principal must have a B.A. degree, plus thirty additional credits in certain courses in administration.

New York City requires, in addition to the above, that every principal have four years of teaching experience and two years as a licensed supervisor (usually assistant principal). (At this writing, the central board has proposed modifying these requirements slightly, but the Council of Supervisory Associations has vigorously opposed any change.)

Thus a New York City candidate for principalship must pass state requirements, city requirements, *and* he must also pass a special examination given by the Board of Examiners. Once this exam is given, all the candidates who pass it have their names placed on a list. No new exam may be given until all the people on the list have been assigned a position as principal. Until recently, local school boards were required to interview and select from the top three names of the list. This is no longer necessary. The lists are now "qualifying," which means that each local board may select any candidate from any place on the list.

* Decentralization Law, Section 2690 (e-2).

ASSISTANT PRINCIPAL

As with principals, the local board may appoint assistant principals, define their duties and fix their salaries, as long as central regulations are followed.*

The chancellor may set educational and experience requirements for this position, which may not be less than state requirements, but may be more.

In New York State an assistant principal is required to hold a B.A. degree, plus thirty additional hours of graduate study. In New York City the Board of Education requires three years of teaching experience in addition to the degree and graduate study.

The Board of Examiners gives an examination to all candidates for assistant principal, and a qualifying list is drawn up. These lists remain valid for four to eight years, and no other exam may be given until all the candidates whose names are on it are given positions.

WHAT IS WRONG WITH
THE PROCEDURE

This highly complicated procedure might be worthwhile if it produced skillful, sensitive supervisors, but the low achievement level of New York City pupils indicates that most of the administrators who do pass the tests do not necessarily know how to do a good job.

Not only are standards and examinations often irrelevant but they tend to act as barriers, screening out many black and Puerto Rican candidates. In our system of nine hundred schools, where 35 percent of our students are blacks and 23 percent are Puerto Ricans, only one regularly licensed principal is Puerto Rican and only nine are black. About thirty-three blacks and four

---

* Decentralization Law, Section 2590 (e-1).

Puerto Ricans, lacking regular licenses, serve as acting heads of schools in our city. Without licenses they cannot acquire tenure as principals, can be replaced more easily and may be paid less. Most (and maybe all) of these men and women meet New York State requirements, but they fall short of the experience requirements set up by the New York City Board of Education.

In fact, the regulations operate to impede the promotion of the more independent applicant, no matter what his race. One of the few white principals who had developed black community support was denied a district superintendency by central authorities because he lacked a required course in community relations. It was only when an enraged community organized and exposed this preposterous technicality that it was waived and his appointment approved.

Although supervisors are required to have previous experience, there is no stipulation that such experience be *successful*. Actually, there are many instances where successful acting principals have been denied principalships because they could not pass the paper examination. When a principal leaves, the parents may want an experienced assistant principal or teacher promoted on the spot. They have watched him perform on the job, and have respect for his obvious ability. But if he is not on the "list," the parents are out of luck—unless they are willing to fight and fight hard. This particular problem has come up again and again in Puerto Rican and black communities where it is doubly aggravating because the candidate "qualified" by the city is usually white, inexperienced, and completely foreign to the neighborhood, and the community choice is a nonwhite, long-time area resident, with many years of service in that particular school.

Local boards are often stymied by another technicality: A principal goes on terminal leave or is transferred to headquarters. However, he continues to receive his pay from his former school, often for a year or longer. During all that time, his position can only be filled by an acting supervisor, who has second-class status. Absurd? Of course. But this is no joke to the parents in Morrisania, which has one of the highest staff-turnover rates in the city, and which recently lost two top candidates for principalships because they refused to accept positions under these conditions.

Although the 1969 Decentralization Law states that each district may set up its own operating budget, parents will really have to fight if they want to pay someone more than the city board has authorized. At present the city fixes supervisory pay rates at a certain percentage over teachers' salaries. Districts which are about to lose some of their best principals might want to offer them a salary increase to induce them to stay, but local boards do not have this power and parents will have to organize and demonstrate very forcefully if they want to see this change come about.

Because the law is so ambiguous, local boards will be faced with many roadblocks if they are serious about tackling the problem of hiring their own school administrators. For example, when Local Board 6 wanted to hire a particular man for principal at JHS 52 in Inwood, the central board objected; it simply removed JHS 52 from District 6, appointed the principal whom headquarters wanted, and a week later, "returned" the school to the district. This has been repeated at several districts throughout the city. Local School Board 2 selected its district superintendent, but the central board decided it needed him to do a job elsewhere; it transferred him out from under the local board's jurisdiction and that was that.

It is important to note that local boards may hire their district superintendent on a two- to four-year contract; but they may not do the same with principals or assistant principals. Now the advantage of a contract, as most suburban towns will testify, is that if the supervisor does not work out in the job, the contract is not renewed when it expires, and embarrassment is minimized. Even where a suburban supervisor is offered tenure rights, he must first serve a satisfactory probationary period in that town, even if he had years of tenure in his former community. After all, each school system has a different notion of satisfactory performance. But in New York City, if a local district wishes to hire someone who had been working elsewhere in the city and he had earned his tenure there, it must accept his tenure status automatically.

For all these reasons it is difficult if not impossible to get top-notch men to administer our schools. The examination system, and the red tape, insure a perpetual supply of second-rate people. Parents will have to insist that they won't play the game by these rules if they want to get supervisors whom they can trust to do a good job, and whom they can hold accountable.

Action Checklist for Parents

HOW TO RECRUIT AND HIRE GOOD SUPERVISORS

Work to abolish the Board of Examiners.

Join with other parents and pressure for the abolition of the Board of Examiners system. More than half a dozen major studies have recommended this during the past ten years, but the supervisors have effectively organized and resisted all change. Even if the law remains on the books, however, there is plenty you can do to get around it.

Demand that the community be involved in the selection process.

When a vacancy occurs in your district or in your school, make sure your local school board involves parents and the community in the entire selection process. It should set up a parent-student-community personnel committee to assist in recruiting, interviewing and selecting the new supervisor.

√Your local board must consult with the parents before it takes any action. Do not permit them to use you merely to ratify their choice.

√A personnel committee does not have to be small. It is more important that it include a wide spectrum of groups and factions so that the person who is finally selected has a broad range of support. It should include parents, students, teachers, paraprofessionals, supervisors, and community representatives.

√You may want to permit your local board to appoint the members of this screening committee, or you may prefer that the board allow each group to select its own representatives. (Parents select parent members, teachers select teachers, etc.)

√A combination of methods is also possible, with some members of the committee selected by the various groups and some additional ones appointed by the local school board.

Discuss the selection process publicly.

The choice of a district superintendent, principal, etc., *is a political and educational choice*. It is perfectly proper for a broad spectrum of the community to participate in this process.

An educator who lacks the trust of the community will not be able to do a job. Several years ago the UFT proposed that teachers elect their principal. This idea is not really outlandish; it just needs expansion to include all the essential groups—parents, students, and others—without whose support he cannot do a job.

The composition of the screening panel should be ratified at a public meeting of the local school board and the public should be invited to discuss interviewing and selection procedures.

Additional nominations should be accepted. Many parents and teachers will probably want to discuss the qualifications they believe a candidate should have. However, many other parents will become impatient with theoretical discussion. They are anxious to get down to interviewing flesh-and-blood applicants. So discuss criteria and procedures, but don't confine yourselves too narrowly too soon.

Advertise the vacancy.

Advertise the vacancy as broadly as you can; encourage many candidates to apply.

√See suggestions for recruiting applicants in the checklist "How to Hire Good Teachers."

√Notify everyone who is on the appropriate Board of Examiners list, but it is certainly not necessary to confine yourself to that list. (Even if you think the list contains some good candidates, you should give yourself an opportunity to compare.)

√Be sure to announce the opening to staff members who now work in your district. It is good for morale when successful teachers and supervisors interested in a promotion are encouraged to stay within the district. Some towns think this is very important and give extra credit to local applicants. (But other towns want fresh blood, and look outside their system too.)

Develop an interviewing procedure.

√—In some towns the local superintendent does the preliminary screening. Then only five or ten "finalists" are seen by the personnel screening committee. But your committee may not want to do this and may prefer to interview everyone who applies.

√Don't settle for less than five or ten applicants to interview. If less than that have applied, *stop* and look at what you are doing. Either you have not announced the opening in enough places; or you are not paying enough, or your timing is wrong, or word has gone around that the central board does not want you to fill the job and will fight the appointment of anyone you select. If this happens, stop interviewing and start organizing to get the money or time or power you need to fill the job properly.

√Every community has its own interviewing procedure, and they vary enormously. Some are rather gentle; others believe that the interview is the time to put lots of stress on the applicant. One excellent supervisor told me, "The harder the questions got, the tougher they made the interview, the more I knew I wanted the job." One system interviews everybody separately, and then, when they are down to six or seven finalists, schedules a public debate between the candidates to see who does the best.

As I write this I can hear some New York City parents saying, "That can never happen here." I don't believe it. *If* you strip the recruitment process away from central headquarters regulations, and *if* you show the applicant that you intend to provide an aggressive and articulate parent body to support him in his fight to improve the schools, I am convinced we will get some wonderful people who want to apply for these jobs. And *if* the supervisor is the most important person for the schools, isn't it worth this fight?

What questions should be asked in the interview?

Develop a list of questions to ask the applicants. Here are some to start you thinking:

- √What do you think makes an outstanding school?
- √Have you ever been involved in marking a tenured teacher unsatisfactory?
- √What would you do to maintain discipline among the students?
- √What would you do if you found out the students were using drugs?
- √What do you think is the main reason black kids so often drop out?
- √What do you think about bilingual education?
- √How would you improve teacher performance?
- √What would you do about a teacher who drinks?
- √What do you think is the role of the parents in a school?
- √If there is another strike, what would you do?
- √Will you be moving into the district? Where do your children go to school?

Be sure to visit the school your candidates come from.

After you have narrowed down your choice to two or three candidates, go see the schools where they are currently working.

This is the only way to find out if a candidate acts as well as he talks.

√Poke around and ask questions. Talk to students, teachers parents, the custodian.

√Take more than one member of the committee to do this. Be sure at least one parent goes on this trip, even if it is several hundred miles of traveling.

Fight for the appointment of the candidate you want.

√Do not submit three names to headquarters and let them choose. That is a weak position. Choose your person and stick with him. If he is not on the "list" insist that an exception be made. Words like waiver, variance, provisional, temporary, experimental, emergency, acting, were all invented to cover this type of situation.

√If your committee has been composed of a broad spectrum of school and community groups, you will have the strength to push for the man you want for the job.

√Your local board has the authority to hire its own lawyers. Undoubtedly you will get involved in some legal maneuvering if you are determined to select your own staff.

√You may have to organize sit-ins, picket lines and other types of demonstrations. At one time, after Newark parents successfully did this, that Board of Education suspended all existing lists and appointed nineteen blacks to supervisory positions. The New Jersey State Education Commissioner upheld this decision, ruling that local boards could violate agreements with teacher organizations for the "public good."

√If you are faced with a charge that you are "racist" because the candidate you have chosen is a particular color, don't be afraid to take up the battle. In some communities the race or cultural background of an administrator will significantly affect the kind of job he will be able to do. In some areas, being black or Puerto Rican or Chinese must be recognized as an asset and a decisive qualification, *among others*, for the position.

Settle community differences privately.

If there is disagreement within your community over this hiring process, and if some parents believe that educators must be selected by professionals, and other parents believe they must be selected by parents, then talk this out and work out a procedure which would give both ideas a chance.

Each district will have several vacancies a year. Perhaps the local school board can agree that half of these will be filled in conventional ways, through the list, and half of these will be filled by community selection, and then the results and the achievements of the various men can be compared.

Don't get bogged down in fighting each other. The education of our children is too important. The bureaucrats at headquarters who oppose change want us to keep busy criticizing and fighting among ourselves. Learn to compromise within your community; learn to try out a variety of approaches so you won't have to compromise when you begin to fight the downtown officials! REMEMBER: Power is never given away. It must be taken. Parents must force their local boards to hire the type of supervisors the schools must have. If our children must go to school, we parents must have the right to help select the people who run those schools.

5·Improving the Staff

HOW PERSONNEL IS CURRENTLY EVALUATED

What is a good teacher? What qualities and characteristics are found in a good principal? The New York City Board of Education does not seem to know, for nowhere has it ever listed any specific performance standards which must be met by its staff. "Rating" is generally considered to be a nasty word; during their first three years in a position, called the probationary period, teachers and supervisors are evaluated by their immediate superiors, but after that, only a superficial one-word rating is sent to headquarters. According to the *New York Times*, during a recent five-year period, out of a citywide teaching staff of over 55,000, only 170 regular and 82 substitute teachers were marked "unsatisfactory."

The evaluation form which has been developed by the Office of Personnel for evaluating teacher performance contains twenty-eight different items on which the teacher is marked. These include such vague and nebulous criteria as: "personal appearance; professional attitude; effect on character and personality of pupils; control of class; skill in adapting instruction to individual needs; attention to records and reports; housekeeping and appearance of room." There are no objective standards suggested anywhere in the evaluation form, except the ruling concerning absenteeism: "If a teacher is absent for ten days during a year's probationary period, he shall have his permanent appointment postdated."

The evaluation report for probationary supervisors (principals and assistant principals) is even more vague than the one for teachers. There are nineteen different items; some of these are: "self-control and manners; supervision over heating, lighting, ventilation and cleanliness of school; adequacy, accuracy and currency of school records and reports; effect on unifying and systematizing work of school, effect on discipline of school; guidance and assistance given to weak or inexperienced teachers; and nature, frequency and effect of school-community activities."

None of these items are further defined or explained in any Board of Education document that I could locate. Nor can I find why particular items were considered important indicators of satisfactory performance instead of others. Why must a supervisor have self-control and manners, for example, but not a teacher? Why is a teacher supposed to show "resourcefulness and initiative" while these qualities are not included in a supervisor's rating form? A teacher is supposed to "maintain good relations with other teachers" but must only make an "effort to establish and maintain good relationships with parents." A supervisor is not required to "maintain" good relations with anybody, according to the form.

During the probationary period, a teacher is supposed to be evaluated at least once each term. His supervisor (department chairman, assistant principal or principal) notifies him *in advance* when to expect the *formal observation*. The teacher then prepares a specific lesson which he presents to the class when the supervisor comes; the supervisor stays about half an hour, and follows this up with a *post-observation conference* and a written report, which goes into the teacher's record folder, after the teacher has read and initialed it.

The tenured teacher is also supposed to be formally observed at least once a year; the form which his supervisor fills out is very short. No specific criteria or performance standards are listed at all; he is simply rated S for satisfactory or U for unsatisfactory.

The UFT contract specifies an appeal procedure which all teaching personnel may follow if they do not agree with the rating they receive. The teacher first writes a dissenting statement, which must be attached to the rating report, and then initiates the grievance process, which can be taken all the way to the chancellor and the State Education Commissioner, if the teacher so desires. For probationary personnel marked "doubtful" the practice in New York City has been to transfer that teacher to another school to see if he improved his competence in a new situation. However, the teacher is given full credit for that year on probation. Thus, a teacher can be marked "doubtful" one year, transferred, marked "doubtful" the next year, transferred, and marked "satisfactory" the third year, at which time he automatically receives tenure. From then on, it is practically impossible to dismiss him.

Under the latest union contract, a new provision has been introduced which calls for the establishment of "objective criteria of professional accountability." During recent years, since teachers have received increased salaries and relief from non-teaching duties, parents and taxpayers everywhere have been demanding reassurance that these increased expenditures are actually producing a better quality of instruction for the children. In response to the demand that teachers be held accountable in some way for performing their job satisfactorily, the union inserted this new, quite vague statement in its contract. When asked what this meant, the union president told one newspaper that once such criteria were worked out, teachers would be told what they are doing wrong, and would then be helped to improve; for those who do not improve after a "period of time" a hearing would be held, and those who are still "found wanting" would be removed. Only time will tell whether or not parents are right when they greet this new provision with distrust and disbelief.

WHAT IS WRONG WITH
THE PROCEDURE

Classroom observation is rarely used by New York City administrators as a tool to assist teachers in perfecting their skills. Instead, principals often use these observer ratings to put down creative teachers, to intimidate teachers who disagree with them. It is symptomatic of its entire approach that the system has only spelled out causes for removal and has never bothered to define positive standards for acceptable and excellent performance.

When teachers first enter the system, they quickly learn that most principals are far more interested in routinizing the classes and establishing discipline procedures than they are in helping teachers improve their teaching performance. Teacher orientation and staff conferences are more concerned with hall routines, fire drills, dismissal schedules, attendance cards, accident reports, etc., etc., than they are with discussions about school policy or professional growth. Teachers are treated as bureaucratic functionaries and child custodians, and so it should not be surprising that these are what they soon become. As the union has become stronger, staff meetings are dominated by worker-management arguments: I visited one junior high school staff conference where the principal and UFT chapter chairman argued for thirty minutes (of the fifty-minute meeting) over the three minutes the teachers spent getting to their rooms between classes —the UFT chairman wanted that three minutes to be deducted from teaching time; the principal wanted it included as part of the preparation period.

In good school systems the initial three years of a teacher's experience—the probationary period—is considered to be the most crucial part of a teacher's training. Many school boards assign lower teaching loads to new teachers so that they will have ample time to learn by observing master teachers. In New York, although the union and the board have given lip service to this internship philosophy, they have not really implemented it. Recently a minimal watered-down experiment was tried, whereby new teachers were given some extra help. But the children were made to suffer for it. Because the principals did not have adequate staff replacements, the classes had to double up while the probationary teachers were out watching the experienced teachers give lessons.

It is not a crime to be told that you are not suited to teach. In decent systems, incompetent, impossible teachers are identified early enough in their teaching career so that they can leave the profession and find a job for which they are better qualified. It is unconscionably cruel, however, to abandon new inadequately prepared teachers to the classroom without giving them any supervision, support or assistance, and then blame them when they fail. In New York City our Board of Education is unbelievably reluctant to ask the bad ones to leave and inexcusably unable to give the average ones help so they can improve.

Certainly a large measure of the trouble lies in the fact that most supervisors are suffering from the same handicaps as the teachers. They do not have the slightest idea of how to effectively supervise or train their staffs. Most of them are rather arrogant about their ability; they feel that the exams they have passed prove that they know what they are doing. They don't ask for help because they don't realize that they need it. Even when they can see that they have problems, they most certainly do not look to parents or students as resources for helping them deal with their difficulties. The Parent Association at PS 90 in Harlem once issued a flyer calling for the removal of their principal. The grounds: "He has downright contempt for parents by not counting on our assistance in solving the many problems at PS 90."

Who should be evaluating staff performance? Teachers seem to feel that they should be judged by other teachers, yet the union has never developed any standards or procedures for doing this. Many school systems have developed a joint panel of teachers and administrators to work out the evaluation process together. But parents are beginning to feel that professionals should not be left alone to do this vital job. It is true that lawyers

and doctors have set up performance standards to police their
own professionals. But if a client does not like his doctor or
lawyer, he may choose another. Our children are often stuck
with highly unsatisfactory teachers and supervisors; many parents have come to believe that we must be allowed to help
develop a procedure which assures us that incompetent teachers
will be removed and that average teachers will be given help
so that they can improve.

When the UFT talks about teacher evaluation, it always uses
the phrase "objective criteria." One can easily and objectively
add up the number of days a teacher is absent, but how do you
measure a tone of voice? How do you evaluate a certain look?
If we don't face up to the fact that many parents are angry
about the failure of the school system to deal with bigoted and
racist teachers, we will be developing totally irrelevant standards
for judging teacher performance.

Many parents feel that teachers should be measured, at least
in part, by the amount of academic progress made by their
pupils. The UFT has recently stated that teachers should be
measured by the amount of progress pupils make, *in comparison
with other pupils of the same socio-economic background.* Not
too many years ago the school system issued something called
a reading index to all principals. Based upon group IQ scores,
which have since been discredited, it assured the supervisors
in nonwhite communities that most of the children couldn't be
expected to read on grade level, and that if only a very small
percent of the students were reading, the school was doing an
adequate educational job. Parents found out about this system
and were outraged. If a teacher's performance is going to be
measured only by that kind of yardstick, we will be no better
off than we are now.

Parents are saying that we believe poor children, nonwhite
children and failing children can be taught. They are saying
that they want to locate the type of person who will have success when teaching those children. Many teachers succeed in a
middle-class community, but are not able to perform satisfactorily in a poverty area. We want to chance to develop performance standards and criteria for our own communities. "Success"

and "desirable teaching traits" for one neighborhood may simply not do for another. Thus, we believe that parents—and students—should have the right to work with teachers and supervisors in setting up performance standards and in evaluating all personnel.

There is no point in developing an elaborate process for measuring teacher effectiveness if we are going to continue paying inferior, average and superior teachers exactly the same salaries. In effect, we are rewarding mediocrity with this system. As the ad for a major airline goes: "A bonus is the oldest idea in the world." Recently the United States Office of Education funded a half dozen experiments where teachers who bring their pupils up to grade level within a specified period of time were to be paid a bonus. Teachers as professionals are opposed to "merit pay"; they claim that it is a divisive, nonproductive mechanism that destroys staff morale. But when teachers are paid $12,000 and $15,000 a year for less than ten months' work and less than six hours a day, and the majority of the children whom they teach fail to learn, what does that do to community and parent morale? Nothing could be more divisive or nonproductive for our nation. We cannot afford to pay those salaries and continue failing our pupils.

In summary, we must develop a longer, more carefully supervised probationary period, with an effective weeding out of those who are unsuited for teaching. Tenure cannot continue to be bestowed in perpetuity. We must establish some legitimate, relevant performance standards for our teachers and supervisors, and these standards must reflect the concerns and needs of our local communities. Professionals, parents and students can work together in setting up these standards and carrying out the evaluations. And in those local school districts where they wish to try it, the merit-pay system must be permitted so that the communities may see for themselves how it works.

Action Checklist for Parents

HOW TO EVALUATE AND
UPGRADE YOUR SCHOOL'S STAFF

Demand that your local school board involve parents in establishing a procedure for evaluating staff performance in your district.

√Perhaps for the first year or so your local board might permit the parents and staff in each school to develop their own evaluation procedure and criteria. If a district-wide formalized rating system is set up too quickly, it might stifle some of the best and most interesting ideas.

√Board of Education rating forms for probationary and tenured personnel should be distributed for community discussion. Perhaps a special public meeting could be held where these forms are debated and new ones developed, or possibly your local board could set up a special staff-parent-student committee to prepare a rating form for your school or district.

√Insist that your local board recognize the right of parents to visit the schools and evaluate the staff, as long as they don't interrupt the teaching process.

√If your local board agrees to involve parents in staff evaluation, make sure your responsibilities are clear. One of the most harmful tricks that is played on parents is to be told to go ahead and do something, and then afterwards to be told: "Oh, you had no right to do that." Will your evaluation committee have advisory status only, or will your local board respect and follow your recommendations?

Even if your local board will not officially involve parents in its evaluation of staff performance, you have a right to set up your own committee and develop criteria for evaluating your own staff.

√Try to get official recognition first; but if you don't get it, go ahead anyway. For the sake of the children, you must do all you can to improve staff performance.

√Get a group of parents together and discuss the qualities you will be looking for in teachers and supervisors. After you have developed a preliminary list, involve staff, students and community organizations. They will have many good suggestions.

√United Bronx Parents (791 Prospect Ave., Bronx, New York) has developed some material to help parents discuss what is a good teacher and what is a good supervisor. In addition, the Educational Research Service of the American Association of School Administrators (National Education Association, 1201 16th Street, N.W., Washington, D.C. 20036), has a booklet *Evaluating Teaching Performance*, which includes ten different types of rating forms used in various systems throughout the country. Although these have all been developed by professionals, many of them are much better than the ones used in New York City and you will get lots of good ideas from this pamphlet.

Once you have agreed on the criteria you will use in evaluating staff performance, decide who will do it, when it will be done, and how it will be done.

√Who will help do the evaluation? A parent committee? Will you include students? Community residents? Staff? Perhaps you want to ask an outside consultant or agency to assist you. Many programs include evaluation funds which might be used for this purpose. The danger with hiring an outside agency is that most of them have a rather "professional" point of view and may not be looking for the same thing parents are interested in.

√When will your evaluation be done? How often? Will you want to give a teacher advance notice that you will be coming into her room?

√How will it be done? Through a formal observation only? Perhaps you might also send a questionnaire home to the parents, or have the students fill out a report card rating the teacher. And won't you want your rating to include more than just what happens in the class? How will you evaluate the teacher's attitude to the community?

√You must decide whether your committee will evaluate only new teachers, only probationary teachers, or all teachers. Will you apply the same standards to everyone? How will you evaluate the supervisors?

Once you complete your evaluation, decide how you will use the findings.

√If a teacher or supervisor is not performing satisfactorily, will you recommend that he be transferred, reprimanded, retrained, given another chance, or dismissed?

√If you decide that a teacher needs more help, will he be removed from the classroom while being trained? What kind of training will he need? Who should give it? Should he get this training during school hours or after school? Should the teacher be paid while being retrained? How much time will you give the teacher to show improvement?

√Will you discuss your findings directly with the teachers involved? Will you submit them to the principal? To the local school board? Will you make your findings public?

You may want to investigate the teacher-training programs.

√Observe the various training and in-service programs in your district and in other districts. Ask your teachers what they think about them and what they would like to see instead. Organize to get these changed so they are more useful to your staff.

Be sure to investigate the help being given to paraprofessionals.

√How are they evaluated? How are they helped to improve? Are they being used effectively? Are they being helped to become teachers?

√In some schools parents complain that paraprofessionals have been "turned around" by the system. If this is the case in your school, make sure it isn't your own fault. Have the parents helped the paraprofessionals get recognition and status in the school? Are they faced with so many problems they are unable to function properly?

√Treat them the same way you do the teachers and supervisors. Evaluate them; get bonuses for the good ones; get extra help and training for the average ones; and for those who you feel are unsuited to the job, give them another chance, and if they don't improve, demand their removal.

You may decide to direct all your actions against the schools of education which has mis-educated so many teachers in the first place.

√Picket lines and demonstrations at the teachers colleges to force them to change their curriculum, methods and requirements are long overdue.

You will find that some of your staff members cannot be retrained, cannot be improved. You will have to insist that these particular people are dismissed.

√If you have a terrible principal, your teachers will not be able to do a good job.

√If you have two or three really incompetent teachers, whom nobody seems to be able to touch, the entire staff will be demoralized.

√You will have to organize to get these people dismissed. The next chapter deals with removal of incompetent staff.

6·Firing the Staff

HOW TO GET RID OF
INCOMPETENT TEACHERS,
PRINCIPALS AND SUPERVISORS

It is slightly less difficult to dismiss a probationary employee than it is to get rid of one who is tenured. The word "fire" is never used by professionals. "Discontinue the services," "remove," "discharge," "dismiss," all are considered nicer terms.

Current Procedure for Discharging
Probationary Staff Members*

Local school boards are authorized to discontinue the services of any probationary employee on recommendation of the district superintendent with the approval of the city chancellor.

—The principal files a report with the district superintendent on any probationary teacher he wants to dismiss.

* State Education Law, Sections 2573 (c-1), 3019 (a), 2590 (j-7); Board of Education Bylaws, Section 105 (a); UFT Contract, Article IV, F-15.

—In some districts the local school boards have also invited parent associations and community organizations to submit their recommendations.

—Before any action can be taken, the employee is entitled to a fair hearing. This is often called due process. The district superintendent may hold the hearing himself, or he may appoint a committee to conduct the hearing for him. (Traditionally he asks other principals or district superintendents to do this but this is not required by law.)

—At the hearing the employee is entitled to bring an attorney or union representative with him. He may call witnesses or cross-examine anyone who testifies. He may buy a copy of the minutes (transcript) of the hearing.

—The district superintendent may accept, reject or modify the findings of the committee which held the hearing. He makes his recommendation to the local school board.

—The local school board, by a majority vote of the whole, then decides whether or not to dismiss the employee. If they decide to dismiss him, they must give written notice of at least thirty days in advance of the effective date of termination of service.

Before any of the steps outlined above may be taken, the city chancellor must be notified. No probationary employee may be dismissed, even after all these steps are taken, without the approval of the chancellor.

This procedure applies to teachers, principals, assistant principals, district superintendents and school secretaries. Paraprofessionals and other part-time employees do not go through probationary or tenured periods, so it does not apply to them. If your local school board does not make public a list of who is and is not on probation in your district, you can obtain the information from the Bureau of Teacher Record, Office of Personnel.

Current Procedure for Discharging
Tenured Staff Members*

The New York State Education Law specifies that "persons who have served the full probationary period *shall hold their positions during good behavior and satisfactory service and shall not be removable except for cause . . .*" Local school boards are now authorized to hold hearings when specific charges are brought against a tenured employee, and under specific conditions and procedures, they may discontinue his services.

—The district superintendent may bring charges against any employee on any of the following grounds: unauthorized absence or excessive lateness; neglect of duty; conduct unbecoming his position; incompetent or inefficient service; violation of any bylaws of the city or community board; or any substantial cause that renders the employee unfit to perform his duties properly.

—No charge may be brought against an employee more than six months after the alleged misconduct occurred.

—Although principals may recommend that charges be brought (and perhaps parents may also recommend this, although no such possibility has ever been admitted), only the district superintendent may actually file formal charges. Before he can do this, however, he must notify the employee, the local school board and the city chancellor of his intentions, and the employee is immediately entitled to a preliminary hearing with counsel and full due-process procedures. (He may cross-examine witnesses, etc.)

—After the preliminary hearing, if the district superintendent decides to continue and bring formal charges against the employee, he must notify the city chancellor, who will decide whether or not the employee will be temporarily suspended from active duty, with full pay, until the hearing takes place. In any event, no employee may be suspended in such a procedure for more than ninety days.

* State Education Law, Sections 2573 (6) and 2590 (j-7); Board of Education Bylaws, Sections 100 (8 and 105); UFT Contract, Article IV, F-15, and Article XX.

—The local school board officially receives the charges, and appoints a trial examiner from a panel of examiners which has been drawn up by the city chancellor and approved by the UFT.

—At the hearing, the employee has the right to be represented by an attorney, to cross-examine witnesses, to call his own witnesses and to get a copy of the minutes.

—After the trial examiner gives his decision, the local school board may reject, confirm or modify it by a vote of the majority of the entire local board membership.

—The local board may then decide on the penalty. It may reprimand the employee, fine him, temporarily suspend him without pay, transfer him within the district or dismiss him.

—The employee may then appeal any of these decisions to the city Board of Education.

—The city Board of Education may review the case itself, or must submit it to arbitration if so specified in the UFT contract.

—After the decision of the city board or arbitration panel, the employee may still appeal an unfavorable decision to the State Education Commissioner.

—If the decision of the State Education Commissioner does not satisfy the employee, he still has the right of appeal through the courts.

WHAT IS WRONG WITH THE PROCEDURE

Before the fight over local control, supervisors often complained that they were unable to fire incompetent employees. The procedures for documenting charges against tenured personnel were so complicated and cumbersome that it wasn't "worth the trouble." When a particular staff member could no longer be tolerated by a principal or parent group, he was quietly transferred. According to the *New York Times*, between 1962 and 1967, out of a citywide staff of over 55,000, only 170 regular and 82 substitute teachers were marked unsatisfactory. *During the entire five-year period, only twelve tenured teachers were dismissed!* There is no reason to believe the pattern since then has changed. This practice has to produce a sizable number of unskillful and incompetent teachers and principals who are permitted to remain in daily, unproductive, sometimes destructive contact with our children.

Several years ago I was shown a copy of an actual file of documents and statements that had been collected by a district superintendent in preparation for a disciplinary hearing involving a tenured teacher. The teacher was charged with corporal punishment—hitting kids. However, before the school system could fire him, a total of twenty-seven separate incidents were witnessed and recorded by various staff members in two different schools! Here are some sample entries in the file which was presented to the trial examiner:

Oct. 21

Letter from junior high principal to district superintendent:

I am reporting Mr. B. for repeated use of corporal punishment. Yesterday for the fourth time this term he was involved in striking a child. I informed him in writing that if he used corporal punishment once more I would report him to you as violating the law . . .

Nov. 18

Letter from the junior high principal to the district superintendent:

This is to inform you that Mr. B. once again struck a child. Towards the end of period 7 he punched Eleanor U—— of Class 6–4 in the stomach and pulled her arm. She went to the guidance counselor who informed me that the child was doubled over in pain when he saw her . . . I hereby request that Mr. B. be immediately removed from his duties at this school because I consider him a danger to the safety and welfare of the children entrusted to his care.

Dec. 21

Letter from an elementary school assistant principal to the district superintendent (The teacher had been transferred from the first school to this one):

When I went into Class 2–3 at about 10:15 this morning I noticed one of the boys holding his face and crying. When I asked him what was troubling him, he and several other children answered, "The teacher hit me." The boy David M—— had left his seat to talk with another child. When he returned to his place, the teacher struck him on the back with the wooden room pass and then grabbed him by the back of his neck pushing his head down so that his face struck the desk . . .

On January 5 the teacher in question was transferred to the district office with pay until the disciplinary hearing could take place in February. I was not able to find out what happened as a result of that hearing.

Now that some measure of "decentralization" has been legislated, the procedure for disciplining or dismissing a New York City teacher has been made even more difficult. What was formerly almost impossible for professionals to accomplish is now absolutely impossible for community boards or parents!

Everywhere in New York State a tenured teacher is protected by the State Education Law, and properly so, or no teacher would have any protection if he spoke out on a controversial issue. In fact, that was the original purpose for most tenure legislation— to protect a teacher's freedom of speech. However, in New York City we now have a double layer of additional "security." Elsewhere in the state the education law stipulates that a tenured teacher is entitled to a fair hearing before either the local Board of Education *or* its trial examiner before any disciplinary action may be taken. In either event, final authority for action is left to the local board, but the teacher has the right to appeal any decision to the State Education Commissioner and then to the courts. In New York City the following procedures have been added:

—Our local boards must obtain prior approval from the city chancellor before they may institute a hearing.

—Our local boards may not hold the hearing themselves; they *must* appoint a trial examiner, but they are not even permitted to make their own choice. They must select an examiner from a list which has been approved by the city chancellor and the UFT!

—After the local board makes its decision, the teacher may appeal to the city board—and then he may appeal again to the State Commissioner and the courts.

Unlike the rest of the state, local school boards in New York City are not permitted the right to temporarily suspend the teacher, with pay, pending the hearing. Instead, our district boards must request the chancellor to approve a temporary suspension. At PS 39 in East Harlem, where the district superintendent had filed charges against nine teachers, the local school board petitioned the city board for permission to temporarily suspend (or reassign) the teachers, with full pay, until the hearing took place. The city board denied their request. While the UFT delayed the hearing's implementation, eighteen policemen were required to protect the presence of the nine teachers reporting to school each day, against the wishes of the school board and the parents—but with the approval of the city board and the UFT.

The city board has further aggravated this impossible situation because it keeps changing its mind, and adds or takes away powers from the local boards almost monthly. At first, for example, it told the IS 201 Governing Board that it could suspend its teachers pending a hearing, but after union pressure mounted, the city board rescinded its decision. How can a local board play the game if the ground rules keep changing?

Even if local boards are given unambiguous authority to discipline their staff members, a "fair hearing" can be useless if the charges which the parents substantiate are considered illegitimate by the teachers' union. When the local board and unit administrator in Ocean Hill-Brownsville brought charges against several teachers in that district, the Board of Education appointed a trial examiner. As far as I can find out, this was the first time the decision of such a hearing officer was ever made public. Studying his findings, it is easy to despair.

Several witnesses testified that a particular teacher had "failed to maintain control of his class." The students were found throwing paint at each other in the teacher's presence, and he had done nothing to stop them. The trial examiner found that since the teacher had performed no better and no worse than the average teacher under similar circumstances, he could not be dismissed, transferred or disciplined! Now, suppose you take over a business that had gone bankrupt under the old management. As you see it, your first job is to shape up the employees who had become terribly lazy and unproductive under the careless supervision of their former boss. You can't very well fire them all, so you decide to take one or two of the worst offenders and make examples of them in order to set new standards of performance for the rest of your workers, to show them that you are not going to stand for any more nonsense. Well, under the rules followed by the trial examiner you cannot do this, because if the teacher you want to discipline is not doing his job properly but if everyone else is not doing theirs either, then he is performing up to "average standards"—never mind if "standard" means "god-awful."

The Decentralization Law permits a local superintendent to bring charges against an employee for "excessive lateness" for class. What is excessive? In Ocean Hill-Brownsville the unit administrator brought charges against a teacher who had been late twenty-two times in seven months but the trial examiner ruled that no evidence had been offered that these latenesses "were more than those suffered by a teacher of a similar status under similar circumstances" and he dismissed the case.

The Board of Education and the union have rather restricted notions regarding "qualified witnesses." For example, in the Ocean Hill-Brownsville hearing, after a principal testified that a particular teacher had failed to perform his job properly, the trial examiner took great care to point out that this principal lacked authority because he had not been appointed through regular channels and that his predecessors, who had been "duly qualified" by the Board of Examiners, had given the teacher "satisfactory" ratings the four previous years—therefore his transfer was not justified.

The Decentralization Law stipulates that charges may be preferred against a teacher whose "conduct is unbecoming his position." In Ocean Hill, when the unit administrator brought one such teacher up for discipline, the main witness against her was a respected community resident who was an educational assistant in that teacher's classroom. She testified to having heard the teacher use profane language to the children on a number of occasions; in actuality the community was seething because of the strong names that teacher had been calling the kids. The unit administrator asked that she be suspended or transferred "in order to maintain a safe atmosphere in the school." The parents were ready to tear the building down if the teacher remained. The hearing officer stated that the parent-witness "holds no license from the Board of Education" and that "I find that testimony incredible and hence give it no weight in this instance." The unlicensed teacher kept her license to teach—and curse—the children.

Recently the head of the city supervisory association charged that 47 school supervisors and teachers had been forced to leave their positions because of harassment. Under the unworkable and unfair "fair hearing" procedures set forth by the State Education Law *and* the Decentralization Law *and* Board of Education bylaws *and* the UFT contract, the system will be lucky if it can "properly" discipline or discharge *any* staff members. Is it any wonder that parents, compelled to send their children to public school, find themselves equally compelled to do everything in their power to get rid of the really terrible teachers and supervisors?

Action Checklist for Parents

HOW TO GET RID OF A TRULY TERRIBLE PRINCIPAL

Until the Board of Education stops fooling around and delegates clear and authentic powers over the hiring and firing of personnel to local school boards, parents must resort to political pressure tactics if they want an incompetent, prejudiced or unproductive principal removed from their school. Since the current procedures for presenting charges against teachers or principals are so cumbersome and impenetrable, parents and local boards are obliged to use these stop-gap methods to force the transfer or dismissal of a staff member who is downright harmful to the children.

It is our fervent hope that businesslike and effective arrangements will soon be established which will provide us with more acceptable avenues for raising legitimate grievances against teachers and supervisors, and with some confidence that we will get a fair hearing and reasonable, *prompt* results. In the meantime, however, if parents are faced with a truly terrible principal, here are some suggestions you might find effective. You can also use them as a guideline if you need to remove a teacher or assistant principal and find all the "proper channels" hopelessly clogged.

Select your target carefully; be sure you have a strong case.

You will have a reasonable chance for success if a sizable segment of the parents, students and community agree that the principal is incompetent or ineffectual. It is particularly helpful if, in addition to a solid backlog of unsettled complaints, a specifically horrendous crisis has recently occurred which focuses attention on the need to remove him. You are more likely to accomplish your goal if you have some substantial (though unofficial) staff support within the school. In many situations, some of the best and most devoted teachers or supervisors have privately complained to parents about the principal, citing numerous examples of misconduct and mismanagement which might normally remain hidden from the community.

It will also ease your task considerably if your principal is either on probation or close to retirement age. Procedures for the removal of anyone who has not yet won tenure are less complicated. And if, on the other hand, he has been around for many years, and although he has tenure, is eligible for his pension, some uncomfortable boat-rocking might encourage him to retire from office ahead of time. (To ascertain the probationary or tenured status of your principal and his proximity to retirement, you may call the Office of the Deputy Superintendent of Personnel.)

If your principal is unhappy at your school anyway, and is desirous of a change to a less "troublesome" community, your pressure may be just what is needed to induce his superiors to grant him his transfer.

WARNING: It is quite difficult to remove a principal if any of the following conditions prevail:

√If a handful of parents can't stand him, but they don't have much support from the rest of the parents, it would be premature to call for his removal. If you believe that the other parents are misguided, then show them why you think the principal is no good, but *don't* isolate yourself at the outset by demanding the resignation of a popular principal.

√ It is very difficult to get rid of the easygoing "good guy" who has no mind of his own and who is willing to bend with every breeze. Since he is usually too weak to demand real work from his staff, he can have considerable support from the goof-offs. It is a measure of how little we have learned to expect from our schools that many parents are willing to settle for such a principal, even though he won't do anything spectacular, because he is easy to manage and can be prevented from taking any unpopular or particularly offensive actions, as at the slightest sign of opposition he always changes his mind. If you should try to organize support for his removal, the invariable reply will be: "The devil we know is better than the devil we don't."

√The hardest principal to remove is the one who treats his school as his personal kingdom. He has been around for years and has no intention of transferring. He has made sure of a staff that supports him by the simple expedient of disparaging or transferring any teacher or assistant who ever disagreed with him. He has co-opted the parent association by giving paid jobs in the school to the most vocal leadership or by placing their children in the best classes. Whenever his authority is challenged, he quickly discredits or isolates the source. He is frequently an influential member of one of the citywide supervisory associations. He is a formidable opponent and you had better know what you are doing if you want to get him out of your school.

Organize a campaign to demand his removal.

Your basic ingredients for success: You must be persistent; you must present your arguments persuasively and clearly; you must build an ever-increasing base of parent-community support.

At first there are usually only five or ten parents who are really outraged at what is happening in the school. They form the nucleus for the initial committee; they must have plenty of determination and energy to keep going in the very tough months ahead. But they must work to get more and more parents interested, involved and indignant. Many wonderful groups fail at the outset because they spend too much time relating to the district superintendent, the local school board members, the officials downtown; they become engrossed in meetings with the "powerful," and neglect the community whose support they absolutely must have if they are to succeed.

This entire operation can take anywhere from four months to an entire school year. In the successful campaigns that I have seen around town, the parents usually start organizing in February or March, after the first semester has demonstrated for certain that the principal is not equipped to handle his job. Starting in the spring also provides good weather for meetings, and ample time to prevent the principal's return the following September.

Call a meeting of the most concerned and angry parents. If you don't have the support of the parent association officers, but you do have many parents who agree that the principal is not performing his job adequately, you will want to form a new group. Call it a Parent-Community Committee, or Mothers Club or a Committee of Concerned Parents. Be sure that some influential parents and community leaders are involved in it from the start.

Draw up a preliminary list of grievances. Everyone who comes to the first meeting will have a particular story to tell about something the principal did wrong. After the parents relate the various incidents, write up a list of the ones which are the most shocking or the ones which seem to occur most often. A sample list of grievances can be found at the end of this chapter.

Call a mass meeting to broaden support. Mimeograph your list of grievances and canvas as many parents as you can personally to get their support. Invite them to add their own complaints, urging them to attend the meeting. Some groups invite the principal to this first public meeting, but many others do not. When parents do invite him it is because they know he won't come, which will further enrage the community, or they know that if he does come, he will only do something foolish or stupid which will add fuel to the fire. If you are not sure that either of these things will happen, don't invite him. You want an atmosphere where parents will be completely free to speak their minds, and his presence might discourage this. It is not necessary, and in fact is probably not even a good idea, to hold these

initial meetings in the school. A local church or community
center is usually smaller, friendlier and more conducive to parent
discussions.

However, no matter where you hold your meetings, the principal will make sure that some spies are present. There are
always parents or teachers who support him, who come to these
meetings to disrupt, or to simply observe and report back all
that happens. Therefore, make sure that nothing is done which
you don't want him to hear. For example, if there is someone on
the school staff who is feeding you important information, make
sure he is *not* at the meeting and is not talked about, unless, for
other reasons, he does not mind exposing his hand.

It is impossible to keep such a campaign a secret, and really
it is wrong to do so. What you are doing is perfectly proper and
necessary if your children are to receive the education they
deserve. If you try to hush it up, talking about the principal
behind the scene, under cover, you will only make some parents
less self-confident about their right to demand his removal and,
anyway, you are bound to be found out. Be proud of your protest
(but don't be naïve either).

*During the public meeting enlarge your list of grievances and
develop an extensive list of demands.*   It is very poor practice to
invite many parents to a large meeting if you don't intend to take
advantage of their presence by involving them directly in the
campaign. Don't waste the entire meeting by telling them what
you know is wrong with the principal. Let the audience tell each
other all the stories and problems they have encountered in
their dealings with him.

If they are dissatisfied with the initial list of grievances which
your smaller committee prepared, don't become defensive. Encourage the parents to draw up their own list. The longer and
more detailed the complaints are, the stronger your case will be.

√A good list of grievances contains many specific incidents that
   can be documented as to time and place, for example: "Two
   third-grade classes were refused lunch as punishment for misbehavior."

√A good list of grievances includes a wide variety of problems which many parents will immediately understand and identify with. "Garbage is always left uncovered in the hallways where the roaches and rats can get to it"; "The principal is never available to parents, and when he does see them he is evasive and uncommunicative."

√A good list of grievances is clear and includes common, very real, down-to-earth problems: "The principal allows the teachers to park in the playground"; "The principal refused to attend the sixth-grade Arista Assembly"; "The principal shouts at his teachers in front of the children."

It may be necessary for you to call several meetings before the parents are ready to start listing their demands. Sometimes only fifteen or twenty parents appear at the first "public meeting"; they talk all night about what is wrong, and want to call another meeting where they can bring more parents. Mimeograph a flyer which includes some of the complaints they brought into the meeting, calling a second and even a third meeting to hear grievances.

But soon (sometimes even the first night if the situation is critical enough) the parents will be ready to make a list of *demands*. Obviously your first demand is for the removal of the principal. However, it is important that you have about a dozen or more supplementary requests that you want the school authorities to provide for your school. (A sample list of demands appears at the end of this chapter.)

In the beginning the district superintendent and the local school board will do everything they can to steer clear of the real issue. They will be willing to offer your school some immediate tangible services in an attempt to divert you from the problem of the principal.

Thus, if you have a list of a number of things parents want, you will undoubtedly get some of them, even though your basic request is ignored (at first!). This will demonstrate to the parents that in unity there is strength, and as they win, for example, some minor repairs, or an exterminator, or a Puerto Rican guidance teacher, they will be proud of their initial accomplishment, and gain courage for the more difficult battle ahead.

A good list of demands follows logically from the grievances. If you are complaining about garbage, you need an exterminator. If you are complaining about the lack of community people employed in the school, demand that a specific number of local men and women be hired at once as teacher assistants.

A good list of demands states clearly that the parents are not "after" the entire faculty. One school stated specifically which teachers they no longer wanted on the staff, and which ones they felt were "retrainable." Since there were black and white teachers in both categories, the parents deflated any charge that their demands were racist. By pinpointing their dissatisfaction, the parents demonstrated that they respected and liked the vast majority of the staff, and thus were able to win unofficial support from many of the teachers and vocal, outspoken backing from several very brave ones. When parents demand the removal of several staff members, the union invariably starts the rumor that "there is a secret list of twenty more who fall next"; this cuts the ground out from under that process, and lets everyone know quite clearly exactly who the parents are holding accountable for the intolerable conditions.

Demand a meeting with the district superintendent and local school board to present your demands. If you are seeking the removal of the principal, there is usually no point in asking to meet with him, since obviously he isn't going to agree to fire himself.

Since you are presenting your local board and superintendent with a written list of grievances and demands, insist that your group receive a written reply, within a specific period of time.

Take as large a group of parents and community representatives to this meeting as you can. The school system frequently tries to restrict unreasonably and artificially the size of a parent delegation. You must avoid this if you can, for it will weaken your group. Of course, a large committee of parents makes the discussion a bit noisier and harder to keep under control. But such a meeting is more than worth the trouble, since it permits all the interested parents to see the official in action and hear the responses directly.

Be alert to any attempt to break your group into factions, to isolate you from each other, to play you against one another. When you appear at the meeting, another group of parents or community people may appear suddenly who have been called in to act as buffers between you and the superintendent. Don't fall into that trap. Always respect another parent or community group and never get into a fight with them in front of the school authorities if you can possibly avoid it. Ask for time to caucus with them before your meeting—or continue your meeting, but don't address your arguments to them. Don't let the superintendent or local board steer you away from the real target—the principal. "We respect these other parents, but we do not agree with them," you might point out. "We have had five meetings and we represent a sizable part of the community. The principal may still have the support of some parents, but his usefulness in our community is at an end because so many others oppose his continuation in office."

Sometimes, the district superintendent will listen to all your grievances and then suggest that each "case" merits individual investigation and attention. He wants to get the various parents into his office separately, ostensibly to give each the help he or she deserves, but too often to intimidate or harass them. You must make clear that you hope he will provide assistance to every child and parent in the school, that these are just examples of what is happening to everyone, and that the difficulties facing the school must be resolved for everyone, publicly, and not just for one or two families behind closed doors. Never reveal the names of particular parents who have individual complaints.

Your superintendent will undoubtedly make some counteroffers. He will ask you to give the principal more time; he may suggest that you go see the principal directly (or he may already have invited him to be present at this particular meeting). Whatever you are offered, don't agree to anything at that particular meeting. Insist that if possible the offer be made in writing, in direct response to all your demands, and insist that you need time to consider any of his suggestions in private and will answer him later. You will avoid much heartache this way, for *some of the most attractive offers can turn into traps upon close examination.* For example, you may be discussing the lack of discipline in the school and the district superintendent may offer to help the principal overcome this problem. As a result, the next week you may find twenty fifth- and sixth-grade boys have suddenly been suspended "at the request of the community."

Be especially careful of do-gooders who come to settle the problem for you. On numerous occasions parent groups invite ministers or social workers to accompany them to these meetings only to find quite unexpectedly that the Reverend is making deals which he was totally unauthorized to do.

If any teachers or supervisors in the school have come to your support, *protect them.* Make certain that the district superintendent or principal doesn't call them in for an individual conference or "off-the-record" discussion without a dozen or so parents present as witnesses. If you aren't scrupulous about this, word will soon get out that it is dangerous to give your group any backing and that you are not loyal to your supporters.

After your initial meeting with the district board and superintendent don't waste any time: Keep the parents involved by making them get more support.

1. Mimeograph your demands into a *petition* and canvas as many parents and community residents as you can for their signatures.

2. Organize a *grievance committee* which collects more complaints and problems every day.

3. Organize a *watch-dog committee* which makes periodic, unannounced visits to the school to see how conditions are and if they have improved. Keep issuing public announcements of "no progress" or new grievances. Of course, if a miracle occurs and the principal improves greatly, acclaim it! But I am assuming that the person you have chosen as the target is far more unyielding than that.

4. If you have given your local board a specific time limit to investigate your demands and give their answers, announce a public meeting for that date, and invite everyone in the community. Don't let your superintendent or board members weasel out of coming to report to that meeting!

5. After you receive their reports, if the local board and the district superintendent still haven't agreed to remove the prin-

cipal, intensify your campaign. (They still won't. They will probably only agree to give some additional services or repairs.) Go see your local elected officials, your borough president, the members of the Board of Education, the mayor, your community planning board, your antipoverty agency—everyone who is concerned about your community and any threat to its peaceful existence. Try not to go anywhere with fewer than fifteen parents and community residents.

6. Try to get a particularly respected agency to publicly announce their support. Once, in the South Bronx, when the parents had organized to demand the removal of a flagrantly unqualified principal, they found out that a local mental-health agency had had a special program in that school but had discontinued it after they found the principal to be destructive and unstable. When some community leaders heard the social workers talking about the principal, they were indignant: "If you really care about our children the way you say you do, put your comments in writing and give us a copy of your letter." The agency was very anxious to develop stronger ties with the neighborhood; it acknowledged the parents' criticisms, and a two-page letter on official letterhead was written to district headquarters, with copies circulated throughout the community. That letter played a key role in mobilizing the neighborhood against the principal, legitimatizing the grievance of the "less educated unprofessional" parents.

7. Call a press conference or sponsor a press tour of the school. Make public a detailed report on each complaint and grievance, and how it is still unresolved. State clearly how you have tried to have the principal investigated through every possible channel, with no success. Spell out clearly the dangerous, unprofessional, unproductive, wasteful job he is doing. Announce your intention of blocking him personally if he is reassigned to the school in the fall.

8. Stage a series of demonstrations to prove you have the strength to support your threat. If you have organized effectively in the community, by now you should have enough parents, students and community people who are willing to physically

demonstrate that they support the demand for his removal. Organize a picket line at the school, the district office or at Board of Education headquarters, whichever seems to make more sense to you. Or call a sit-in in the principal's or district office. The more local you can keep the demonstrations, the more support you are likely to build from your community. People will see you marching in front of the school and join you. This is less likely to happen downtown. On the other hand, you must do something to get attention. If you confine your demonstration to your local community, you will have to think up a particularly newsworthy twist—for example, at P.S. 175 in Harlem the fact that the demonstrators wore African garb got plenty of press attention. United Bronx Parents members washed diapers and cooked arroz con pollo at a memorably picturesque sleep-in. When the Lower East Side began to block a street with cement bricks, the cameramen appeared in force. Use your imagination and ingenuity, and you can turn a local demonstration into a real confrontation.

9. Naturally many groups will want to call a boycott for one day or longer. But don't do this until you have tried everything else—successfully. A boycott must be almost 100 percent effective. If your previous meetings and demonstrations failed, don't resort to a boycott, for it is bound to fall flat also. Instead, start over again. However, if you have prepared your case properly, it is quite possible that the parents will want to organize a one-day boycott to further display their determination and solidarity before school lets out for the summer.

10. Pursue the campaign during the summer. Tragically, the technique most favored by the school system is to wait parents out, to let them wear themselves out, to never give an answer in the hope that the problem will simply fade away. It may be that you never received a direct reply from your local board or headquarters in answer to your demand for the removal of the principal. They will tell you it is still "under investigation." Therefore, during the summer keep up a steady,

irritating series of smaller battles to let them know you have not forgotten the issue. For example, you might picket the principal at his home, his summer home or his church. Let him—and his neighbors—know you do not want him. I know some people consider this a terrible invasion of privacy, but what the devil to they think is fair about twelve hundred semi-illiterate, cruelly undereducated students?

Whatever you do, remember that you must be prepared to carry out your threat to block him bodily if the authorities dare to keep him assigned to your school in the fall. If the downtown officials know that you are serious about this threat, that you are organized and prepared, albeit reluctantly, to carry it out, they will more than likely avoid the confrontation and move him someplace else. Then you can begin your fight to get him replaced with someone who was worth the battle.

You will never get an out-and-out admission that you were right about him. They will simply transfer him to another school to harm some other parents' children. Many of us throughout the city have worked out an underground communication system where we try to keep track of where these "floaters" are being sent so we can warn the parents there, but it isn't always possible.

The entire procedure *does take time and careful organization.* It rarely can be speeded up although in some cases I have seen parents succeed within a four-month period. But it is worth it if the time is spent building a unified parent-community organization. If you are determined and persistent, you will wear the system down, and the authorities will finally give in just to get rid of you!

SAMPLE LIST OF GRIEVANCES

We, the parents of PS ____ demand that our
children get a decent education. They cannot
get educated under the conditions that are
permitted in our school. Here are some of the
intolerable things going on right now:

1. Too many good teachers are allowed to leave
   each year and no one cares.
2. Last week the principal dragged a crying
   small child by the ear down the hall into his
   office.
3. Garbage is constantly left uncovered in the
   hallways. We have many roaches, waterbugs
   and rats.
4. The principal is unavailable to the parents.
   If any of us do get in to see him he is
   always evasive and uncommunicative.
5. The principal refused to make reading scores
   available to the parents.
6. When one fourth-grade teacher sent a child
   to the office to be reprimanded, the principal pushed the child away, saying, "I don't
   want to be bothered."
7. Children who have trouble reading are not
   given adequate help.
8. The principal shouts at teachers in front
   of the children.
9. The principal refuses to permit any teacher
   assistants from our community in his school.
10. The principal failed to attend sixth-grade
    Arista Assembly.

11. The principal plays black and Puerto Rican parents against each other.
12. The principal has set up no supervision of the playground during lunch period.
13. The principal allows the teachers to park their cars in the playground.
14. Two third-grade classes were refused lunch as punishment for misbehavior. When parents complained, the principal just shrugged.
15. The principal gives a biased description of children to new teachers.
16. Children are permitted to fight in halls with teachers ignoring them.

SAMPLE LIST OF DEMANDS

We the undersigned demand that immediate steps be taken to correct conditions at JHS___. We further demand that the principal be replaced with someone more attuned to the needs of our children. We are willing to meet and discuss any point in our demands, except the removal of Mr. ___. We give the local school board and the Board of Education the balance of the school year and the summer recess to make necessary changes. We want:

1. A more available and capable principal.
2. More reading teachers.
3. Control of teacher absenteeism. If a teacher must be absent, arrangements must be made so that the same substitute goes to a class each time.
4. We demand that a committee of parents and

teachers be immediately set up to develop
standards for teaching. All teachers who
can't or won't conform to these standards
should be replaced.

5. Our children should be considered just
"children" without any disparaging
adjectives.

6. An exterminator must come to our school
regularly until the roaches and rats are
gone. Garbage should be covered and put
away properly.

7. Fifteen teacher assistants to be immediately
assigned to our school for thirty hours a
week each.

8. The reading scores for our school must be
made public at once and a program for improving the reading of the children worked out
by the teachers and supervisors.

9. In addition to removing the principal,
Mr. ____ and Mrs. ____ must be immediately
removed from our teaching staff. We will not
prejudice their future employment elsewhere
by stating our reasons here.

10. The following twelve teachers must be required to take a sensitivity course and a
teaching-skills course this summer if they
are to remain in our school [Names follow].
Failing this, grant them transfers to
schools more suitable to their talents.

11. Parents should be made welcome in this
school by principal and staff.

12. Necessary repairs be immediately attended to
in the library, lunchroom and gym.

13. That a written reaction to these demands be
received before our next general parent
meeting in May. This must be sent to us no
later than ____.

7 · Reporting to Parents

THE REPORT CARD

Once when I was visiting a third-grade classroom I saw this composition on the bulletin board:

I WORRY

I worry when I get my report card. I don't
really have to worry when I get my report card.
If I do good work in school and have good
control in school I won't have to worry.

Every mother knows that most kids get very tense around report-card time. At the end of the year, they become more and more anxious—"Will I pass?" "What class will I be in next year?" "If I get Miss —— I will absolutely die." And many kids pretend not to care and say nothing. They are so sure of failure, so sure that nothing good can possibly happen on the report card—or next year in school. Any educator who thinks that the children don't realize that the school groups the "bright" kids separately from the "slow learners" should stand outside a school on the last day in June. "Did you make IGC?" little girls will shout out to each other. Or, if the school has no such special class for "intellectually gifted" children, the kids still know which one is the best. "Did you get Cooper?"—everyone knows that Cooper teaches the smart kids.

And yet, if you eliminate report cards altogether, whom are you fooling? Colleges still require high schools to tell them what marks the student made. And the war will still take those boys who don't make college. So even if the school doesn't give the student any grades or report card while he is in school, the ax falls anyway.

Should there be report cards? Should they be different from what they are now?

The Current System in New York City

There is no state law requiring a school system to issue report cards. Every school district in the state has developed its own method for reporting to parents. Some give marks and some don't. Most schools do send home a written report evaluating the pupil's performance several times a year. This is what is done in New York City.

ELEMENTARY SCHOOLS

Kindergarten and first-graders do *not* receive a written report card. Instead, their parents are invited to meet with the teacher in an individual conference twice a year.

Children in the second through sixth grades receive a written report card three times a year, usually around Thanksgiving, mid-March and at the end of June. They are rated excellent, good, fair, or unsatisfactory in the academic areas (reading, oral and written English, math, social studies and science). They are marked satisfactory or unsatisfactory in music and art. The specific *results of the math and reading standardized tests* are supposed to be entered on the report card. If a child's work is below grade level in reading or math, the teacher is not supposed to mark him "good" or "excellent" in these subjects.

Children are rated in "personal and social development" indicated by such remarks as "Shows respect," "Obeys rules," "Shows self-control," etc. Students are given a mark for "work habits" ("Follows directions," "Works neatly," etc.) and Homework.

The report card indicates special health needs and the number of times the pupil was late or absent during the marking period.

The final marks in all these areas are supposed to be entered on the pupil's cumulative record card.

There is space on the report card for the teacher to write a personal note. In some schools the principal also records a comment. The elementary report card is in Spanish in some parts of the city.

Parents are supposed to sign the report cards and return them to school. They may keep the report card when it comes home the final time in June. There is space for the parent to write in a personal comment just above his signature.

When the report card comes home the final time, it tells the parent whether or not the child has been promoted. If a child is in danger of being left back, a warning is supposed to appear on the report card at the end of the second marking period, and the teacher is supposed to invite the parent in for a special conference at that time. The final report card usually indicates which class (and sometimes which teacher) the pupil will be assigned to next term.

JUNIOR HIGH AND INTERMEDIATE SCHOOLS

Students in these schools receive a report card at least four times a year, at approximately ten-week intervals. Some junior highs send home the first report card after six weeks.

Students are given a *numerical rating* in all subjects. The report card interprets these ratings to mean: below 65—little ability; 65—below average ability but passing; 90—outstanding ability.

Reading and math standardized test scores are supposed to appear on the report card.

The pupil is marked in the area of "personal adjustment," which includes "courtesy," "effort," and "self-control."

The report card indicates the number of times the pupil was absent or late during each marking period.

There is space for the official (homeroom) teacher's comment.

There is no space for the other teachers or for the principal to make a comment.

Parents are supposed to sign and return these report cards. They may keep the final copy. There is no room for the parents to make any comment.

Teachers are instructed that "pupils should not have their marks lowered for poor behavior." Teachers are also told that they should inform the parents if a child is doing poorly "before the issuance of a report card."

All the marks may be entered in the pupil's record folder; in many schools only the final mark is entered.

HIGH SCHOOLS

Every high school issues its own type of report card. Most high schools send home report cards three times a term, or about every six weeks. All high schools mark the students in subject areas (math, English, etc.), citizenship, and attendance.

Parents are supposed to sign and return the cards; they may keep the final report card.

As in the junior high schools, no mark is *supposed* to be lowered because a pupil misbehaves; parents are supposed to be "*warned*" beforehand if the pupil is doing poorly; and all marks may be entered in the pupil's cumulative record card, although usually only the end-term marks are actually recorded.

WHAT IS WRONG WITH
THE REPORT CARD SYSTEM
IN NEW YORK CITY

Standards vary from teacher to teacher, from school to school— so parents don't really know what "excellent" means. Some teachers will give a pupil a high mark, even though the child is reading *below* grade level "because that is very good considering that child's potential." Other teachers will give a child a poor mark, even though that pupil is reading above grade level "because that child is not working up to his ability." Now, that might not seem so bad, but parents and teachers often disagree about a child's true ability. And many studies have shown that teachers generally *underestimate* the potential and the intelligence of children who are poor or who are black or Puerto Rican. Thus, a teacher may not have taught such children very much all year long, and the children, therefore, may not have learned very much, but the teacher justifies herself, and tries to fool the parent, by sending home report cards marked "excellent"—even though the children really read quite poorly compared with national standards.

Compare these printed, official messages on two different high school report cards.

Morris High School—a predominantly black and Puerto Rican student body, with very few children receiving diplomas— adds this notice on the report card for parents to read: "New York State Regulations require all students to achieve a reading grade of 8.0 or higher in order to receive a high school diploma beginning June 1968."

Stuyvesant High School—a predominantly white student body, with 98 percent of the students receiving diplomas— admonishes in large print: "Most colleges require 80 percent average."

The one high school stresses and expects the *minimum* requirements; the other, the *maximum*.

Report cards reward students who accept the teacher's opinions and values, and penalize students who reject them. Although teachers are instructed *not* to lower a pupil's grade for misbehavior, parents and students know that this happens all the time. A great deal of stress is put on self-control, getting along, neatness, obedience. If a child knows his work but keeps a sloppy notebook, he is marked down. If a pupil is bright and talkative, her brightness is ignored, and her talkativeness is punished. If a child is creative, energetic, shows initiative—but disobeys rules and does not line up properly, does not sit up straight in his seat, forgets his white shirt on assembly days, constantly loses his pencils—his teacher will make sure that the parent realizes the seriousness of this misbehavior, and the child's marks will reflect her displeasure.

Report cards often make children competitive and interested in studying for marks only. Many students believe that the marking system is artificial and harmful. Parents will tell a child that he will get a dollar for every A he receives; other children will be beaten if they bring home a bad report card. Many thoughtful educators believe that neither of these is helpful to the child. Many older students are now asking for less emphasis on grades and more attention to learning. Many school systems have eliminated grades altogether and have substituted "evaluations"— some of these are written by the teacher; in some communities the student evaluates his own progress, by setting his own standards and marking himself.

Report cards have far-reaching consequences for students, and yet they have no way to appeal an unfair grade. Poor marks mean that a child will not be placed in one of the "top" classes; poor report cards will affect the student's chances of going to college, being drafted, getting a good job. And yet if a teacher if unfair, bigoted, or has a very narrow set of values, and gives a student an unreasonable grade, or makes a derogatory comment about his "social adjustment," there is really nothing that either the parent or student can do. Sometimes, if he fights hard enough and has enough connections, a parent can get a report card changed. If your child is one of the lucky ones, only a few of his teachers will treat him unfairly, and you can hope that the poor marks will be disregarded in the total picture. But what if your child is one of an entire group of students who are misunderstood, underestimated, disrespected, and generally disliked by almost all teachers and supervisors? Many black and Puerto Rican parents, and particularly parents with noisy, energetic, lively boys and girls, feel that their group of youngsters *is* generally mistreated and misgraded—and miseducated—by the current staff of educators. What recourse do they have to appeal an unfair report card? None.

Report cards often mystify parents and rarely inform them

of their child's actual status in school. Most parents, remembering their childhood days when a child was promoted only if he had satisfactorily completed the year's work, believe that this is still true today. When their child is marked "promoted," they breathe a sigh of relief, and think all is well. There is nothing on the report card, particularly in the junior and senior high schools, to warn the parent that the pupil is not in the academic program, that the minimum course requirements for college eligibility are not being met. For example, the ninth-grade pupil receives a mark for *general* math—his parent does not know this means he has not been given algebra, and therefore will not be allowed to receive an academic diploma four years later. A student, in the general track, works on a magnificent social studies project; he spends weeks creating a three-dimensional model of New York City, laboriously delineating the rich and poor communities, the businesses and industries, subways, parks. And he only receives a C—for in that school, children in a general track can never get a higher mark, no matter how excellent their work is. Furthermore, teachers' comments are often fatuous and irrelevant: "Johnny dresses beautifully," "Jane has lovely eyes." So what!

Teachers often disregard the system's own instructions. Very often children's test scores for reading and math are not entered, as they are supposed to be, or false marks are recorded—the teacher's "estimate" of the child's ability, rather than the test scores themselves. Rarely does a parent receive any warning before report-card time; inevitably the first time parents find out that a child is doing badly is when the report cards are brought home.

Under local control each district may now develop their own report-card and marking system. It will be up to the students and the parents who don't like the way it is now to force their local school board to improve or radically alter the current system.

162

Action Checklist for Parents

HOW TO IMPROVE—OR CHANGE—
THE REPORT CARD SYSTEM

A committee of parents, students and teachers should look over the report cards as they are really filled out now, and recommend changes. Here are some things you may want to consider.

If you think that report cards are important, but you want to improve them:

√How often do you think they should be issued? Until 1936, New York City issued monthly report cards. Now some schools issue them three times a year, others four and six times a year.

√What items do you think should be marked? Academic subjects? Citizenship? Social development? Work habits? Attendance?

√Do you think a child should be marked "excellent" if he is doing very well, considering his own ability, or only if he is doing very well compared with the rest of the class? or compared with the rest of the children in his grade in the city?

√Do you think that a child who reads well and does well on all his tests should be marked "good" even if he cuts class a lot?

√Do you think that a student who does well in science should be marked "good" even if he talks a lot in class?

√Do you think standardized scores for reading and math and other subjects should appear on the report card?

√Do you think the teacher should make personal comments on the report card? And if so, what kinds of comments do you think are appropriate?

√Do you think a parent should receive any warning on the report card if the child is not going to receive a diploma in junior or senior high school? if the child will not be eligible for the academic track? If so, how early in the child's school career should such a notice appear?

√Do you think the parent should receive the report card *before* teacher conference time, *during* the conference, or *after* the conference is over?

If you think that report cards and grades are harmful in their current form, and you want to radically alter the marking system:

√Do you think that parents should receive any written report from the teacher at all? If not, why? If yes, in what form?

√Some systems have the teacher write a letter or hold a conference with the parent in evaluating the pupil's work. Do you think this would be better?

√Some systems are permitting the pupil to evaluate his own work and grade himself. What do you think of that?

√Perhaps you believe that some areas should be marked but not others. Do you feel that "citizenship" and "pupil social development" are appropriate subjects for a report card?

√Some students and teachers believe that attendance should not be compulsory and that, therefore, absences and latenesses should not be recorded on the report card. What do you think?

Once you and the other parents and students decide what kind of reporting system you want, organize a campaign to get it.

HOMEWORK

A few years ago I remember coming home from work late, to find a panicky nine-year-old pacing the floor. "Where have you been?" She grabbed my arm. "We have to go to the library right away. I need a picture of a Haitian flag for homework." I don't have the slightest idea, to this day, why she needed that particular flag, or why it was assigned for third-grade homework. I only remember how upset she was and how tired I was. At first I refused to be moved; I was sure we must have a picture of the flag in one of the encyclopedias or dictionaries we had at home. But her older brother had already looked and the flag was not in any of them. I tried to convince her that she could go to school without her homework, that I would write a note to the teacher, that she could do something else as a substitute assignment—nothing I said worked. Finally, we got into our car and drove to the library, and located the book with the flag.

At that moment, I hated the school and the teacher—but especially I hated homework. Our family was spending several hours every night doing homework. Our daughters were over-conscientious about it; our son couldn't care less. And each evening, my husband and I took turns pushing and helping until the homework got done.

Two months later, our two older children transferred to a Harlem school. And overnight, our homework problems were over. The fifth- and third-grade teachers in that school assigned almost no homework at all, or only a few spelling words or math problems as a drill. At first it was wonderful. Free evening, no pressure, no tension. The kids loved it. But soon I began to get a little nervous. How can they learn anything if they don't have homework? I asked my husband. I went to see one of the teachers. She was sympathetic, but told me that most of "these children" had no place to do homework, could not be depended upon to study much at home, had too many chores to do for their families after school—and so the school gave very little homework.

Which school was right? How much and what kind of homework should children get, or should homework be abolished altogether?

New York City Policy on Homework

ELEMENTARY SCHOOLS

In January 1964 the Elementary Division issued a statement on homework which has never been updated, and which is still considered basic policy, although most schools completely disregard it. That directive states:

—Kindergarten and first grade should *not* have *written* homework, but they should have about fifteen minutes of home study each night (reading, finding pictures, visiting places, listening to the news, etc.).

—Students in second, third and fourth grades should have between twenty and thirty minutes of homework each night.

—Fifth- and sixth-grade students should have approximately forty-five minutes of homework nightly.

—Homework, after the first grade, should be at least partly written, should be related to classroom instruction, should be definite and clear.

—Homework should never be given as a punishment.

—Homework should always be checked and returned by the teacher.

—Homework should be "adapted to the needs, interests and abilities of *groups* of children." (This means, states the directive, that some groups of children would have different assignments than other groups of children, and that some children would have individual assignments.)

JUNIOR AND SENIOR HIGH SCHOOLS

There is no central policy statement regarding homework in the secondary schools; each school sets its own homework policy.

In one manual for new teachers, the board suggests that homework papers be collected daily, reviewed by the teacher and
returned to the pupil, after the work is "credited" in the pupil's
records.

In the orientation booklet distributed to Morris High School
students there is no reference to homework requirements. In a
similar booklet issued at Stuyvesant High School students are
told that homework assignments should consume about three
hours each night.

WHAT IS WRONG WITH
HOMEWORK

The range is from excessive amounts of homework to almost
none, depending upon the school's expectations of the youngsters' abilities! Occasionally an individual teacher gives some-
what unorthodox types of homework, out of educational conviction, or does away with homework altogether. But most of
the time, in New York, schools in middle-class, college-bound
neighborhoods assign an inordinate amount of homework; and
schools in working-class, poorer communities assign very little
homework on all grade levels. This, despite the fact that several
studies have shown that "slow learners" benefit the most from
homework assignments; brighter children the least.

Homework is frequently given as punishment for both individual and group misbehavior. Two boys get into a fight; the
teacher asks the class who started it; the class clams up—so the
entire class is punished and must write compositions on "How
I should behave in school," or "Why fighting is dangerous" or
"Ways I can help my teacher do a better job:" For some classes,
in some parts of the city, homework is given *only* for punishment.

Homework is often unclear, and uncorrected. In several
ghetto areas, parents have insisted that their children receive

homework. Sometimes the school will react to this pressure in an almost childlike fashion: "All right, we'll show you that your children can't do homework properly." Homework is assigned, often in great abundance, but it is not explained, so that the children come home bewildered, and are unable to complete it. Or some parents will work very hard with their children, helping them to figure it out, insisting that they do the work neatly, and the teacher never looks at it, never corrects it, never comments on it.

Particularly in desegregated schools, students who come from poorer homes are actually penalized by the homework assignments. Where teachers have pupils from middle-class and poor communities in the same classroom, they usually assign a great deal of homework in order to placate the ambitious parents who want to see the "standards" kept high, even though the school is "mixed." But many of the assignments require a parent's help. Maybe the mother won't have to jump on a bus and go to the library, but she will often have to correct spelling and punctuation, reinterpret an unclear assignment, help a child find the right reference book in his home library so he can "look something up." But what if the parent did not go very far in school herself? What if she cannot speak or read English very well? And what if she isn't able to buy a lot of reference books?

"Tell the parents to be sure to have a quiet, well-lighted corner for the children to do their homework," the principal exhorts the parent-association president. Fine—if you have only one or two children and you live in a decent-sized apartment. But what if there are six or seven or more of you, in three or four rooms? (The seven of us live in five rooms, and I know how impossible it is to locate even one quiet corner for homework— and I know the tension we build up while we yell at each other to "Shut up, I'm doing homework.")

"Don't interrupt the child to send him on errands while he is doing homework," says the teacher. But what if you run out of milk? What if you must take the baby to the doctor and need your big boy to watch the other children? And who's to say which assignment teaches the child more—doing the math problems or cooking dinner?

Homework often encourages kids to cheat: "Don't copy from each other, children," warns the teacher with a tight smile. But what do you expect? A student is given twenty-five dull math problems, plus lots of homework from his other teachers. Is it realistic to believe that he will do all those dreary repetitious calculations without trying first to copy from a friend? And why is it called *cheating* when students *help each other?*

Action Checklist for Parents

HOW TO IMPROVE—OR CHANGE— HOMEWORK POLICIES

If you believe that homework is important, get together a group of students, parents and teachers for discussion.

√What kind of homework do you think is worthwhile?

√Should every child and every class have homework?

√Should every child in the class have the same assignment or different ones?

√Should children take books home from school in order to do homework?

√How long do you think homework should take for each grade?

√How much help should parents give? How little?

√Should the teacher correct homework? Mark it? How often?

√Should homework ever be given as punishment?

√If you think every class of a grade should have the same amount of homework, how will the principal make sure this is done? What record will be kept?

√Whatever policy you set, get together again in six months to see how well it has worked and to make changes.

Do you think homework should be completely changed or abolished altogether?

√Some educators believe that what cannot be done in school should not have to be done at home; others feel that kids learn the most when left alone to explore the world around them in their own way. What do you think?

√If some of you feel this way, form a group of students and parents to demand that homework be abolished altogether for all classes, or perhaps you believe homework should be made voluntary, permitting each student to use his imagination and creativity in choosing what he would like to do as "homework."

√Some schools set up an after-school homework period so that all homework can be done by everyone in school, with the school library open, and with all teachers present to help those students who wish the help.

THE PARENT-TEACHER
CONFERENCE

In New York city, parents are officially invited to come to school and "confer" with the teachers twice a year. If a child is having trouble in school, his parents may be asked to come in for an additional conference. These parent-teacher conferences *ought* to result in greater understanding and cooperation between the child's family and his school. Unfortunately, this rarely happens.

At United Bronx Parents we conduct parent education classes. In the fall, before conference time, we hold discussions with many parents, urging them to visit the teachers, suggesting that they talk to their children first and prepare a list of specific questions to ask each teacher. After her visit to IS 38, one mother brought in this report:

I attended a conference with my boy's teachers. Miguel's English teacher gave him an F. When I asked why, he told me Miguel did very poor in some tests. I told him what my son told me, about him not checking homework and not explaining the lessons clearly, and how my son dislikes that class. The teacher tried to change the subject, telling me of the remark he made on the report card that "Miguel is a boy of great values." I asked him what he meant because I knew of my son's values, but that will not help his English.

His math teacher did not invite me to sit down. He was doing clerical work and he stood up and told me that Miguel was a fine boy. When I asked about his math level, he showed me his record, but he was looking at another boy named Miguel. I noticed this and I told him. He then said he was sorry but that he has about two hundred children during the day and some of them are Miguels. We then discussed *my* son and he assured me that Miguel was doing fine work.

What Is Wrong with the Parent-Teacher Conference

There is too little time. The system sets aside two specific sessions for conferences each fall and spring. On the day of the afternoon conferences, classes are dismissed at noon, and the children are sent home. This frees the teachers to meet with parents, although it may not free the parents to meet the teachers. If you are a working parent, you are supposed to come to the evening conference, which takes place at the end of a regular day of classes. Elementary, junior and senior high schools all have different conference days, supposedly for the convenience of parents who have children in several schools.

Each conference session lasts approximately two and a half hours. An elementary school teacher has about thirty children; if the parents are orderly, half of them will come in the daytime, and half of them at night. If they all come, that means that fifteen parents must be seen in a hundred and fifty minutes— exactly ten minutes per parent. In junior and senior highs, each teacher has about a hundred and fifty students a week. If all their parents dared to come, each conference would be exactly two minutes long!

The National Education Association suggests that the average parent-teacher conference should last about thirty minutes, and should take place four times a year. For parents whose children are experiencing difficulty in school, the association recommends that an hour, at least, will be required for an adequate conference to take place.

There is no privacy. Parents enter the classroom and are usually given a number, or they sign a visitors' book. There is often a student monitor who asks them to wait. Although you may have to sit around a long time before you can meet with the teacher, you are not bored because you can hear every word the teacher is saying to the parent whose turn has come. "Johnny needs to work harder . . ." "Your daughter is talking too much . . ." "Are you having trouble at home?" By the time your name is called, you are only anxious to see how fast you can get away, and most of the time you have completely forgotten everything you meant to discuss.

There is too much double-talk—parents rarely learn anything specific or useful, and they are often lectured, or asked embarrassing questions. The Board of Education instructs teachers to use these conferences to find out "whether the family is insecure economically to the extent that the child reflects insecurity." The teacher is told that she will want to learn "whether members of the family are qualified to help the child." Use "infinite tact," cautions the board, "but find out whether the child follows a routine that is wholesome . . ."

So the conference starts. The teacher tells one mother her child goes to sleep too late at night. Last year's teacher had told her he should spend more time with his father; this year, when he watches TV with his father, the teacher is angry.

The teacher tells another mother she should help her daughter with her math. Last year's teacher had said *not* to try to help, because she would only get the child mixed up since the school used different methods.

A mother tries to get up her courage to tell the teacher that the welfare cuts have fixed it so the children haven't got enough clothes and she can't get the two younger ones to school at all. Just then the teacher asks if there is an adequate desk in the house for her big boy to do his homework on. "Be sure you have

enough light and a quiet corner for him," she says. The mother
shuts her mouth and just nods.

"How is my child doing in school?" asks the parent. She
means, How is he doing in *reading, math, spelling.* "Fine," answers the teacher. She means that the child is behaving himself
and not causing any trouble.

But some parents are more aggressive. "How is my child
doing in his reading?" they ask. "Fine," they are told. "What is
his reading level?" "We aren't allowed to discuss the records
with you; you will have to make an appointment with the principal for that," says the teacher. The parents are not shown any
official records; in fact, in many schools they do not even see
any samples of the children's work!

The conference is totally unrelated to reality. If you do not
speak English, you are out of luck, for there is no one there to
translate what you or the teacher is saying. If you do not have
a maid to take care of your children, and you dare to bring them
with you, you are frowned upon; the teacher often doesn't know
what to do with a mother who is talking and balancing a crying
baby at the same time. Is it surprising that mothers would rather
avoid all the embarrassment and stay home?

And what about the teacher who wants to do a really good
job. . . . how can he possibly handle five, ten or even twenty
parents intelligently, comprehensively, patiently all in the same
afternoon or evening? Is it surprising that most of them don't
even try? ⸱

Teachers frequently will tell you that "the parents of the
children who are doing fine always come—the ones who really
need to come stay away."

Yet the entire procedure almost guarantees that a parent
whose child is having trouble will *not* come. The child is handed
a mimeographed notice. If he is having difficulties in school, he
knows it; and he is going to try to lose that notice so he won't
have to give it to his mother or father. Even if his parents do
find out about the conference, they are going to be most reluctant to come. *If* they can get off from work early enough, *if* they
can get someone to take care of the other kids, *if* they don't mind
talking to the teacher in front of all the other parents, they *might*

decide to come. But who would want to sit down and face the inevitable lecture? Who wants to be made to feel even more guilty and baffled? Who wants to come to a setup like that, where there is almost no opportunity to ask real questions or get real answers?

And then the teacher enters a note in the child's permanent record folder: "Uncooperative parent—refused to come to see me at conference time."

Or if the parent *does* go? And he dares to ask, "What are *you* doing to make sure that he learns?" For this the teacher has her instructions: "Don't ever argue with a parent; allow the parent to let off steam." And after the parent has left, the teacher picks up her pencil, and makes an entry in the student's record folder: "Hostile, uncooperative parent; has chip on his shoulder; does not want to help the child succeed in school."

Thus the conference process helps the system excuse its own failures. Their premise is that "children who are not succeeding in school have uncooperative parents," and the parent-teacher conference is set up to prove that their reasoning is correct.

If parents are fed up with the conference process, they should pressure for changes, but first they might ask, Shouldn't a school be able to educate the kids even if it does not get parent cooperation?

My friend Evelina Antonetty often tells parents: "What happens to orphans? They learn, don't they?" If the school system believes that the child cannot learn unless his parent behaves "properly," mere procedural changes will not improve parent-teacher conferences. If school officials set up these sessions so they can bulldoze the parents, lecture the parents, remake the parents, and blame the parents when the school fails to reach or teach the children, then most parents will, quite sensibly, continue to avoid them.

However, if the system should decide that *schools* are what needs to be remade, changed and drastically improved, and if the teachers recognize that they can learn a great deal from parents which will enable them to teach more effectively, then within that context, procedural changes *are* important and will help enormously to bring more and more parents—willingly— into a closer relationship with the schools.

Action Checklist for Parents

HOW TO HAVE A GOOD
PARENT–TEACHER CONFERENCE

In order to help the *schools* to improve, and in order to help the *teachers* do a better job, parents should demand the following changes in the parent–teacher conference procedures:

Children should not be dismissed from school to make time for parent conferences. Most New York communities have many working parents; when children are sent home early, it completely disrupts family schedules. When elementary, junior and senior highs are each dismissed early on different days, it is even more troublesome for the already harried working mother. Schools must make arrangements to supervise the children (in assemblies, in gym programs, in classes with other teachers) while the regular teachers are meeting with parents.

All the conferences should not take place on the same day. If the children are not sent home, the teachers can take turns scheduling parent conferences. In any event, it is too much to expect any teacher to prepare and think straight for more than four or five parent conferences at one time.

When conferences are scheduled, they should be at the parent's convenience; parents should be given a reasonable length of time and a reasonable amount of privacy.

Part of the teacher's job responsibility is, or ought to be, seeing the parents. The parent has to take time off from work, or make special arrangements to come to school. Whenever possible, it should be the *parent's* convenience which is sought, and not the school's or the teachers'.

At a minimum, thirty minutes should be set aside for each conference. If conferences are not scheduled one on top of another, it would allow the parent, and the teacher, to take more time if it is needed.

There should be a room set aside where the teacher and parent may talk privately, where the class won't be listening and other teachers won't be constantly interrupting.

If a mother brings smaller children with her, a staff member should be assigned to watch them for her, so she can give her complete attention to the teacher.

Teachers should be prepared to present complete and detailed information. The State Education Department recommends that the following material be presented to the parent:

—All information in the cumulative record folder, including test scores, health and attendance information, the anecdotal record, and anything else in the pupil's record.

—All materials, workbooks and books which the child uses and samples of his work.

The State Education Law (Section 7611) specifically states that all this information must be made available to *parents and students* at their request.

The teacher should interpret the records to the parent in a nontechnical, straightforward fashion. He should give the child's test scores without waiting to see if the parent asks for them. He should not try to "fool" the parent, talk down to the parent, browbeat the parent, nor should he use so much professional jargon that the parent is made to feel ignorant and foolish. For example, this kind of statement would be helpful to a parent: "Your daughter is reading 4.5. That means she is almost one and a half years behind grade level, and she will not go into the academic courses in junior and senior high school unless she improves."

The parent should be able to get complete information about the child in one conference. He should not be told that he must also go see the principal, the guidance counselor, or someone else. Every staff person who knows the child well or has particular information about him should be included in the conference. If there is a paraprofessional in the classroom and the parent would like her to be present, she should be there too.

If a translator is needed, or would make the parent or teacher more comfortable, he should be there *from the start*. Of course, having so many professionals at a parent conference could prove overwhelming. But, remember, this is all within the assumption that the staff is *not* there to embarrass or browbeat the parent but to learn from her!

If the teacher wants to ask any questions about the child's home life, she should explain why. If the parent believes that the question is a *relevant* one, he will answer it. For example: "Many employers and colleges ask us if a student is dependable. Dependability means to us that a child follows through and completes his work. Your son is not completing his work in school. Do you find that he is dependable at home?" If the parent believes some questions are personal and none of the school's business, he should stop the teacher's probing.

The teacher and the parent should decide what things the school will promise to do to help the child and what things the parent will do at home. If the teacher promises extra help for the child, she should put it in writing.

Parents often have ideas about what the school could do to help the child, but they are usually not asked to give their opinion, and sometimes when they offer it anyway, they are rebuffed. A *follow-up conference* should be arranged to see if the school is keeping its promise and actually giving the child the additional help he needs.

Parents should get a copy of any conference record and an outline of the teacher's requirements for the term.

If the teacher writes up any comments on the conference, a copy must be given to the parent. It is important that the parent co-sign this report, if she agrees with it; and then it could be placed in the pupil's record folder. If the parent does not agree with it, she should be permitted to write her own comments and insert them in the record folder also.

Many parents like to leave the conference with something in writing. In some school systems the conference takes place over the child's report card; in other systems, there is no report card, but at the end of the conference the parent and teacher fill out a joint progress report evaluating the child's work. In New York I have heard parents plead for a written memo from the teacher outlining her homework requirements, and a brief summary of the work and books she will be using that year.

If the school system permits extra help for the child, get such assurances in writing.

Student-teacher conferences and parent-student-teacher conferences should be encouraged, especially in the junior and senior high schools. In several school systems each student has a private conference with his teacher and parent four times a year. Some teachers may object, saying they can't discuss problems in front of the child. Why not? Doesn't the kid know there is a problem? The teacher could probably learn more about the student from the student himself than he could learn from the parent anyway, if the teacher sets up the conference in such a way so that the student feels free to really talk. After all, the law states that the pupil's record folder *must* be made available to the *student* as well as to his *parent*.

Parents must be welcome to come to school and to contact the teacher all the time, and not just when the child is in trouble.

Every school must immediately remove those large warnings: "All visitors report to the office for a pass immediately." Parents should be encouraged to drop into the child's classroom at any time and should not require a special permission slip or pass.

Teachers should start telephoning parents. And it would be wonderful if they would give their home phone number to the kids and parents to use in an emergency. (Once, one of my daughter's teachers did this, and I still haven't recovered from the shock.)

When parents drop off the children or pick them up, they should not be required to remain outside the school building. They should be encouraged to come inside and wait next to the classroom door so they can say a few words to the teacher if they want to.

Teachers should practice writing home notes and telephoning parents when the children do something *good!* Preston Wilcox suggests that the school will know it is really part of the community when the parents start dropping in when their kids are *not* in trouble!

Finally, parents should have the right to stay *uninvolved.* There will always be some who simply believe that what happens in school is between the school and the child. This parent should be allowed his privacy. Reaching parents is not the main job of the schools; educating children is!

8·The Cumulative Record Card

As soon as a child starts school, the system begins to compile all kinds of personal and confidential information about him. This data is added to each year as it is passed along from teacher to teacher, following the child throughout his school life. When the pupil transfers or is promoted to another school, these records go with him. Once a student graduates or drops out of the system entirely, his cumulative record folder, which is what it is called, is not destroyed; it is retained, completely intact, by the Board of Education for the next fifty years!

Teachers are permitted to make any entries they feel are pertinent or appropriate; there is no procedure for ascertaining the veracity or objectivity of the material in these files. Thus, for example, in one Bronx junior high school, teachers received the cumulative record files from the feeding elementary schools which included comments such as these: "Draws well but is restless and uncooperative"; "Resents correction; stubborn"; "Needs constant supervision"; "Temper, possible truant, needs to be watched."

These files have an enormous impact on the child's life both in school and afterward. The teacher's opinion of the child influences the child's success in school, for if the teacher expects the child to fail, he almost always does. The cumulative record card is the system's technique for making sure that teachers will inherit someone else's evaluation—and expectation—of their pupils.

Current Procedure

These folders must be kept in a gray file drawer in the school or guidance office. They may be delivered to teachers by other teachers or by "trusted monitors." (Knowing my own children, I seriously doubt whether any child—or adult for that matter—could really be trusted to resist the temptation to take a quick look!) Inside the folders are the following items:

PERSONAL AND EDUCATIONAL RECORD CARD

This is a four-page buff-colored card which includes information and teacher opinions concerning the pupil's family background and attendance, and academic, personal and social behavior. There is space for the teacher to include his impressions of the parents after he meets them. If there is additional information which the school considers to be of a "highly confidential nature," it is noted on this record, but the information itself is kept in another file in the principal's office and must be sent for separately. (Of course, many teachers jump to conclusions when they note the existence of such a confidential file; they don't bother sending for it—they *know* what it means: another bad kid.)

HEALTH RECORD

This salmon-colored card contains medical information, such as a description of the child's dental and hearing needs, the condition of his eyesight, his previous illnesses.

TEST RECORD

This blue-green card has a record of the child's scores on all standardized tests. (If the parent could see this card, she could tell immediately what tests were lacking, what progress he was really making, and could ask the school authorities some sensible questions.) If the test results do not conform with the teacher's judgment, there is additional room for the teacher to write her own comment about the child's achievement and reading ability. (Until a few years ago, Intelligence Test Scores were also entered on this record form. These tests are no longer given by the New York City system.)

READING RECORD

This is a four-page white card in which the teacher is supposed to record each time the child progresses from one reading "level" to another, what books he is using, what reading skills he has mastered. Since this card is not mandatory, many teachers do not bother filling it out. If the child's bilingualism is considered "pertinent," the teacher indicates it here. Again, there is space for the teacher to enter her own opinions about the pupil's progress, strengths and weaknesses.

ANECDOTAL RECORD

If a teacher considers a child's "misbehavior" to be serious, she is supposed to keep a "detailed and objective" account (daily and sometimes hourly) of his behavior. This document is most often used to support the child's suspension or transfer to a "600 School for Socially Maladjusted Children."

MISCELLANEOUS MATERIAL

There are no restrictions on the extent or nature of the information which may be included in this folder. Teachers and supervisors are encouraged to add "any other data that will aid in the understanding and guidance of the pupil." In particular, reports of parent conferences or interviews with private or public agency personnel regarding the pupil are enclosed.

THE STATE EDUCATION LAW AND PUPIL RECORDS.

Parents used to be told they could not see these "confidential" record folders. However, a few years ago the State Education Department issued a booklet entitled *Manual on Pupil Records* which has slowly but surely come into the hands of a number of parent groups in New York City. Clearly, the professionals in the system have been acting illegally when they denied parents and students the right to this information.

There are two specific laws which are applicable. The first* states that all district records and books and papers are public property and open for inspection by any qualified voter and any such voter may make copies of these records. Thus all data about finances, salaries, achievement scores, etc.—indeed all records and reports—are, according to state law, available to the public.

However, there are certain records which are considered "qualified." In this category are the personal and scholastic records of individual pupils. This information may not be made available to the public, but it must be made available to the *parents*.† *The Manual on Pupil Records* is an important document for all parent groups to obtain. It places great emphasis on the right of parents (and students) to see this information and to understand it. At one point the State Education Commissioner announced that not only must all records be shown to parents but also a specialist must be made available to interpret the record to the parent. Thus, in dealing with a psychiatric report, the psychiatrist who wrote the report should be available to explain it to the parent.

WHAT IS WRONG WITH
THE SYSTEM

During the fight for a student grievance table at George Washington High School, the parents requested the right to take down the name, address and phone number of each student

* State Education Law, Section 2116.
† State Education Law, Section 7611 and Commissioner's Decision 6849, Sept. 22, 1969.

who made a complaint so that his family could be contacted and involved in the parents' committee. The school authorities refused to permit this, issuing this written "explanation":

> The Board wishes to emphasize and underscore a funda-
> mental principle of operation of our public schools, namely
> that any student records, including addresses, telephone num-
> bers, draft status, past record, family status, be kept con-
> fidential. Such records are not made available to anyone other
> than the pupil or parent himself. Even college authorities,
> employers, the police, Welfare Department officials are not
> given such information except on a court order or at the
> request of the pupil or parent.

On the face of it, this is a fair and proper policy. But in actual fact, no one in the system pays any attention to it, and if the board members were serious about its implementation, they would have spelled out procedures for making sure that this policy is enforced. The professional staff continues to send confidential pupil information to the Welfare Department, the Housing Authority, the Police Department, and other public and private agencies. And the professional staff continues to keep most pupil records locked up when a parent or student requests the right to see them! Thus if parents ask for information in order to help their own child, or in order to organize other parents, they are denied it. But if agencies ask for information— no matter what their purpose—it is automatically sent to them. Just one week after the board issued its statement about "confidentiality," a 17-year-old student at George Washington told me that the Welfare Department had denied her application for financial assistance because the school had told the department that she was a "truant." In actual fact, she had applied for help because she had no family and was working thirty-five hours a week and going to school. As a result of the pace, she was absent a great deal; if she got help from the Welfare Department, she could work fewer hours and attend school regularly. But the school never asked her why she was absent. When the school got the letter from the Welfare Department, it never asked her permission to send an answer. It mailed a routine reply: "Truant." And the student, denied welfare assistance, had to quit school in order to hold down a full-time job.

According to its own teacher manuals, the board instructs its staff to use the information in the cumulative record file to help them decide whether or not the curriculum will have to be modified (watered down) or enriched (upgraded) for the particular pupil. The teacher is told to examine such factors as the child's "social and economic status," "the number of rooms in which the family lives," "the nature of the parents' supervision of the child," "the economic conditions of the home," "whether the pupil's out-of-school activities are wholesome," etc., etc. Teachers are urged to study the contents of the folder *before* they meet their official class for the first time in the year.

The contents of the file are used to determine whether the child will be assigned to an advanced or "slow" class. But beyond this the material provides considerable weight in suspension hearings; it is frequently used to substantiate the principal's decision to refer the child to a mental health agency, to a special school for the emotionally disturbed or to a class for disruptive youngsters.

Considering the use to which these files are put, one would think that the Board of Education would be anxious to make certain that all entries are highly accurate and fair. In a few cases, where parents have become adamant and insisted on looking over their contents, the most damaging information about the child has been removed *"to protect the informant"*! If highly derogatory information exists in the student's records, they are effectively prevented from challenging it since neither the parents nor the students have usually seen it; there is no procedure for a parent to use to contest the contents in the child's records. In fact, even if certain things happen which later prove that entries in the folder were incorrect or unfair, there is no regulation stipulating that these harmful and untrue statements must now be removed from the permanent record. In one Queens high school, a student was found to be illegally and unfairly suspended, and was reinstated in the school; six months later the father and the lawyers were still trying to force the

Board of Education to remove all mention of the unlawful suspension from the student's records.

Now that more parents have learned about the provisions in the state law, undoubtedly more of them will begin to ask to see their children's records. We have already begun to do this in the Bronx; it is, however, a tedious process. First the principal tells the parent that she is incorrect; the records cannot be seen. We then pull out a copy of the law (it has been excerpted and mimeographed by United Bronx Parents). The principal then calls his district superintendent for confirmation. Usually he then agrees to show the parent the information, but only when a "specialist" is available to interpret the data. Since there is a shortage of specialists, the parent is asked to wait or come back some other time. If she sticks to her guns, eventually she will be shown her child's complete folder. However, the top-echelon official who "explains" it to her uses so much double-talk and educational jargon that she becomes confused or overwhelmed. Parents are permitted to bring their own "experts" or even friends to go over the records; and, of course, parents are now also allowed to obtain copies of these records. If they do this, they can show them to people they trust and get their interpretation.

Although many parents have found out about the existence of these important documents, many more have not. If a parent or a student does not know that they are being kept, they do not know they can ask to see them. And if they do not see them, they cannot challenge their accuracy.

What is needed is an automatic process, which guarantees that every parent will see her child's full record at least once a year. A procedure, such as the one that has been won by the teachers, would be very helpful. If any statement is to be placed into a teacher's record folder which might be harmful or might in any way adversely affect his career, the teacher has the right to read it and initial it *before* it becomes a part of her record. In a number of cases, the full record does not accompany the teacher when she is transferred to another school. Teachers have the right to challenge what goes into their file, and if they prove the information is incorrect or exaggerated, all such reference must be removed from the record. The fact that everyone knows the teachers will see their files is often enough to guarantee that statements are made more carefully and with greater accuracy.

Finally, I don't understand why a full cumulative record need accompany a child when he is transferred or promoted to another school anyway. It seems to me it would be much fairer, and would really guarantee every child a fresh start if the only information that was sent was a list of the courses which he successfully completed and his end-term marks.

Action Checklist for Parents

HOW TO CHANGE THE CUMULATIVE RECORD SYSTEM

Demand that your principal and/or local school board immediately review and clarify the procedures for keeping and using cumulative records.

√A parent-student-faculty committee could be set up to investigate the problem and to learn about the law.

√A public hearing might be held to broaden the discussion.

√The types of things which should be investigated are:

Exactly what forms are in these records.

How they are used.

Who sees them. Can agency officials obtain copies without parental permission?

What information is included in these records which is really none of the school's business and should no longer be asked?

√At the end of this study, a new record form should be developed for your district with a clear public policy regarding the use to which these records may be put.

Demand that a procedure be established so that every parent knows about the existence of these records, and is able to see and challenge their contents.

√This does not have to wait until your local board investigates and revises the contents of the records.

√Parents now have the right, under law, to see these records at any time.

√Insist that your school automatically send a complete xeroxed copy of the child's full cumulative record card to the parent at least once a year.

√Parents should be given the right to initial all potentially damaging or adverse entries *before* they are placed in the record. (Teachers have this right.)

√Parents should be told that the law permits them to challenge any material in the file which they believe to be libelous, false or misleading. Parents should be provided with an effective appeal procedure for making such challenges. (Teachers have this right.)

√Any information which is found to be false or wrongly stated should be completely removed from the record. (Teachers have this right.)

√Parents should have the right to attach their own comments or explanations to the child's record. (Teachers have this right.)

√Parents should be informed that they have a right to obtain a copy of this record at any time; they may bring in their own friends or experts to look it over with them and to help them understand it.

Insist that no information about any pupil be given by the school to any public or private agency without the parent's permission.

This is especially important in terms of police, courts, and the welfare department.

Insist that the school officials establish a time limit after which no material may be placed in a child's folder. (Teachers have won the right that any incident which has not been entered into the file within three months of its occurrence may not later be added to the file.)

Frequently a teacher will be getting along fine with a pupil, will be satisfied with his work, and then something happens which causes the teacher to radically alter his opinion of the child. In his anger, he goes back in memory and suddenly "remembers" and writes up incidents which supposedly took place five or six months earlier.

No anonymous material should be permitted in any file. (Teachers have this right.)

An effective grievance procedure must be established so that parents and students may challenge or contest any entry in their file.

Parents or students should be able to appeal to a committee which is not composed of school-system employees, but which is composed of parents, students and other community representatives, and is perhaps appointed by the local school board.

If a student transfers or is promoted, the material in his file should not follow him to his new school.

√Let the staff in that school form their own opinions of the child without any "help."

√If the law states that records must be kept, let them be kept behind lock and key in a district office somewhere, only to be released with the parent's permission.

√All that is really required to accompany the student are his end-term marks and a list of the courses he has successfully completed.

√If the child did get into some real trouble at his first school, he must be permitted to live it down and start over again, without the staff in his new school reading about his "background" or without their receiving this very subjective evaluation of his ability and performance.

The cumulative record card must not remain an unregulated abused tool of the system. It is too important and parents must be allowed to examine, challenge, and control this material and its use!

9 · Student Suspensions and Student Rights

THE RIGHT TO
FAIR TREATMENT

"If you lived in a community where you saw people being destroyed by drugs, welfare, unemployment and hunger, you would become terribly angry or terribly apathetic. Thank God, the kids are angry." Thus spoke a young teacher from Brooklyn at a recent Board of Education public hearing on student rights. But the members of the board showed no sympathy; in fact, they were so frightened and upset by the anger and emotion displayed by the students who had come to testify that they suddenly adjourned the hearing and walked out on the pupils.

Boys and girls in our city schools, and particularly in our high schools, have been trying to get adults to listen to them for years. They describe the conditions in their schools as "inhuman," "jail-like," and "irrelevant"; but the grownups rarely hear or believe them. During the teachers' strike of 1968 the students witnessed the adults fighting over the school system; law and order was brushed aside by principals and teachers who participated in the strike. When the strike was over, the students proved that they were not slow learners. They began to organize, protest, picket, march, demonstrate—and even strike. The adult response was to punish the students who protested; policemen and security guards were stationed in the schools; students were forced to carry identification cards at all times; law and order was going to be had at any cost. No matter if the children were repressed in the process. They were complaining about things which were really unimportant—weren't they?

What are the students complaining about? What are conditions like in our high schools? Throughout this book I have described what happens inside the schools—the overcrowding, the poor teaching, the irrelevant curriculum, the outdated books, the poor lunches and, most terrible of all, the vast number of students who have not been taught even to read. When you have had enough you can put the book down. And I can get angry and protest. You and I are not students who are compelled to go to those schools day after day after day!

Skim quickly over these statistics:

—There is an overload in our academic high schools of more than 40,000 students.

—There are probably more than 10,000 suspensions a year.

—Most of our high school students have tried marijuana; and perhaps as many as 10 percent in some of the schools are using heroin.

—Anywhere from 30 percent to 60 percent of our students drop out of high school.

—Of our school population 55 percent are nonwhite; 80 percent of the students in the academic track in our high schools are white.

—The majority of the nonwhite pupils are in the general track.

—Less than 20 percent of the nonwhite students go on to college.

See. It took you less than two minutes to read those lines. But how would you feel if you were forced to spend five and a half hours a day inside those schools, where these were not cold facts on a piece of paper, but were the hot hard facts of life? All around you, each day, you would watch your fellow students taking and pushing drugs; you would see teachers pretending nothing was wrong; you would see policemen brought into the schools—not to stop the drug-pushing but to force the *students* to behave. Nobody seems to want to know *why* the children are using drugs. And nobody is forcing the teachers to behave; nobody is forcing the Board of Education to provide adequate space; to improve the curriculum; to set performance standards for its staff; to deal with teacher prejudice; to order unbiased books; to provide decent lunches. The children must obey the law and be orderly, but the school officials are able to flout the law—and continue to collect their salaries.

Why are we so afraid of the students? Why are we so angry when they protest? If the school system treats the children with indifference and hostility, is it surprising that the students treat the schools the same way? Don't we realize that the failure of the schools to teach and the failure of the pupils to behave are directly related?

The Public Education Association has issued a small but excellent pamphlet entitled *Student Grievances in the New York City High Schools*. In it they quote one high school pupil who is trying to describe why the students behave the way they do:

> I know why those guys throw rocks and set fires. They found out there's no way they can make it. They know that's not right but it's true, and they don't know what to do about it. If you try to change things, you get put up against the wall for that, too. So finally you get mad. That's just human.

When students react to these terrible conditions, the conditions are rarely changed; the students are simply punished. What are the regulations concerning suspensions? Why are students suspended? What is the law, and what is wrong with it?

Suspensions: The Rules and Regulations

THE NEW YORK STATE EDUCATION LAW*

The law specifically states that all children between the ages of five and twenty-one years of age are *entitled* to attend public

* State Education Law, Sections 3202, 3206, 3214.

school. Children between the ages of seven and sixteen *must* attend school. In order to be sure that "children shall not suffer through unnecessary failure to attend school *for any cause whatsoever*," the law provides that the school system must employ attendance teachers who are to make certain that every child is provided with an opportunity to go to school.

The law recognizes that there may be certain youngsters who cannot be taught in a regular school situation. These children may be suspended but they still have the right to a public education. The law is very clear about this. *At no time and under no circumstances may a child of school age be deprived of his full educational opportunities.* There are four grounds for suspension. A child may be suspended (1) for being disorderly; (2) for being insubordinate; (3) if he is dangerous mentally or physically or (4) if he is feeble-minded.

If a student is arrested for a crime committed outside of a school, he cannot be suspended merely because he was arrested.* We still have a code of justice whereby a person is innocent until proven guilty. Once that student comes to trial and is found guilty, he will receive his punishment via the courts. Suspension is not supposed to be used as a punishment. This is terribly important. The law says that some children simply cannot function in a conventional school setting; therefore each board of education must establish special schools or educational programs for these children. A suspension, under the law, is *not* supposed to be a punishment; it is supposed to be a technique for *helping* the child, for resolving the child's problems.

Students and parents who have firsthand experience with the New York City suspension process do not believe that it helps the child. They have seen too many principals use suspensions to harass students, intimidate parents and to get rid of those pupils they simply do not want or can't handle. Before describing these abuses, let me outline the Board of Education suspension process.

* Howard V. Clark 299 NYS 2d 65 (Sup Ct., Westchester County 1969).

NEW YORK CITY BOARD OF EDUCATION SUSPENSION PROCEDURE*

"Prevention" Procedures: The circular tells the principals that they are supposed to "help children resolve their adjustment problems" long before suspension is considered. This means that the school staff is supposed to obtain extra "support" and "special services" for those children who need them.

When a "serious problem" arises regarding a pupil's behavior, the principal is to call a *pre-suspension conference* with the parent and staff and the student. The parent is to be notified of this conference in writing. The school system terms this a guidance conference to enable the school to "plan educationally for the benefit of the child," and therefore the parent is not permitted to bring an attorney at this time.

Parents who are contesting a suspension should take the time to find out if these "prevention" procedures were really followed. Frequently a school official will hold a meeting with the parent and will suggest that the child needs "special help," but more often than not, that help is never actually made available. The referral may never be made. Or if it is made, the waiting list for that service is so long that the child is never seen. Or an appointment is set up, but when the child reports, the person he is supposed to see is so overworked and rushed that he can barely pay any attention to what the child tells him. If the pupil doesn't come back a second time, everyone is too busy to notice. Months later, when someone remembers to inquire about the child, there is no record that he came. It is assumed that the child was uncooperative and did not want to be helped, and that is the notation placed in his file.

Principal's Suspension: If a principal decides that a child's "overt behavior" prevents the "orderly operation of classes or other activities" or "presents a clear and present danger of physical injury" to staff or students, the principal has emergency power to suspend that student. The following procedure must then be observed:

* Board of Education Special Circular No. 36, 1969–1970, Nov. 12, 1969, and State Education Law, Section 3126.

The parents are to be telephoned immediately and sent a letter by certified mail. This letter must tell them why the child was suspended, and asks the parents to call the office to make an appointment to discuss the suspension.

The child is not to leave the school until his parent arrives to take him home. If no one arrives, he is to remain in school until the end of the school day.

An emergency suspension may not exceed *five days,* and therefore the meeting with the principal *must* take place within that time.

The parent is permitted to bring two persons to act as "advisers" but "who may not act as attorneys." The principal is also permitted to bring two assistants to the meeting. If the parent and the principal agree, they may increase the number of people who are present.

The hearing is conducted by the same principal who suspended the child. The parent is permitted to ask questions of the complaining witnesses; he and the student are allowed to tell their side of the story.

This meeting *cannot* take place unless the parent or person in parental relation is present. If the parent does not come, the principal may simply reinstate the pupil, or may refer the case to the district superintendent "who shall take such action as he may determine."

A pupil suspended by the principal must be returned to the school no later than five school days after the day of the suspension. There may not be two consecutive periods of suspension; and there may not be more than two emergency suspensions for any one pupil in any one year. The suspended pupil is marked absent during the period of suspension.

If, after the meeting, the parent believes the suspension was not justified, he may appeal first to the supervising assistant superintendent and then to the school board. (Appeals from elementary and junior high school students should go to the district superintendent and then to the local school board; appeals from high school and special-school students go to the supervising superintendent at headquarters and then to the central Board of Education.)

After a decision on an appeal is reached, the parent must be informed of the decision in writing and the reasons therefore. In any case where the suspension was found to be unjustified, the student must be exonerated and any record of disciplinary proceedings against him removed from his record.

After the conference, the principal may either return the child to the same class or a different class in the same school. Or the principal may request the district superintendent to suspend the pupil for a longer period, in which case the district superintendent must observe the procedure described below.

District Superintendent's Suspension: If a principal believes that a student is too "disruptive" or that he "would benefit from an alternative educational experience" he is to refer the case to the district superintendent, giving him a "brief summary of the student's behavior."

The district superintendent schedules a hearing. At this point the student may or may not be already suspended. If the student has been already suspended by the principal, the district superintendent must call the hearing quickly and must notify the parents by telegram. He must however, give the parents at least *four days' notice* in advance of the hearing. If the student is attending school, however, and the hearing is to determine whether or not he should be suspended, the parents are to be mailed a certified letter, giving them *no less than ten days' advance notice* before the hearing takes place.

The telegram or letter must designate the date, time and place of the hearing and contain a statement of the parent's right to be *represented by an attorney*; this notice must also include a listing of the charges against the student and the possible *consequences* which might follow the hearing.

The state law, and therefore the board regulations, provide that the pupil shall have a "fair hearing." This includes the right to question witnesses who had made complaints against the pupil.

If the parent fails to appear, the superintendent must reschedule the hearing, but he may suspend the pupil pending the new hearing. At the end of the hearing, the superintendent must make a *written statement of his findings and recommendations*.

As a result of the hearing a child may be reinstated in the

same school, transferred to another school, referred to a Special School for Maladjusted Children (600 School), or referred to the Bureau of Child Guidance or other "suitable" agency for "study." If there is a waiting list at the alternative educational institution, the pupil may be kept suspended "pending his placement." The suspended pupil is marked absent during his suspension.

The parent may appeal the superintendent's decision. Elementary and junior high school students are to appeal to the local school board. High school and special-school students are to appeal to the central Board of Education.

WHAT IS WRONG WITH SUSPENSION PROCEDURES

They are unjust and undemocratic. And they are not helpful to the child. They are used as weapons to harass, intimidate and punish.

The Regulations Are Often Ignored. Because so many groups had protested the unfair procedures, in late 1969 the Board of Education modified them and introduced a number of reforms. (Actually a state law had been passed which forced the board to make these changes.) However, the most serious weakness in the new procedures is that there is no mechanism for parents or students to bring charges against those supervisors who disobey the regulations. There is no process set up by the Board of Education to monitor the hearings, and nowhere has the board specified whether and in what way staff members will be disciplined if they fail to obey the new rules.

And they have a history of ignoring regulations. Parents are supposed to be notified the day the child is suspended so that they can come to the school to pick him up. But in many cases the teacher or dean or assistant principal will simply scream at a student, "Get out of my school!" Consider what happened at Franklin K. Lane. Almost seven hundred parents were notified on a Friday that they had to come to the school or their children would be suspended. Monday morning, before a single parent could even attempt to comply, all the students were suspended!

The rule most often broken is the one which states that principals may suspend children for no more than five days. Over 80 percent of the five-day suspensions are stretched into seven days, ten days, and longer. During that period the child is denied access to public education, with no hearing, no opportunity to ask why, no chance to challenge the charges.

Teachers and supervisors have demanded and won extensive protection; the procedures which must be followed before they can be disciplined or dismissed are complicated and extensive. But they deny similar rights to the students.

The Hearings Are Often Unfair.   The principal or his immediate superior conducts the hearing and renders the verdict. And yet he is often the same person who brought the charges against the child in the first place. Thus he is the arresting officer, the judge and the jury. And there is no procedure which would permit a parent to challenge the bias of the principal, or of any of the other school officials who are present.

As the hearing proceeds, all kinds of "evidence" are introduced. Since an attorney is only permitted at the district superintendent's hearing, most of these remarks are permitted to go unchallenged. The child's cumulative record card is produced; many of the statements in that record are unverified anecdotes, written up over a period of time by a variety of teachers. These statements are introduced into the hearing as if they were the complete, objective truth.

Often the family background is delved into far more than necessary. Although too little is said about what the school has failed to do, much is said about the failure of the parents. It is embarrassing to listen to the professionals talk to the family: "I notice your child's last name is different from yours. Do you have a husband, Mrs. Garcia?"

And finally, there is no official transcript of the proceedings, although lawyers and community groups have pleaded for this rather simple and obvious guarantee of fairness. Sometimes a secretary will be called in to take minutes; sometimes only summary notes are written. Thus, it is very difficult for a parent to appeal the decision. It is only her word, against the "evidence" of professional, educated school officials.

The Rules Are Erratic, Inconsistent and Secret. In many cases students are accused of breaking rules they have never heard of before; parents are rarely shown any written regulation which their child has been accused of violating. "Excessive" cutting can mean five times, ten times, or twenty times, depending upon the individual principal. Even within the same school, two students with the same record are treated quite differently, because the staff "likes" one of them and considers the other one "arrogant."

In one district "offensive language" is considered normal; in another, it is grounds for suspension. In neither case, however, is the parent or the student told about this regulation in advance. I know of one *second-grade* boy who had been suspended for "indecent exposure"—his fly was open and the teacher was furious. If that criterion was applied consistently, there would be very few little boys in our public schools.

In some districts, when a child is suspended, his entire record for all the years he has attended school is submitted as "proof" that he has been bad for a long time. In other circumstances, where a child has a good attendance and academic record over the years, it isn't referred to at all, and instead they speak only of the terrible thing he did *this* time. In January 1969, a large number of students were suspended from a Brooklyn high school, allegedly because they had been truant for thirty days or more. The fact that many of them had no record of truancy prior to that term, and that the UFT had been on strike for thirty-seven of the ninety-day term, was not considered at all when the decision was made to dump those children. The parents went into court, however, and the judge, citing the extenuating circumstances, ordered the board to reinstate the pupils. He suggested that the school system could be considered responsible for the overcrowded situation and overlapping sessions which contributed to the disorder and truancy.

Suspensions Are Often Used to Push Kids out of School. Children are legally permitted to go to public school until they are twenty-one, but they are only required to go until they are sixteen. Very often a seventeen-year-old will be helped to decide to quit school through the suspension process. When the parents arrive at the hearing, they are told, "He's past the legal age for school; why not let him go to work?" Pregnant girls are also advised to leave school, although the fact that only girls are suspended for this offense shows how little the school authorities know about sex. And frequently the system will suspend a pupil because they learn about some allegation against him in family court that is totally unrelated to his conduct in school.

Sometimes Suspensions Are the Result of a Political Disagreement Between the Student and School Authorities. Students are suspended for distributing "unauthorized" leaflets or newspapers, refusing to say or stand for the Pledge of Allegiance, picketing, etc. Students believe that these suspensions are used by the administration to isolate the radical leadership from the other students. Since the high school principals' association have issued a statement telling its members to do just that, it is quite possible that the students are correct.

At Brooklyn Technical High School, for example, one of the city's specialized high schools, with extremely high academic entrance requirements, three black students were suspended for putting up pictures of Malcolm X and Eldridge Cleaver in the cafeteria. White students had posted pictures of Marilyn Monroe and the Beatles, with no complaint from the administration. After the three black leaders were suspended, one hundred six other students demonstrated in protest; as a result, they were *all* suspended!

Although a Suspension Is Supposed to Help a Child, It Almost Always Harms Him. The suspension and the hearing can have grave consequences for the child. Parents are often tricked into believing that their child will be helped. The referral which is being made is spoken of in glowing terms, but the following is what can really happen.

A child is referred to the Bureau of Child Guidance, a division of the Board of Education, for testing. That agency has a six-month waiting list; the student remains out of school all that time. He is finally examined, and they decide that the child should be institutionalized. Most of these institutions are totally inadequate—the newspapers are often filled with sensational stories about the awful conditions at agencies such as Spofford House. But if the parent refuses to accept the verdict of the bureau, and won't let her child be placed in such an institution, she is considered a lawbreaker, and the Bureau of Attendance takes her into Family Court. If the parent retracts and gives her permission, but if the child refuses to be committed, the child is the lawbreaker, and the Bureau of Attendance takes *him* to court.

If the child and the parent don't protest, and agree to the institutional placement, they will soon discover that there is a ten-month waiting list or longer. So the district superintendent may recommend that the student receive home instruction during that time or, more likely, the student will simply be "exempt" from public education until placement becomes possible.

If the child is sent to a "600" school, the consequences are just as severe. There are many reports that have been made criticizing the services, staff and stability of these schools. And yet the "600" schools and the Bureau of Child Guidance placement institutions continue to be the only educational "alternative" available to the child who cannot function—or is no longer wanted—in our public schools.

Arrests and Police Actions Are Becoming as Common as Suspension. Someday they will write about the war in our city—the war between the old and the young. I don't know who will win the war, but I certainly know who is suffering the most casualties right now.

As principals have been required to conduct "fair" suspension hearings, they have found a new way to circumvent the regulations. Instead of suspending the children, they call in the police and have them arrested. Our daily papers report that plain-clothesmen, disguised as students, have been assigned to many of our high schools. Security guards, not very carefully chosen and even less carefully trained, have also been assigned to many schools. If a child gets into trouble, it is easier to arrest him, remove him instantly, and let the courts handle the whole mess. If the parent is thus forced to hire an attorney, if the child misses days of school while waiting for court action, so be it.

Thus, when our schools fail with the children, they have found a new scheme to avoid dealing with the problem. Instead of asking: Why are the children misbehaving in school? What should our schools be doing that they are not doing now?— instead of changing, the school officials simply refer the entire problem to the police and the courts.

The Board Keeps Totally Inadequate Records on Suspensions. The new regulations require the principals and district superintendents to keep full details about every suspension, what caused it, and what was done about it, but to date no detailed information has been released to the public.

Parents believe that some schools and teachers cause more student "disruptions" and suspensions than others. But the system has, up to now, kept no records which would help them analyze the problem or the contributing factors. There are no data about the types of referrals that are made, and absolutely no information as to whether the children are helped by these referrals. Where a child has been accepted by a special institution, does he improve? No one knows—or maybe it is because they *do* know, that they don't make anything public.

The board claims that there is no budget for adequate educational facilities for children who are in trouble. But the system is callously neglectful when it does not provide information about the extent and nature of the problem, so that the public will be informed and will see to it that adequate services and funding are provided.

It should be noted that the Decentralization Law provides that community boards will be given the authority "to maintain discipline in the schools and programs under their jurisdiction."* Although the high schools remain under the jurisdiction of the

---

* Decentralization Law, Section 2590 (e-8).

central board, the elementary and junior highs do not. This might very well mean that the regulations described here will be revised by each local board. I certainly hope so.

Action Checklist for Parents

WHAT TO DO IF YOUR CHILD IS SUSPENDED FROM SCHOOL

The Board of Education has very unfair, probably illegal procedures for handling school suspensions. These rules are being appealed through the courts and by the time you read this, the law may have been changed; if it has not, however, parents should be organizing to achieve a just and proper policy. Meanwhile, if your child is faced with a suspension, here is a list of some things you can do to make sure his rights are protected.

How to prepare for the hearing.

Do everything possible to get him back into school at once—don't wait until a hearing takes place. It is absolutely essential that your child not be out of school. It is not fair to suspend a child *before* a hearing takes place. This is the same as sentencing a man to jail before he has a trial. Unless your child went completely crazy in school and actually socked a teacher or another child, there is absolutely no reason why he should not be permitted to remain in school until a hearing is held. The law says all children have a right to a public education. Don't let them deny this to your child!

Talk to your child and trust him—don't start blaming him. You must get your child's side of the story. And you ought to believe him and want to fight for him. You are the most important thing he has going for him. Ask him what happened, and why he thinks it happened. Find out what he wants to do next. Does he want to go back to the same class, or does he want a different teacher or perhaps a different school?

Get a lawyer or someone else with experience to help you— never, never, never go to a conference or hearing alone. The school officials may try to convince you to come alone. They will call it a guidance conference for the "educational benefit of the child." Just remember, these are really hearings, no matter what name they give them. They can have very serious consequences for both you and your child. You must have someone with you who knows the ropes and who will make sure your rights are protected as much as possible. If you need help, go to the New York Civil Liberties Union, 156 Fifth Avenue or Citizens Committee for Children, 112 East 19th Street.

Get as much information as you can—get a copy of the charges against your child so you can study them in advance. You may also want to talk to some other teachers whom your child likes and trusts. You might want to see the school or district guidance counselor to find out what they say, and to see if you can find out what the authorities intend to do next. Be sure to talk to other parents and children in the class. If many other children are having trouble with that same teacher, you should find it out. Maybe it is the teacher and not your child who is at fault.

Make sure they schedule the hearing at a time when you can come. If you are commanded to appear on a date when you must go to work, or cannot come for some other reason, insist that they postpone the hearing to a more convenient date. If you receive a notice only the day before the hearing, insist that you need a little time to get prepared. Under no circumstances should you let them rush you into this unprepared. They are not allowed to conduct the hearing without you!

If you do not speak English easily, bring your own translator. Even though they may be prepared to supply a Board of Education translator, you can be more certain that you will not miss anything that is going on if you bring your own.

At the Hearing.

Insist that they present their facts clearly—you have a right to question all their witnesses.

√If your child is accused of a specific act, insist that the person accusing him be present. You have a right to question him.

√If the child's story and the teacher's story are different, insist that witnesses be called in and questioned during the conference.

√If they tell you the child has broken a particular rule, ask to see a copy of the rule he is supposed to have violated.

√Insist that the staff give you *specific facts*. A vague statement, such as "He doesn't behave" or "He always talks back," is not good enough. It would be inadmissible in a courtroom. Tell them to describe exactly what he did and didn't do, when, where, and how often. Ask as many questions as you need to; make sure you understand exactly what they are saying about your child.

If a teacher testifies against your child, request information about that teacher's background, experience, length of time in that school, whether he or she has been involved in other such incidents, etc. Very often a child gets along fine with his regular teachers, but a substitute or a teacher from another class gets angry at him and starts a feud. If this is so, point it out.

You have a right to call your own witnesses to speak in your child's behalf. If your child wants to tell his own version of what happened, make sure they let him do it, and make sure they listen to him. Don't let them ignore your child.

If your child gets along fine elsewhere—in other classes, in church, in a community center, at work—call in witnesses from those places to present his side of the story. If the children in the class want to speak on behalf of your child, call them in to testify also.

You have a right to show that they have not tried to help your child before this crisis occurred. The school is supposed to speak with the parent when a child first begins to get into difficulty, first begins to be absent too often, first begins to fail in his work. If they did not call you in before, as is very often the case, be sure you point this out. Sometimes they will talk about a number of things they have done to help your child; if these things are not true, don't be afraid to say so. If the help they gave was no good, talk about it. If the agencies they sent you to for help never gave you an appointment or frightened you, say so. If you requested special help but they did not give it, remind them of this. If there is something you think should be done right now to help your child, speak up.

They may ask you or your child to leave the room for part of the hearing, but if you do not want to go, you should not go. In a fair hearing, everything is out in the open; nothing is secret. However, if there is something you are afraid to say because a certain teacher or supervisor is in the room, you have the right to ask that he leave, and he must go. This hearing is supposed to be for your child's benefit, and they should do everything possible to make certain you are not afraid or uncomfortable.

If they start talking about your personal family life, do not be afraid to object. Of course, you want to do everything you can to help your child. But when a child is suspended it has to mean that *the school has failed your child,* and your discussion should mainly be around what the school will do to help him get on with his education.

Remember that anything you or your child says may be used against you in court after the hearing. One junior high school child had been involved in setting a fire. It was her first offense. The guidance counselor promised her that if she wrote down what she had done and said she was sorry she would not be punished. The next morning, when the mother came to a guidance conference at school, she began to reprimand her daughter. Suddenly she found that the fire marshal was present, had listened to and seen everything, and he proceeded to arrest the child for arson!

Be sure you get a list of the names and titles of everyone they bring to the hearing, and the names of all their witnesses.

Keep your own notes during the conference. But also demand that the school system provide you with a complete copy of the transcript.

Most times they simply call in their secretary, who just makes a summary of what takes place. That is not good enough. A "fair hearing" means that a full and complete transcript must be taken of the entire proceedings; it must be available to you in case you want to appeal.

Don't agree to any recommendation unless you are absolutely certain that you understand what it will mean for your child. A principal renders his decision right on the spot. You should request a written copy. A district superintendent is supposed to put his decision into writing and you must be given a copy. You may be asked to make a recommendation. Hopefully you and your child talked this over beforehand and decided what you want to ask for—that he go back to the same class, transfer to another class, or to another school.

But if they start talking about a "600" school, or if they want to refer him for "testing" to the Bureau of Child Guidance or transfer him to some program you are not absolutely certain about, *don't agree* and don't sign anything until you have a chance to think about it. Talk to your child about what he wants, investigate it for yourself, and come to your own conclusion.

Remember that you have the right to appeal whatever decision is made. And you should insist that your child return to his school while you are making the appeal. If the principal gave the decision, you may appeal to the district superintendent and your local school board. And then you may still appeal to the city Board of Education.

Don't be ashamed to go after community support. This entire procedure must be changed, and your child's story may help the campaign. In one Manhattan district, when a determined and energetic mother was unable to get her boy reinstated in school, she told her neighbors, and a large group of them organized a petition campaign, sent telegrams to all the local politicians and Board of Education members, and conducted a sit-in in the district office *and* at a local school board meeting, until finally the Board of Education itself took up the matter and ordered the boy put back in school.

In Brownsville not only did parents and the community organize to get their suspended children back into school but they also initiated a court suit to force the Board of Education to pay the children damages for the time they lost while out of school.

Until children are guaranteed a fair hearing, and the right to remain in school until *after* a hearing takes place, it will often be necessary to organize a political campaign to obtain justice.

Educators believe that if they cannot get along with the students they have to change the students. Parents and students suspect that it would be much more practical to change a few of the teachers and principals.

Action Checklist for Parents

DEMAND NEW SUSPENSION REGULATIONS AND A BILL OF RIGHTS FOR STUDENTS

The High School Student Union and the New York Civil Liberties Union have both prepared excellent documents advocating and justifying a bill of rights for students. I am indebted to them both for most of the following ideas and, in particular, to Ira Glasser, Associate Director of the New York Civil Liberties Union.

Immediately declare an amnesty and reinstate all suspended students in your district. Give all students who have been transferred to "600" schools an immediate opportunity to return to regular schools in your district.

Since so many pupils were suspended unjustly, and because the "600" schools almost never thoroughly review the status of their pupils in order to permit them to return to regular classes, it would be dramatic evidence of the vigor and determination of your local board if it agreed to start from scratch, and immediately reinstate all suspended or transferred students.

Establish a community committee of parents, teachers and students to determine and define *responsible pupil and teacher behavior*. Hold a public hearing on their recommendations and then adopt and publish the behavior code. This committee should be composed of a *majority* of students, preferably including a number of those who were formerly suspended. It may also want to write guidelines to help the teachers teach in a manner least likely to evoke disruptive behavior.

Appropriate penalties for misbehavior should be established and made uniform for the district and published for all to see. Once the joint committee agrees on what is acceptable student and teacher behavior, it must also establish a description of the penalties for each type of misbehavior. Naturally there will be some flexibility, but it must be clear, for example, that a child who swears faces specific minimum and maximum penalties. Let the community decide what punishment fits which "crime" so everyone will know what is expected and they will also know that the rules will be applied fairly and equitably to all.

Establish an independent review board where students, parents and teachers would have the right to file complaints. In particular, this panel would permit parents and students to bring complaints against school officials without any fear that they will be hurt.

Announce that no student would be suspended, transferred or discharged *prior* to a hearing. This policy must be clearly and forthrightly announced and enforced by your local school board.

Establish procedures to guarantee that the hearing is fair. Your local school board should hold a public discussion to make certain that all opinions about what constitutes a fair hearing are really adequately discussed.

√*Who should conduct the hearing?* Many students believe that all disciplinary hearings should be conducted by a group of students: a student court, a jury of peers. The New York Civil Liberties Union suggests that an impartial hearing examiner should preside. Certainly the current procedure is terribly unjust whereby the principal, who often is the same person who is bringing the charges against the child, conducts the hearing.

√*The right to a lawyer.* Of course, students and their parents should have the right to be represented by an attorney of their own choosing, but many families cannot afford a lawyer. Therefore the local boards must figure out a method to provide every student who needs one with a *free* attorney in such hearings.

√*The right to see, copy and challenge the cumulative record folder, anecdotal records and all pupil behavioral cards.* Teachers have the right to challenge any material in their files; pupils and their parents should have the same right.

√All the rights guaranteed on paper by the current Board of Education should be reinforced and really carried out: *the right to cross-examine witnesses and call friendly ones; the right to see the charges before the hearing; the right to an effective appeal,* etc.

√In addition, further protection should be guaranteed, such as: *the right to a free copy of the transcript of the hearing; the right to be free from being forced or tricked into making self-incriminating statements*—both before and during the hearing; *the right to a translator; the right to challenge a hearing officer or witness for bias.*

Demand that your local school board publish a monthly fact sheet on suspensions in your district. This fact sheet should include full information on the number of suspensions or transfers, from which school, which class and for what reason. Who held the hearing? What penalties were imposed? If the child was then transferred or referred to another facility, there should be follow-up information in the next month's report. All of this can easily be done without naming names, thus protecting the privacy of the child and his family.

All suspension procedures developed in your community in this manner should be applied to your local high school. Once the parents, students and teachers establish a fair and just suspension policy, you must not let the high schools go by default, just because the Board of Education says they are retaining "jurisdiction" over them. These schools all belong to the community; the central board has no right to arbitrarily remove them from the proper jurisdiction of the community board.

Demand that your local school board establish *fair* procedures regarding the use of police and security guards by school officials. Many students find themselves or their lockers searched arbitrarily in school. Children are being called into offices to talk to police without any crime having been committed. Students are being removed from school and taken to a police station without the parent's knowledge or permission. *Your local board must forbid this type of violation of the First Amendment.* Work out discipline procedures for your schools with your students, teachers and parents—and not with the police.

Demand that your local board reemphasize that students have the right to express their political and social views during school hours and that students have the right to participate as equals in the operation of the schools.

The Constitution of the United States and the Bill of Rights are not restricted to adults only. Students have the right to freedom of speech, freedom of assembly, freedom of the press, just as grownups do. And if we want our children to grow up knowing how to govern themselves, our schools will have to teach them how to do that by permitting them to participate in making decisions right now about how their schools are to be run. Your local school board should establish a student–parent–teacher committee which develops, holds hearings and publishes a bill of rights for students. This might include:

√the right of students to elect their own student government and spend their own funds. All students are to be permitted to vote and run for office.

√the right of students to publish their own newspaper or flyers and distribute them in and outside of school without prior authorization or censorship.

√the right of students to hold meetings in the school without the presence of teachers.

√the right of students to participate in screening, hiring, evaluating, and dismissing teachers.

√the right of students to review curriculum requirements and to participate in setting standards and selecting textbooks.

√the right of students to establish and maintain rules concerning attendance, discipline, etc.

√the right to dress as they wish; the right to wear political armbands and buttons and to have all other rights guaranteed in the Constitution and Bill of Rights.

√the right to criticize school policies and school officials without fear of repression or punishment.

The word "participate" would have to be debated and argued and defined in each district. Students are asking for more than merely an advisory role. Like their parents, they are tired of being manipulated, talked to, and then ignored. Participation, to most students, means an equal partnership. I think that many local school boards would be ready to give our students just such an opportunity, if only we parents will lend our support to these demands.

If our local school boards will give our students a chance to bring their own experience and imagination to bear on the school situation, if we parents will allow our childen to help us run the schools, we may very well do away with school suspensions entirely, and we may find that there are actually very few children who are troubled or disturbed, after all.

10 · Public Hearings

Probably the most unyielding puzzle that faces anyone who wants to exert specific influence over the public schools is how to locate the official who would have authority to make the appropriate decisions.

How would you feel if your child's school was suddenly rezoned, so that it meant he would have to travel twice as far to school each day, and no one had told you about it until the decision had been made, and there was no procedure to appeal the ruling? You go to your principal, who tells you the policy was decided "downtown." You call your local school board member who tells you he is just as angry as you are but that "headquarters" mandated the change. Who at headquarters? You are given at least three or four different officials to see, and each of them stalls you, or when you finally do see them, they blame someone else.

There is no official procedure for parents who wish to appeal such decisions. Under decentralization, the buck-passing is even more maddening. A fine guidance teacher is "excessed" from your school. That is a fancy professional word which means transferred. Your district superintendent blames city headquarters personnel policies. You organize and go downtown to protest. Once you get there you are told, "That decision was made by your local school board." You go back to your board, which denies it had anything to do with it—and in the meantime the teacher is gone, and no one will admit responsibility for the transfer.

Parents have discovered that all the top-echelon staff and Board of Education members gather together in one room regularly each month, and conduct Public Meetings or Hearings. Here ordinary mortals are free to come and actually see and hear the powers-that-be in the flesh. Sometimes, on specially "important" subjects like the construction or expense budgets, integration, decentralization, student rights and Title I monies, all-day hearings are scheduled. These meetings appear to offer the only direct access to the people in power, and many parents try to use them to confront the board members with questions and problems. Fathers take time off from work; mothers hire baby-sitters. Community groups will often prepare their testimony with painstaking care. The people come in large numbers and often have to wait around hours for their turn to speak.

Sitting on raised platforms in huge soft chairs, behind enormous mahogany desks, the board members read newspapers, eat, chat, doze, and rarely put questions to the speakers or respond to their inquiries. If a parent is persistent and demands a reply, the voices from the podium are often harping, sneering, condescending or critical. "You have your facts wrong," the parent will be told, with a wave of dismissal. Or a lesser staff official will be called to the microphone to be asked about the charge. "Oh, we have checked into that and we have that problem under control" will be the bland self-assured response. You know they have done nothing of the sort, but unless you are ready to call them liars, you nod meekly and return to your seat.

Many opportunities to start a serious discussion, or to forge a direct link between the parents and the people in power are ignored or lost. Is it any wonder that parents become so aggravated that they begin to heckle, disrupt or shout in a pitifully inadequate attempt to force those in charge to listen and respond? From the parents' point of view, the real story of these meetings rarely appears in print or television. Sometimes, after an especially stormy evening, the *Times* will report, "Militants Disrupt Board Hearing," but the story *behind* the disruption is never told.

A classic example took place several years ago during an ordinary Board of Education all-day expense-budget hearing. As one three-minute speaker followed another, the board members took turns at duty, and the reporters went home early, disappointed by the uneventful, dispirited testimony. A small delegation was present from Harlem, waiting to speak about the needs of its schools, but most of the audience was composed of middle-class white parents from Queens and Staten Island. Suddenly, about two thirty in the afternoon, a black mother approached the microphone: "My name is Mrs. Wagner. I'm president of JHS 267 in Brooklyn and I want to know if I can speak now, since I have to go pick up my younger children after school." The board chairman replied, "I'm sorry, but you are out of order. You have to wait your turn." Mrs. Wagner tried again. "Please, I've waited here all day. I just want to ask for—" But before she could complete her request, again and more sharply she was asked to sit down. "Your name isn't even on the list of speakers," helpfully chimed in another board member. "Didn't you write in to request time to speak?" The question was condescending and Mrs. Wagner began to get angry. "I didn't know I was supposed to write in. My principal and the other parents just told me to come down and talk, and I'll only take a few minutes."

By this time, the audience had picked up interest. The mothers, black *and* white, understood, and the next speaker, who was from Staten Island, generously offered to give Mrs. Wagner her turn. But the rules could not bend. "I'm sorry," said the chairman, "but unless she is scheduled, she must wait until everyone else is heard, and then, if there is still time, she may speak." Mrs. Wagner, miraculously, stood her ground. And the parents from Harlem, who had never seen her before in their lives, recognized a kindred spirit, and began to shout: "Let her speak! Let her speak! Let her speak!" After five more minutes of glaring at the immovable parent, the board members got up and walked out.

At first no one could believe it. Everyone waited for the members of the board to return. But when it became obvious that they were not coming back, one parent shouted, "Let them go. They never listen to anything we say anyway." And a young Italian mother quipped, "Why don't we listen to ourselves?" She strode up to the platform, plopped herself down in the president's chair, pounded the gavel and gravely announced, "The *real* hearing will now come to order." Within minutes nine others had joined her there, and that was the birth of the Peoples' Board of Education. For three days and nights, under the glare of television lights and newspaper coverage from all over the world, those parents remained in that room, joined by hundreds of others from every part of the city. Later that first night they elected a more representative board, composed of black, Puerto Rican and white parents from a variety of communities, and named the Rev. Milton Galamison its chairman and Mrs. Evelina Antonetty, vice-chairman. I am proud to say that I was there and was among those chosen to serve.

A Quaker group came down to lend us a mimeograph machine, and we wrote and mimeographed our own budget proposals on the spot. And for seventy-two hours we conducted a hearing the likes of which was never seen before, or since, in that sacred hall. The Board of Miseducation—for that is what we began to call the group who had walked out—tried everything to get us to leave, and even turned on the air-conditioning system, although it was late in December. Finally we left only when we were all arrested. None of the media ever believed that it all happened spontaneously. Most of the education experts confessed to their readers that the "plot" had been hatching for weeks. Only those who were there and participated knew that if it had been planned it could never have happened. The rigidity and stupidity and arrogance of the official board unified all of us more effectively than we could ever have done on our own.

What are these public meetings and hearings held by the Board? How often do they take place? What are they supposed to accomplish? How can parents use them to promote local needs?

Types of Hearings

There are several types of hearings which take place regularly throughout the school year:

BOARD OF EDUCATION MONTHLY PUBLIC MEETINGS

These meetings take place several times a month, usually on the third Tuesday or Wednesday evenings. Sometimes they are held in the hall of the Board of Education; other times, when a very large crowd is expected, they are conducted in a bigger auditorium in some other part of the city.

Until recently there was only one public meeting each month, and the agenda (or calendar) for that meeting was rigidly determined by the professional staff and the board members. Parents jammed those meetings, often interrupting the procedures, since they had no other mechanism for introducing items which concerned them. In an attempt to "improve communications" the board decided to change the format. Two monthly meetings were scheduled, starting mid-1970. For one, there is no agenda; parents and others may simply write or phone headquarters and ask to be put on a speakers list. They may then spend four minutes talking about any subject they choose. For the second meeting, the board provides the agenda. It usually consists of fifty or more different items, and is mailed out four or five days in advance. Parents may request that they be put on this mailing list, but of course the majority of parents don't know they can do this and, therefore, never see these important agendas. It is not necessary (so far) to reserve speaking time for these sessions; when the item is called, you are supposed to indicate that you wish to speak and, theoretically, you will then be heard.

The UFT, the supervisors' associations and the major city-wide pressure groups, such as the Public Education Association and United Parent Association attend these meetings regularly. So do many neighbhorhood groups from all parts of the city.

BOARD OF EDUCATION SPECIAL ALL-DAY HEARINGS

These are scheduled at various times in the year to discuss particular issues. The expense budget, for example, is usually "heard" in December; the construction budget in September. There are no agendas because the entire hearing is devoted to one topic. However, usually a proposed budget or policy statement is made available on which the public is "invited" to comment. These documents are invariably long and technical and are released usually only a week or so prior to the hearing. Usually speakers must write in advance, requesting speaking time.

SPECIAL HEARINGS ON EDUCATION CALLED BY OTHER AGENCIES

Several times each year other city departments schedule public meetings to discuss education issues. The City Planning Commission holds a hearing on the construction budget every December; the Board of Estimate and City Council hold a hearing on the same subject at City Hall each February—this same body holds a hearing on the expense budget in April. On occasion the Commission on Human Rights, the Council Against Poverty and various city, state or federal legislators will decide to conduct public "investigations" of a particular facet of the schools. Some of these, especially the marathons held at City Hall, are as tedious and unrewarding as those run by the Board of Education, although no individual who has been elected dares to be as rude to the parents as the school officials are. But sometimes, as in the case of the hearings run by Congressman Powell or the Commission on Human Rights, they offer a startling contrast to the board's procedures and also provide a showcase for the presentation of community concerns.

WHAT IS WRONG WITH
MOST PUBLIC HEARINGS

The most obvious thing that is wrong with these hearings is that the officials who conduct them rarely listen. They have usually made up their minds beforehand, and in many instances have already taken a vote in a closed session prior to the public meeting. Furthermore, some of the most powerful and most influential pressure groups never appear at public hearings. They do their lobbying and influencing behind the scenes. Sometimes the public never knows who has been manipulating these decisions; other times, a large delegation will testify effectively at a public meeting, but they are effective simply because their appearance there is the climax of a well-organized, thorough series of private meetings with all the top-ranking officials. Those parents who don't know the ropes, who come innocently to the hearings thinking someone will hear them, are sadly mistaken, and it is heartbreaking to watch them try to get attention at these overly long, often noisy sessions.

Although the new rules now permit parents to bring their own concerns to the attention of the board, it remains to be seen whether or not these sessions will be anything more than a public catharsis. The board, particularly the headquarters staff, still determines whether any action is to be taken. If community groups pour out their hearts at these meetings but if no meaningful resolutions are voted, "reforming" the hearing process will soon be recognized as fraudulent.

Many of us, however, have learned to be quite inventive; we find numerous ways to bend each agenda item, so that we can use it to introduce issues which are of grave concern to us and our neighbors. For example, if one item specifies the approval of an annex for a school in Brooklyn, we might go to the microphone and state, "We are glad the parents in Brooklyn are getting relief for their children, but our school in the South Bronx is also terribly overcrowded and our annex has been delayed for months. What kind of help are you going to give us, and when?"

If the chairman of the hearing is flexible, or has eaten a good meal that evening, he may let us get away with this and we may get an answer. If he has had a fight with his wife, or if he wants to reassert his importance, he may call us out of order, and then we have to decide on the spot whether we will insist or sit down. Often parents who do insist are thrown out by the police.

Another difficulty with these hearings, and especially with the regular monthly meetings, is that the calendar is made public only three or four days in advance. If a parent group wishes to research a particular item, it is extremely difficult to do so. Sometimes, it is apparent, unbelievably, that the board members themselves do not know what they are approving. When the Council of Supervisory Associations won its first collective bargaining agreement, the matter was placed on the calendar with no copies of the contract made available to the public. One parent, however, had obtained a copy from her principal, and was shocked at a number of the provisions. Many far-reaching educational policies were included, and were being approved without any discussion either by parents or local school boards who would be expected to implement them under decentralization. When she began to read aloud those portions she found most outrageous, the board members expressed their amazement; they had not even realized that their staff negotiator had agreed to their inclusion. Believe it or not, despite these revelations, the contract was approved that same evening, because the supervisors convinced the board that "irreparable" damage would be done to their pension rights if passage were delayed.

Only very occasionally do the Board of Education members publicly disagree and split their votes. This does happen frequently, and usually along party lines, in the City Council and Board of Estimate, and alert parent groups learn how to play these factions against each other in order to gain the most for their community. But the Board of Education usually presents a unified, unbreakable and inhuman front. They rarely use public meetings to focus discussion on policy alternatives, as is the case in federal legislative hearings where Congressional members argue and debate with the witnesses. The list of items to be approved is always so long that the board members are usually visibly anxious to "get on with it" and try to complete the agenda so they can get home as quickly as possible. If a storm develops over a particular issue it is sometimes "laid over" or postponed, only to be routinely approved at a special meeting called later, when the protestors are not present.

Under decentralization it is unlikely that anything described here will change. The central Board of Education retains control over the expense and construction budgets. Local boards are supposed to hold hearings on these matters also. So now parents will have an additional layer of meetings and public hearings to go to. If anything, matters will be worse because so much of the law is ambiguous. For instance, local boards may now order textbooks if the central board has approved the books and has authorized funds for their purchase. It is not unlikely that the local board will hold a local hearing on textbooks and adopt a resolution, only to find that at a subsequent meeting of the central board, the books they recommend were not approved, or the contract they needed was not signed.

Nothing makes parents so angry as when they find out they have been wasting their time. We will testify at a local board hearing, urging our school board to approve a specific block in our neighborhood for a new school; our local board will listen and endorse our position; then later the central board will hold a second hearing where they can, and often do, invalidate the local recommendation, selecting an alternate site which meets "citywide standards."

It is one matter to know you are powerless; however it is far more degrading, and dangerous, to have them tell us we have power, and then each time we attempt to exercise it, slap us down, overrule us, or invite us to another hearing. The city is simply too large; the educational problems are too varied and too complex. Even the most knowledgeable and sensitive public official is not wise enough to make decisions for so vast an area.

Unless the Board of Education decentralizes responsibility, genuinely delegating authentic authority to the local board, the chaos can only increase.

If communities find out they have real responsibility, they will quickly learn how to behave responsibly. If public hearings are for real, if our opinions are being honestly sought and seriously listened to by officials who have the power to act and who feel themselves accountable to us, then these public hearings will be a marvelous and important vehicle for public expression. But if we in the communities are denied these rights, if we are continually manipulated and fooled and ignored and used, if the Board of Education and its staff continues to treat us as if we were untrustworthy and lawless, we will react accordingly.

Action Checklist for Parents

HOW TO USE A PUBLIC HEARING FOR YOUR OWN PURPOSES

Learn to make use of public hearings to highlight your local needs, to expose local problems and to focus attention on concerns that are important to you and your neighbors.

Use a public hearing to culminate a campaign.

The most common reason for attending a hearing is to pressure for more money or services. Large delegations attend *capital-budget hearings* to press for new schools in the construction budget; equally strong groups come to demand additional school programs or staff at the *expense-budget hearings*.

To have any real impact, these appearances must be preceded by a carefully prepared community campaign and by a great many informal meetings with various public officials. The testimony at the public hearing is merely "window-dressing."

Use a public hearing to obtain an immediate solution to a "simple" problem.

For example, if a child has been suspended but all the local officials have been torturing you with their usual display of buck-passing, you might get immediate help by finding some way to raise this problem, emotionally, as part of your testimony at a hearing.

Parents in one Harlem school had tried for months to get the fire-alarm system in their obsolete building repaired. When they were testifying at a Board of Estimate budget hearing, one mother described the broken-down alarm box. It happened that a former fire commissioner was sitting in for the mayor that day, and within five hours he had inspectors on the spot, and the needed work was completed.

Use a public hearing to block a bad decision—at least temporarily.

If a site is being selected which will force the demolition of some decent, locally owned homes, or if a contract is about to be approved by a firm which has a history of inferior and tardy deliveries, an indignant, articulate delegation may be able to force the issue to be "laid over."

Unfortunately, it takes more extensive power to successfully block such actions permanently. The officials will find some way of passing the item, probably on Christmas Eve or the hottest day of the summer, when your guard is down. *If* you are really organized and determined, perhaps you will be one of the few groups able to get them to change their minds and delay the offensive decision forever.

Use a public hearing to expose the professional staff when it has lied.

Left to their own devices, the professional staff will often assure the board members that all is well in the communities and that there is "overwhelming support" for whatever item is on the agenda. Local groups have been repeatedly successful in breaking through these deceptions.

For example, when the UFT and headquarters staff told the board that the public was unanimously in favor of the More Effective School Program, a series of hard-hitting, accurate presentations by a variety of groups pointing out the shortcomings of the program, the high costs and relatively low results caused several members to reconsider their support.

When the professional staff assured the board that every parent had been consulted before the students had been suspended from Franklin K. Lane, several groups produced live parents who testified that they had never been notified or consulted. The more the communities can do to expose staff inadequacies, the better.

Use a public hearing to make valuable connections.

Quite often these hearings will afford parents an opportunity to make contact with a particular staff person who has been "unavailable" by phone.

These hearings provide parents with a unique opportunity to meet parents from all over the city. Once, when some Bronx parents were testifying against a Title I proposal, they described an especially inadequate principal, whose supervision was so weak and ineffective that the Title I programs in his school had proved to be worthless. They demanded his removal or else an admission by the board that the Title I program was a farce. Later, several parents from other parts of the city approached the Bronx group and said they had similar difficulties. The groups kept in touch with each other, and over the next months succeeded in obtaining the transfers of three of the principals involved. (Unfortunately, the tenure law prevented them from seeing to it that these supervisors were dismissed.)

Use a public hearing to educate those officials who are still educable.

Some of the officials conducting these meetings are new to their jobs; some are anxious to learn from community groups. Forthright factual presentations by parents will sometimes grab their attention. If the chairman of the hearing steps on you and does not permit you to complete your testimony, the less callous members may come to your defense, and after the hearing you can hang around to talk to them and win yourself a sympathetic ear.

Don't pin too many hopes on this approach, however. Within a couple of months, something happens to almost all board members and public officials. Constantly fed "facts" by a professional staff that keeps them too busy to go see for themselves, they become corrupted by the air at headquarters, and quickly learn to tune out the complaints of local parents.

Use a public hearing to educate and learn from other parents.

Many times parent groups and community leaders will attend hearings and not testify at all. They circulate among the other people who are speaking, talk to them, hear about their problems, exchange mimeographed flyers and information. This is a real opportunity for parents to meet each other.

If you are looking for specific issues that are angering parents, hearings and public meetings are the best place to find them. At several times in recent years, when it came their turn to speak, a number of speakers have actually turned the podium around, addressing the parents, rather than the public officials.

Use a public hearing to go on record.

If you are planning to appeal or protest a decision taken at these hearings, you should testify to go on record. Even though you are sure you cannot influence the officials, you should present your case so that you can go back to your community and show your neighbors how local needs have been ignored.

Use a public hearing to force a confrontation.

If every effort of your group meets with resistance, if you cannot get an appointment to discuss an issue, or if you cannot get an answer to a request for action, then you may want to use the public hearing to force a response.

For example, *fight back.* A group of black construction workers who were trying for months to get the board to pass an on-the-job training program for school-construction jobs, finally had to sit-in and threaten in order to force the resolution onto the calendar, and then they had to disrupt the meeting itself to get the item approved.

Use a public hearing to ridicule and deflate the professionals.

Most board officials take themselves far too seriously. If you are attending a meeting where foolish, pompous and totally irrelevant nonsense is continuously being spouted, don't just sit there burning up silently.

Once at a meeting the Superintendent of Schools proudly described his new sex education program: "We have assigned a committee of important professionals to develop the syllabus." One mother, who wanted parents involved in developing curriculum, came forward to the microphone: "Mr. Superintendent, I can understand it if you set up a professional committee to develop a reading program. But when it comes to sex, I think I am just as professional as you are."

Some parents may be ready to bomb board headquarters, but if they can arrange to laugh them out of business it would be neater.

Action Checklist for Parents

HOW TO PREPARE
FOR A PUBLIC HEARING

Find out all you can about the hearing in advance.

√*Who is conducting the hearing?* Get the names of the officials who will be in charge. Will they be attending themselves or will they assign staff assistants to sit in for them? Is there a minimum number (quorum) required to preside? Do you know any of the officials fairly well? Are any "on your side"? If so, try to arrange to see those members beforehand to discuss your position and the procedure. They may make several helpful suggestions to you. (Of course, if you are planning something slightly irregular, don't tip your hand even to "friendly" officials.)

√*Where will the hearing take place?* Is the room small or large? If it is small, will this mean you will have difficulty getting inside? If you are not familiar with the meeting hall, go see it in advance. You will need to know exactly how to get there, what the neighborhood is like, what the layout of the building is.

√*When will the hearing take place?* What time of day? How many hours will it last? How many days? Will you have any control over the precise time your group will be called? Or will you have to be prepared to hang around for hours? If so, think of something "creative" to do during that time. If some of the officials who support you will only be present for part of the hearing, find out when and try to arrange to speak when they will be present.

√*Who has been invited to the hearing?* Is it a *public hearing?* If so, how was the public notified? Do people in your community know about the hearing? If you feel it is important that your neighborhood appear, you may have to take responsibility for making sure they get notified, and with sufficient advance notice to allow them to make arrangements to come. Is it a *private hearing?* If so, who has been invited, and who has been left out? Decide what you want to do about this.

√*What procedural rules will govern the hearing?* Must you write in advance to reserve speaking time? If so, and if you want to organize a large number of speakers, then try to get many members of different organizations to write in separately requesting time. Often groups will make up organizational names just for this purpose, e.g., the Fox Street Boys Club, the Second Avenue Civic Association, etc. Will there be a time limit for the speakers? Must you submit written testimony? Who will be in charge of scheduling the speakers? Will certain types of groups be given any special priority? Will the speakers' list be available in advance of the hearing, and if so, when? It is very helpful to know who else is scheduled to speak, and this list can also assist you in estimating approximately what time you will be called.

√*Is there a calendar or other document available in advance?* When and where is it available? Can you get as many copies as you need? Is there any way for your group to influence the agenda? How can you get an item put on the calendar, tabled, laid over? How much time is there between the date the calendar is made public and the date of the hearing? Is there enough time to properly study the document?

√*Will the press be permitted to cover the hearing?* If so, do you know any of the reporters who will have this assignment? Will there be an opportunity for community groups to hold a press conference outside the hearing room? Will you want to bring special press releases to hand out? Will the hearing be broadcast over WNYC or some other station?

√*Will signs be permitted inside the hearing room?* If not, you may want to arrange a picket line or poster demonstration outside of the hearing hall for the benefit of photographers. Or, as many groups do, you may decide to smuggle your signs into the hearing room in shopping bags to use them when your turn at the microphone comes.

√*When and where and by whom are the decisions made?* Are there informal sessions scheduled before or after the public meeting where the actual decisions are made? Can you find out more about these sessions? Do all the officials conducting the session have an equal vote in the final decision, or are some officials more "influential" than others? Is there a specific date by which the decisions must be made? Will the vote be made in public, and if so, when? Is the group which is holding the hearing empowered to take action, or is it only an advisory or investigatory group?

√*Will a report and/or minutes be made available after the hearing?* Will the proceedings be taped? How can you get copies? Will there be a charge?

Decide if you want to attend the hearing, and if so, for what purpose.

√If the rules are tight and crazy, or if the agenda is totally irrelevant, you may not want to bother attending. If the officials conducting the hearing are really horrible, you also may not want to bother with them.

√However, you may decide you want to go anyway. If so, sit down with the other parents involved and decide together how much time you want to put into preparing for the hearing and agree on what you hope to achieve.

√Many parent groups simply plan to go, without much advance preparation, just to see what happens, "playing it by ear." This does not require much work, and often presents some unexpected opportunities for presenting local issues and confronting public officials.

√At other times, however, everyone may agree that the hearing is a crucial one, and in that case much careful groundwork must be laid. You should set up a *planning meeting* to help you prepare properly. Some groups even role-play (practice) what they think will happen in order to feel better prepared. If parents are carefully involved in the advance preparation, they will feel confident when the time comes for the real thing.

Prepare your group well in advance of the hearing.

√*Are there some friendly staff members or other officials whom you should meet with in advance?* If you are going to present a simple problem (e.g., an overcrowded situation or lack of books), you might want to talk to a staff person in advance so that they will be prepared with information when you speak. Their answers will probably be totally inadequate, but at least you will hear their "excuse" at once and be able to go on from there. Otherwise, you are likely to be told by a presiding official, "We will study that and let you know next time." You are apt to be told that anyway, so be prepared to deal with it. Sometimes, of course, you want to take them by surprise, and in that case you won't want to contact anyone in advance.

√*Who and how many parents and community people do you want to come?* If you want many people, you will not get them simply by issuing a flyer two days before the hearing. You would then be just as manipulative as the Board of Education. If you are in the midst of a campaign and many people are deeply involved already, short notice may be all right. But otherwise, plan to give your neighbors ten days to two weeks to get prepared, informed and involved if you really want them to be able to come.

√*Who is going to speak?* Do you have to write letters in advance? Keep a copy of every letter—they may lose it and you will not get on the speakers list.

√*Will you be able to charter a bus?* Or set up a car pool? Or will you arrange for everyone to meet and go down on the subway together?

√*What time do you want to get there?* If you have written in early, you may be scheduled to speak early. But if you are not scheduled to testify until late in the day, you may want to get there early anyway to attract attention from the press. TV and radio look for stories during the first hour or two of these hearings, if they cover them at all. You could set up a colorful demonstration or picket line or press conference early in the day, even if you are not speaking until later.

√*What kinds of posters, badges and other material will you want?* If you do charter a bus, decorate it with eye-catching signs and slogans. Prepare an attractive, identifying cardboard lapel-badge for your entire delegation to wear. One group designed miniature outhouses to dramatize their school's plumbing deficiencies; a group of parents protesting lunchroom conditions carried large garbage pails. You should write a brief flyer which tells your story; bring enough copies for all the officials, the press *and* the audience.

√*What will you do about the children?* We usually plan to bring all the small children with us. Their faces attract television cameras and their noise often encourages the city officials to permit us to testify early. However, for night-time hearings, or bad-weather days, you may want to set up a baby-sitting center in your local church or community center.

What to do on the day of the hearing.

√Bring pencils and paper to write down the names and addresses of the other parents you meet.

√Bring your flyers and other literature.

√Bring your posters. If you are going on a chartered bus, take poster paper (oak tag) and magic markers with you and make up slogans on the bus ride. Some of the best signs get made this way. My favorite, written on the way to a school-lunch demonstration: "If you want to get rid of your principal, feed him a school lunch."

√Bring dimes for emergency phone calls and a list of key-leadership phone numbers in case you need to get more people down quickly.

√Walk around in the lobby and outer halls while waiting your turn to speak. You can see lots of politicking going on, and will get a chance to do some too.

√When your group gets a turn to speak, make sure your speeches are short, emphatic and never dull or repetitive. Don't read long statements. Schedule some factual and some emotional speakers.

√Be prepared for surprises—and take advantage of them. If a group from another community disrupts the hearing or tries to change the agenda, see if there is some way you can support it and broaden its demands to include your own. Don't fight another community group, no matter what. Next time you may be in their spot.

234

Action Checklist for Parents

HOW TO FORCE YOUR LOCAL SCHOOL BOARD TO HOLD GOOD PUBLIC HEARINGS

Force your local board to develop procedures which meet your needs.

√How often do they meet? How often do you want them to meet?

√Where do they meet? Is it easy to get there?

√When do they meet? At the staff's convenience or the parents'?

√Are *agendas* public? Who controls the agenda? The local board or the parents? *Minutes?* Is *voting* always public?

√Are *minutes* always available?

Form a parent committee to advise your local board on meeting procedures.

√Do the meetings seem a waste of time? Or is a lot of important information given out to parents? How do you feel the meetings could be improved?

√Get together with other parents and analyze the meetings. Perhaps you will want to visit other local board meetings. How do you think they can be changed? Make a list of suggestions and demand that your board institute some changes.

Do parents attend your local board meetings? If not, there is probably a good reason.

√If parents feel manipulated or used, they do not come. If they feel that the professionals are doing all the talking, or if they believe that all the decisions are being made privately, they will stop coming.

√Think about some of these alternatives: *open executive board meetings; meetings run by parents* where local board members listen; *meetings run by students.*

√If decisions taken by your board are changed downtown, there may be no reason to attend. Perhaps if your local board became more militant and less defensive, more parents might come and participate.

11·Parents' Rights

THE NEED FOR AN EFFECTIVE GRIEVANCE MACHINERY

One of the main defects of the school system is the fact that the rules are not written down anywhere—at least not anywhere the average parent can read them. Contrast what happens in housing, for example. We all know that the landlord must provide heat in the winter. If he does not, there is an official complaint form to be filled out, and a specific process for the tenant to follow in making his protest. After a certain amount of time, if the landlord does not respond, he is fined and the city provides the heat. The procedure may be slow, it may not always work well, but there *is* a procedure. Tenants are informed of their rights under the law, and they have very tangible machinery at their disposal if these rights are ignored.

With the school system this is simply not the case. In most instances the regulations are not readily available. Thus, if your child is failed for "excessive cutting," and you go to complain, the principal sighs, "I'm just following regulations." What regulations? Where is this particular regulation written down?

Who has decided that this is grounds for failure? The principal?
The Board of Education? The State Education Department?
Where can the parent—or student—go if they want to appeal
the decision? I have tried to get all these questions answered,
and each place I ask, I get a different answer. The simple truth
is that each principal seems to decide for himself what is
"excessive," and then he protects himself from all criticism by
citing nonexistent regulations and the parent is stuck.

Sometimes regulations *are* written down, but the average
parent never gets to see them. Board policies come from numerous sources: the State Education Law, rulings of the State
Education Commission and the Board of Regents, bylaws of the
Board of Education, staff directives, union contracts, local school
board resolutions—a multitude of places. These are not compiled in any one place; they are certainly not available to parents.
Thus, how can you insist that your rights be honored if you
do not know that these rights exist?

Tragically, even when parents do learn the rules, they find
that the professional staff is adept at ignoring any regulation
it does not like. For instance, several civic organizations have
been publicizing the board's suspension procedures. The suspension policy states clearly that no student may be out of school
for more than five days without a hearing. Yet hundreds of
suspended students are out of school for as long as five *weeks*,
and when parents complain that this violates the regulations,
they meet a cold wall of indifference.

There is no channel for a parent or pupil to follow if they
wish to file an official grievance against a staff person. If a
parent makes such a protest unofficially through a letter or personal visit, there is no provision for an automatic investigation
of that complaint. And even if the board admits that the staff
member was wrong in doing what he did, in most cases no
penalties are levied and no action is taken, so there is no reason
why the staff should not continue to disobey the regulations.

For years the system misused teachers in this same way.
That is why the teachers fought so hard for a union and a contract. Now all the rules which they are supposed to follow are
spelled out—and so are their rights. These rules and rights

were negotiated between the teachers and the system. They were not unilaterally imposed. No longer can a supervisor impose his will upon the teachers. If a principal does something which a teacher believes to be unfair, there is an effective and powerful grievance machinery. The teacher files his grievance, gets a hearing, and may appeal any decision which he believes to be unfair.

Parents and students need to have their rights established in this same way. In an earlier chapter I have discussed some of the rights which I think ought to be guaranteed to students. Undoubtedly they will add to that list. But as a parent, I wish to discuss in some detail the rights which ought to be assured to parents. Some of these are really quite primitive. The right to be treated courteously, for example, seems almost too obvious to be included. But it is a right which frequently is denied us.

I believe that it would be easy to organize parents in a struggle to win them rights. Some of them, undoubtedly, have been "granted" in a few of the "better" schools. Others may already exist in an obscure law or regulation. But for most parents, at least in New York City, these rights are nonexistent.

Here are some of the rights I think parents should be guaranteed. I'm sure that every parent who reads this will add many more suggestions.

The Right to Be Treated Courteously

—Parents should be able to see the principal without too much delay. They should not be subject to rudeness from clerks and secretaries.

—Parents should be able to see their child's teacher without a lot of red tape.

—A parent's schedule should be considered just as important as a teacher's or principal's schedule. Parents should not be "summoned" to school. They should be invited, and should be asked to come at a time which is convenient to them.

The Right to Know the Rules

—Parents should receive in writing at the beginning of each term a booklet which outlines all the rules which they, their children and the school staff are to follow.

For example, parents should be told about the *health and medical regulations*. What days are medical services available? What happens if a child gets sick in school? If a child is exposed to a communicable disease, parents should have the right to be informed.

This booklet must clearly state the *attendance regulations*. How many days may a student be absent or late without a penalty, for example? Will the school inform the parent if a child is absent? The schools are supposed to send home a postcard if a student is absent, but they rarely do this. Perhaps the regulation should be changed, so that if a child is absent for more than three days, a postcard is sent home. And if such a regulation is adopted, parents have the right to expect that the staff will obey this rule. Too often parents don't know if their child is truant until it is too late to do anything about it.

This booklet should clearly state the *behavior standards*, *dress codes* and *grounds for suspension*. And naturally, the *procedures* which must be followed in any *suspension hearing* should be included.

—Parents should be given a *schedule for the school years*, which should include dates of parent-teacher conferences, half-days, holidays, parent meetings, report card dates, and citywide test dates.

Whenever a rule is stated, its *source should be clear*. Is this a state law, followed by every school in the state? Or is this just a policy of this school's principal?

Parents should be told exactly *how they may appeal* each rule listed in the booklet. The *grievance machinery* which is available to the parents should be clearly explained. (A suggested grievance machinery appears at the end of this section.)

I wish all parents had desks and secretaries, but the facts

of housekeeping are such that we inevitably misplace vital information the school sends home. The booklet should nevertheless be sent home at the beginning of each term, and *plenty of extra copies* left out in the school office for parents to take whenever they need one. We should not be told, when we ask for an additional copy of the regulations, "You already got one." There is plenty of money for paper when the bureaucracy needs to duplicate many copies of whatever they need—let parents have the same privilege.

The Right to Know about Academic Requirements

—Within the first two weeks of the term parents should be automatically mailed an outline of the *curriculum requirements* for their child's grade. This outline should not be written in educational double-talk, but should be a clear, straightforward statement of what the child is expected to learn that term.

—This statement should include a list of the *books* he will be studying, *homework regulations* and *standards for promotion and acceleration.*

—If a student must meet certain *requirements* at the end of that grade in order to qualify for a particular academic program, such as IGC, or the test for Hunter, parents should be notified at this time, early enough in the year so they can help their child get accepted if he so desires.

—Fifth-grade parents should be notified at the beginning of the term to prepare their children for special junior high programs; eighth-grade parents should be fully informed about the requirements for placement in special high schools and for placement in the academic track of academic high schools. High school parents should be told exactly what courses their child must complete in order to graduate. At George Washington High School, one parent who asked this was told, "Oh, about five credits more." Obviously that was a non-answer.

The Right to Know about, Apply for, or Refuse Special Programs

—Parents should have the right to be informed about all special school programs and services. (Head Start, language classes, talent classes, remedial services, etc.) Parents should be told in *clear, written and unambiguous language exactly what each program or service is supposed to do for the child.*

—If a parent is interested in placing her child in a particular program or service, she should have the *right to apply for it, even if her child's teacher does not recommend it.* At the same time, if a teacher thinks that a child should be in a particular program, parents should have to *give their permission before such a referral is made.*

—Whenever a parent's application is rejected, she should be notified in writing along with the reasons for rejection. She should then be able to appeal this decision. This right should help prevent principals and teachers from giving special preference to any favorite children.

The Right to a Meaningful Individual Teacher Conference Several Times a Year

—Parents should have the right to meet with their child's teacher *at least twice a year, for at least thirty minutes each time,* if necessary. If there is a special problem, then parents should have even more time.

—Parents should have the right to have this meeting in *privacy.*

—The parent should have a right to a *baby-sitter* arrangement if this is required to enable her to attend the conference. If the only way the parent can meet with the teacher is to have the teacher make a *home visit,* this too should be arranged.

—Parents should have a right to a translator at these conferences if one will make the parent more comfortable.

The Right to Information about your Child's Progress

—The parent should be sent a *copy of her child's full cumulative record card* at least once a year.

—Parents should have the right to initial all potentially damaging entries before they are placed in the record. Parents should be told that they have the *right to challenge any information* contained in the record.

—If the parent makes such a challenge, and if the material in the file is found to be false or misleading, it must be completely removed from the child's file.

—Parents should have the right to attach their own comments to the cumulative record folder.

—Parents should be able to obtain a copy of the record's contents at any time during the year.

—The cumulative record card should *not* go with the child when he is transferred or promoted to another school. All that should accompany the child are his marks and the list of courses he has successfully completed. Anything else should require the parent's permission.

The Right to Get Help for a Child Who Is Not Doing Well

—The parent should have the *right to appeal grades and marks* received by his child.

—The parent should be *notified in writing* at least three months before the end of the school year *if his child is functioning below grade level* in any major subjects.

—If a child is functioning below grade level, the parent should have the *right to request—and be given—additional tutorial services* for that child.

—If a child is functioning below grade level, but the school wishes to promote him to the next grade anyway, the parent should have the right to be notified of this decision in advance, and should have the right to appeal it.

—If a child is going to be left back, the parent should be
notified in writing at least three months before the end of
the term, and should have the right to appeal this decision.

—A parent should have the right to be telephoned and/or
notified through the mail whenever her child has been considered "disruptive" or is in the slightest danger of being
suspended. Parents would, of course, like to know these things
before they get out of hand.

The Right to Privacy and
Protection for Your Child

—If a child is placed in a special program with the parent's
permission, all reports, records and recommendations which
result from such a program or service should be shared first
with the parent; *the parent should have to give permission
before any of these reports can be given to anyone else* in
the school system or to any other public or private agency.
The parent should have the right to refuse such permission.

—*No child should be questioned by a policeman* or any other
agency representative in the school *without the parent's
permission.* No child should be asked to make or write self-
incriminatory statements nor any statement which might be
damaging to any student or teacher without the parent's
permission. This may seem like an obvious right, but I assure you that in many schools guidance counselors will ask
students to "write down what Janie did to Dick" or to "put
down on paper what you said to that teacher to cause her
to hit you."

—*No child should be removed from the school premises without the parent's permission.* This includes those instances
when the police want to remove a child. If the parent cannot be immediately reached, and if the police insist on
taking the child out of school, the administration should
assign a teacher who must stay with the child until the parent
arrives. Too often, children get beaten or insulted in police
precincts while waiting for their parent to arrive.

—*No agency, public or private, should see a child's record without permission from the parent.*

—Children receiving free lunch should not be identifiable in any way whatsoever.

—Parents should be asked to give their permission before any questionnaire asking about home or family life is distributed to the children. Similarly, before any guidance person can interview a child and ask such questions, the parent's permission should be obtained.

The Right to Appeal Administrative Decisions

—If a child does not want to be in a particular teacher's class, his parent should have *the right to appeal that placement.* I know this stirs a hornet's nest, but the fact is that many children really hate their assigned teacher and spend a miserable year because the parents are not given any opportunity to request a transfer. If a parent is vocal and influential, she knows how to change her child's teacher; otherwise, she is out of luck.

—*If a parent wants to send her children to a school outside her official zone, she should have the right to make that request,* and should be assured that it will receive serious consideration. For example, many working parents prefer that their children go to a school near their jobs, instead of the one near their home. Or sometimes an older child is placed in a special class in one school, and the parent would like to have all her other children attend the same school so she won't have to get to know more than one set of staff, schedules, etc. As it stands now, that parent hasn't a chance, unless her district superintendent is in a good mood. There should be an official channel for such requests to come through, and they should be expeditiously handled. The governing philosophy should be: Let's try to do what makes sense for the child, instead of Let's do what makes it easiest for the system.

The Right to Receive Notices without Fail

—School authorities often say that they have "notified" a
parent that the child was absent or doing poorly, but the
parent will just as frequently deny ever receiving such notices.
Parents should have the right to be sure they will receive
important information. All too often schools have incorrect
names and addresses for parent. Therefore, if the school
sends home a communication but the parent does not respond, it should be assumed that the mail did not reach
the parent, and *a staff member should be sent to the home*—
in the evening, if that is the only time the parent is home.

—In schools where a large percentage (20 percent or more) of
the students do not speak English, *all* written information
should automatically be *translated*.

—Parents should have the right to obtain information about
school programs, overcrowding, rezoning, etc., *without attending meetings*. Whenever such information is given out
at a meeting, a written summary must be made available
by the school administration and sent home to all parents.

The Right of Access

—Parents should have the right to visit the school and classes
whenever they wish, as long as they do not interfere with
school operations. Parents everywhere have this right. In New
York City, however, the UFT is afraid of public scrutiny and
it has pressured to have this right restricted.

The Right to a Full Day of Education for
Your Children and the Right to
Choose Sessions

—If a school is going to go on short-time or double session,
parents should be notified at least three months in advance.

—All decisions as to which classes or grades should be put
on short time should be approved by the parents.

—Parents, including kindergarten parents, should have the right to apply for a particular session or schedule, and if their application is turned down, they should have the right to an effective appeal.

—If a school goes on short-time, all parents should be given the option of sending their children by school bus to another school where full-time classes are being offered.

The Right to Assist in Interviewing and Selecting School Personnel

—Whenever a school is getting a new supervisor, the parents should be invited to help in the recruitment and interviewing process. Although the official parent association should be informed, other parents who may not be in the association should have the right to volunteer for such a committee.

—Parents should also be invited to participate in the recruitment, interviewing and selection of teachers and paraprofessionals.

The Right to Participate in Staff Evaluation

—Parents should have the right to be informed if their child's teacher is absent for more than five days. Parents should have the right to know what the school is doing to compensate for this situation.

—Parents should be routinely invited to participate in staff evaluation. They should be asked to submit their own estimate or *rating of the teacher's performance* at those times of the year when such evaluations are being prepared. Parents and teachers could develop such rating forms together.

The Right to Initiate a Grievance Against a Staff Member

—Parents should have the right to initiate a grievance against any staff persons in a school. They should be automatically informed of this right and the procedure to follow at the beginning of every term.

—Whenever a parent initiates a grievance, *a hearing* should be held automatically. Parents should be allowed to present their charges, bring their own witnesses, get a transcript of the hearing, and they must be allowed to appeal any decision that is made.

—Parents should have the right to demand an *immediate suspension of any teacher charged with striking a child*. Pending the hearing, such a teacher could be assigned to the school office or district office and not to the classroom.

The Right to Information about School Policies

—*Parents should have the right to a clear and truthful answer when they ask a question.*

—Parents should be given, in writing (a) the name, address and phone number of the parent association officers, (b) the school phone number and an emergency night-time phone number (either the child's teacher's phone number or the phone number of a staff member in charge of community relations), and (c) the names, addresses and phone numbers of the local school board members and district superintendents.

—Parents should be given *ample notice about important meetings* where decisions and policies which affect them and their children will take place.

—Parents should have *ready access to basic information about the school*. They should be able to go to their own school library for such crucial data as school and district utilization, descriptions of courses in junior and senior high schools, pupil-achievement data, data on student ethnic background, budget information about per-pupil expenditures, and staff salaries. If parents request additional information, every reasonable effort should be made to make it easily available.

—All Board of Education circulars, reports and meeting agendas should be posted and put on file in the school library or office where parents can get to them easily.

—Job openings and other opportunities should be posted where *all* parents can see them—not only a select few chosen by the principal.

The Right to Organize and Participate in Parent Organizations

Parents must have the right to choose their own representatives without school personnel present.

Parents should have the right to vote on all school issues without having to pay parent association dues. Voting hours should include daytime and evening hours to permit working parents to vote.

Whenever there is an election or other issue requiring a parent vote, there should be provision for an absentee ballot procedure. Parents should not have to attend a meeting in order to vote.

Parents should be allowed as many votes as they have children in the school.

Parents should be able to meet in school at their convenience without any charges or fees.

Parents who want to hold a meeting in a school to talk with other parents need not be members or officers of the parent association.

Parents should have a bulletin board which they can use.

Parents should have the right to distribute their own flyers and newspapers without censorship.

PARENT GRIEVANCE PROCEDURE

A procedure for making an effective appeal should be established. It might be something like this, which is adapted from the UFT grievance procedure.

Step 1   Parents appeal first to their principal who must render his decision in writing within five days.

Step 2   Parents may then appeal to the district superintendent who must schedule an appeal hearing within ten days after they request it and who must render his decision in writing within five days after the hearing.

Step 3   Parents may then appeal to the local school board which
          may set up an appeals committee. No school employees
          may serve on this committee. It should consist of par-
          ents, community residents and students selected by the
          local school board. This group must schedule an appeals
          hearing within ten days after one is requested, and must
          render a written decision within five days after the
          hearing.

Step 4   Parents may still want to appeal to the local school
          board as a whole. Some groups may want their griev-
          ance process to then go downtown to central headquar-
          ters and/or to the State Education Commissioner.

Should There Be a Parent Union?

I don't honestly know.

I think that I am against a parent union for the following reasons:

I am suspicious of citywide movements. They seem to be easily taken over by nonparent groups who have their own agenda and their own axe to grind.

I am convinced that our school system will only be saved when the vast monolith is broken up into viable local segments with educational policy directed by each local community. (I also believe that all city services—police, fire, sanitation, etc.— would benefit from such complete decentralizing.) A citywide parent union seems contradictory to the philosophy of community control. It would certainly tend to distract parents from their local areas and local concerns.

A citywide union would require funds. And in going after funds, parents are liable to be taken over or manipulated by groups which have money: foundations, colleges, agencies. If the parents were to raise their operating budget from among themselves, it might possibly mean that those parents with financial resources would be able to dominate the organization.

On the other hand, I am cynical about our chances without some kind of coalition so that parent pressure can become more effective.

Our good will and determination are not good enough to guarantee that we win. The supervisors and teachers and other forces are strongly organized, financed and staffed. We should not underestimate their power.

Unless we develop some kind of on-going structure, we will keep going around in circles. We win concessions, but we lack the mechanism to force compliance and follow-up. Parents in one part of the city have no way of finding out what victories have been won by parents in another part of the city. We need to pool our knowledge and know-how and experiences.

So I abstain from making a definite recommendation. Throughout this book I have tried very hard not to theorize. All the stories and suggestions I have outlined are based upon very real personal experiences. Therefore I am refraining from taking a position about a parent union simply because I do not know what it might mean, how it might be financed, how it might work, or how it might help, or hinder, the battle for community control of our schools.

In Conclusion

I hope that parents can find a way to negotiate a "contract" with the Board of Education (or with their local school boards) so that their rights can be guaranteed. Such a contract should include a grievance machinery so that parents may appeal any actions they consider to be unfair. And, of course, for such an agreement to work, there must be a provision for the imposition of penalties if the professional staff ignores stipulations in the contract.

A contract is a mutual agreement between two parties, each of whom promises to give something in return for something. When the teachers sign a contract, they agree to work in return for certain financial benefits and working conditions. What will the parents give if they get these rights? It is quite simple really. The school system is not able to function today because the parents no longer believe in it. The community has lost its trust in the schools. Professionals are seen as the enemy—targets to be attacked and cut down. If the educators want parents to cooperate with them, if they want the community to support and promote the schools, then they must "buy" our trust. They must establish a climate in our schools where parents are respected and not snubbed; where our contributions are welcomed and not disregarded; where our questions are answered and not ignored. Maybe if this happens, our schools will begin to change for the better. For maybe then the schools will begin to serve the children—instead of the system.

12 · Organizing Against the System

THE TACTICS OF THE SYSTEM

I was originally going to call this book "How to *Beat* the School System." But the more I wrote, the less optimistic I became. I decided I had chosen too arrogant a title. We parents will be lucky if we can learn how to fight the system. I am not so sure that we can ever beat it.

Let me describe some of the basic tactics that are repeatedly used by the school system to divide us, defeat us or, quite simply, to wear us out. We must learn to recognize these techniques and develop counterstrategies for dealing with them.

Making Simple Problems Complicated

The Board of Education is quite skillful at this. For example, a group of parents get together and want to know more about reading scores. They might first ask their childrens' teacher, "What is the average reading score of this class? How many of the children are reading below grade level?" Now, the teacher has that information at her fingertips. But she invariably gives the parents the run-around: "Our principal feels that reading scores should not be discussed with you—it is a technical and complicated subject." Immediately the parents have been put in their place. This is a professional topic, they are really being told.

If the parents persist and obtain an appointment with the principal, he will try to give them vague answers, generously laced with multisyllabic educational jargon. If the parents pursue their quest, they may finally be given some specific data about their own school. If they then dare to inquire, "How do these figures compare with the rest of the district?" they will be sent to the district office, where the entire scene will be repeated— *if* they get an appointment. And if they ask how their district compares with the rest of the city or state, they will be told they must go to headquarters for *that* type of information (with a slight sneer, which implies, of course, that *that* type of information is worthless and unimportant anyway). Then if they ask, "Whom should we see at headquarters?" they will be advised, "Write the Superintendent of Schools."

At one of our training programs at United Bronx Parents we do the following "exercise." Several parents, who are completely inexperienced in dealing with the system, are assigned a very simple question to "research." Once, for example, they were told to go see their principal and find out what an SAT teacher was. (In schools with a large number of Spanish-speaking students there used to be a "Spanish Auxiliary Teacher"; recently this position has been renamed "Bilingual Teacher.") Ten parents, all from different schools, were given this assignment. Only *one* of them was able to get the information on her first trip to the school office. And she was kept waiting for forty-five minutes before she saw the principal, who told her that the secretary should have answered her question immediately. (But the principal did not tell this to the secretary, who kept another parent waiting in the same way the following week.)

Mrs. Toby Sanchez, an enterprising and efficient Bronx parent, who helped me enormously in gathering background data for this book, spent days at 110 Livingston Street trying to obtain statistics. After two weeks at headquarters, she wrote me the following memo:

> When I went to 110 Livingston Street for the first time in search of a few particular offices, such as Educational Research, and Teacher Recruitment, the Directory in the lobby gave neither direction nor help. It is a list of personal names and room numbers without mention of function. One small corner of it lists a few departments, but not all are listed, nor does the Directory indicate the large number of important offices that are located in other buildings. It is obviously designed for those who know exactly whom they want to see. It's for insiders, not outsiders.
>
> There is an Information Window on the other side of the lobby, but if there were a complete directory of all the offices of the Board of Education by function and in alphabetical order, there would be no need to employ two people in an Information Window.
>
> I have found that when I ask for a copy of a form or a report written by staff members, the most frequent responses are a blank look with an apologetic "I've never heard of that," or a huffy shrug with a loud-voiced "I know of no such circular," or righteous incredulity: "Do you think we can just give out that sort of information to anyone who walks in here?" If you go away and agree to write a letter or look elsewhere, you have lost. Stand still and tell them that you were referred to their office by someone inside the system or remind them politely that you are only seeking public information. . . . After running out of lame excuses, they will tell you with great exasperation to go see their superior.

At no time was Mrs. Sanchez looking for confidential data. For example, one of the statistics we needed was the most recent information on the total number of tenured teachers in the system. At first she went to the Professional Library on the second floor at headquarters, thinking she could find everything in the files and could avoid bothering people with her questions. "The most recent entry was dated 1965," she wrote me. "When

I asked the librarian why current research was not in the files, I was told that there was no one to do the cataloguing."

Nobody at headquarters answers, "I don't know." Instead, everyone assures you that what you are seeking is not available, or is not public information. They tell you this *automatically* and *authoritatively* without bothering to find out if it is true. The number of tenured teachers in the system was finally supplied to us by the deputy superintendent for personnel; he earns over $35,000 a year. Not one of his subordinates was authorized or able to answer our inquiry. The deputy superintendent assured us that the information was "readily available," but one of his inferiors had originally told Mrs. Sanchez, "We don't have statistics on tenured teachers in our files. You would have to sit in this office for ten hours a day for six months to dig out the answer to that question. With all this decentralization, we no longer keep records like that here." Since all personnel records *are* still kept centrally, either that employee didn't know, which seems incredible, or he was deliberately lying.

At a monthly Board of Education public meeting I once raised the problem of getting information. The secretary to the board replied, "Ellen, you've known me for years. Why didn't you just pick up the phone and ask me for the data. I would have sent it to you at once." This is precisely what is wrong with the Board of Education. People in the city who know insiders are not required to use the "proper channels." And so they don't realize that those channels are hopelessly clogged. The average parent, who has no connections and simply wants to obtain a few facts so she can work more intelligently in her parent association, or so she can present a problem more clearly to her local school board, is totally blocked by this system. Unless she is fantastically persistent and determined, she will not get the information she wants. In fact, if she insists and *does* manage to secure it, she is usually labeled some sort of a nut or troublemaker.

Passing the Buck

Nobody at the Board of Education ever gives you an out-and-out "No, we will not do what you want." Instead you are told, "I wish I could help you, but I am powerless to change this situation"; or "I agree with you completely, but that matter is out of my hands."

Parents are told to take their complaints through "channels." But it is frequently unclear just where those channels lie. The person who has real power in a given situation is not easily identified. Not knowing this, parents waste invaluable hours and energy talking to underlings—lower-echelon people who have no authority and who cannot, or will not, make decisions.

Instead of decentralization simplifying things, it has made this entire process even more complicated. All the laws are so vague and ambiguous that each person you go to can readily tell you to go see someone else. Parents are sent from their principal to the district office to central headquarters—and then back again. For example, some Bronx junior high school parents were angry about their school. They spent a few weeks taking turns staying home from work, walking around the school building, talking to students and teachers. Finally they agreed that there were three important problems which had to be resolved: the lunchroom conditions were horrendous; the overcrowding was beyond belief; and the sale of drugs in and around the school was flagrant. They decided to tackle these problems. The principal agreed with them, and sent them to the district superintendent. He agreed also, and showed them copies of letters he had written to headquarters asking for help.

Within the next four months these parents were sent to the Division of School Lunches (in Queens), which told them the school needed new lunch facilities and sent them to the Division of School Planning (in Brooklyn), which told them that the City Planning Commission (in Manhattan) had stopped the money. They were then sent to the Zoning Division to discuss overcrowding. There they were sent back to their local school board, which told them it had requested an annex—which was bottled up by the Division of Construction and the Department of Real Estate. They went to the local police precinct to talk about drugs, and were sent to the mayor's Drug Addiction Services Agency, where they were told that their budget had been slashed and were sent to see their local politicians, who were all in Albany at the time, fighting over abortion reform and welfare cutbacks.

Every single person they saw agreed with them that the conditions in that Bronx school were terrible—altogether they met
with seventeen different officials, and attended more than 33
different meetings. At the end of the school year, five months
later, they had accomplished next to nothing.

The trouble was that the parents were altogether too cooperative. They respected the authorities too much. They believed
that going through channels would work. There *are* some effective ways for dealing with buck-passing—but I don't believe that
going from one official to another is one of them.

Negotiates in Bad Faith

Labor unions are skillful at recognizing the signs when management is bargaining in "bad faith." Parents are less knowledgeable
about identifying the signs. We hate to believe that we are being
given the run-around.

For example, we make an appointment to discuss a problem,
and then we are kept waiting for an hour. When we are finally
ushered into the room, the official we have waited to see is in
a hurry and can only spare us a few moments. Most of us are
too polite to force him to stay longer. Instead, we rush into our
presentation, "making do" with the pitifully brief time allocated
to us. We don't do our cause justice, but he isn't listening to us
anyway. He has managed to put us off; he has given us our
appointment, and now he is free of us.

Sometimes we arrive and find that our appointment has been
broken altogether; they "tried" to reach us but were unable to
catch us before we left home—we will have to come back another day. Or we are promptly ushered in, but the official we
had planned to see had an "unexpected" emergency and cannot
join us; his assistant is there instead. Each of these techniques
is calculated to wear us out.

While pretending that they are "trying to work things out,"
they are actually doing nothing of the sort. We may finally get
a real meeting, with the person who is really in charge; the
appointment, praise be, is not broken. We sit around the table,
and make a careful, well-documented presentation. We make

several recommendations. The officials nod knowledgeably; they may even congratulate us on our thoughtfulness and thoroughness. Then they tell us they must "look into the situation" for themselves. Sometimes, in extremely tense situations, they appoint a special "fact-finding" committee, which is charged with investigating the problem all over again. Since you and your fellow parents cannot be considered "disinterested" parties, you are usually not included on the fact-finding committee. And of course, while that committee is studying the situation, nothing can be done at all.

During the past fifteen years this particular tactic has been repeatedly utilized by all the different boards of education. Parents and other laymen complained about the Board of Examiners. The Board of Education paid first one outsider and then another to come in and restudy the problem. Their recommendations almost paralleled those of the parents, but each study gained more time for those opposing change to gather strength. Parents complained about segregation and the Allen Committee was formed. Outsiders who were not part of the struggle were brought in as "consultants." Money was made; months passed by and the same facts that had been found by the parents were, not surprisingly, found by the experts. The educational park, the comprehensive high school, the 4-4-4 complexes, decentralization, community control—all these reforms were originally demanded by parents, and were then put into the hands of "professional investigators," who studied, analyzed and talked them to death.

Frequently we parents unwittingly contribute to our own defeat. When we do get a meeting with an official, we are sometimes so frustrated and filled with pent-up anger that we spend the entire session pouring out our hearts, screaming and ranting about the problem. At the end of the hour, we have done all the talking. Our time is up. And we have not forced the official to respond to us at all.

And sometimes we will be told that we are raising a crucial and very difficult problem. They will offer to meet with us and negotiate a solution. "While we are meeting," they will suggest, "we must be certain that there will be no disruptions or demonstrations. After all, negotiation cannot take place in an atmosphere of coercion." We forget that the teachers' union negotiates while it is on a strike. We submit to the board's request, and we spend hours and weeks talking with the officials down-town. Meanwhile we lose all contact with our fellow parents back in our neighborhood. Rumors fly that we have "sold them out." We are too busy to keep everyone informed, and the anger in the community either turns against us or cools altogether, because the most articulate leadership is being kept occupied far from home. Suddenly the board breaks off the negotiations with us, and when we go back to our neighbors we find that the momentum is gone and we cannot pull them back together; we are unable to pull off any sort of demonstration because we have lost our following.

The most frustrating example of bargaining in "bad faith" is this one. *The officials will sometimes agree to do what we ask.* We think we have won an enormous victory. And then the weeks and months go by and nothing happens. The promise is never implemented. They blame this agency or that official. They tell you it is "in the works." And a year or more passes. Soon the parents who won the first victory are no longer in the school; the new parents don't know what was promised before. The board has managed to win by default.

Thus, just as important as finding out how to win a victory is learning how to follow up and enforce compliance. When a trade union signs an agreement they spend months and years forcing management to comply with their part of the bargain. Parents, lacking a union and staff, have not yet been able to do this.

Parents Are Forced into Winning the Same Thing Over and Over Again

We parents are just learning to demand that all promises be put into writing. For years we trusted board officials to do what they said. But since we did not have any written agreements, an official might promise to do something and then someone else would take over his job and tell us that he didn't know anything about any such agreement. We would be right back where we started.

More commonly this is what happens. Parents win an issue in one part of the city, but have to win it all over again in another. A child is suspended in Jamaica, Queens, for sitting down during the reciting of the Pledge of Allegiance. His parents contact lawyers and successfully plead their case. The board is forced into reinstating the pupil. But two weeks later another student, this time in Coney Island, is suspended for doing the same thing. As a rule, unless the case has received an unusual amount of publicity, the Brooklyn parents don't know what happened in Queens. Another lawyer is found, and often another fee is paid. The fight must be fought and won all over again.

The Board Keeps Us Busy Responding
to Its Issues

South Bronx parents were preoccupied with improving the school lunch program in their community. They organized several very successful demonstrations and were about to run a large rally exposing the conditions when the Board of Education scheduled two public hearings for their area—one on district lines and the other on school construction.

Several principals and district superintendents called in the parents and persuaded them to postpone their school lunch rally until after the hearings took place. One principal told some parents that unless they attended the budget hearing they might lose their new school. Several teachers told other parents that if the district boundaries were changed their school would lose its Title I reading program. In both cases, the parents were not being told the truth. The new school was already under construction; the district lines had nothing to do with Title I funds. But the parents felt they could not afford to take the risk. They stopped what they were doing in order to attend the hearings, and they postponed their lunch rally because they were simply too tired to do both.

A variation on this tactic occurs when parents demonstrate for a particular change and the Board of Education responds with a totally irrelevant solution. For example, parents at Stitt Junior High School had protested its overcrowded conditions for years to no avail. Finally, they decided that the real issue was the principal of the school. They organized a campaign for a new principal; they interviewed and selected their candidate; they ran a very effective boycott. Then the Board of Education responded. It solved the overcrowding—but did not hire their candidate for principal.

A similar situation followed after black high school students demonstrated throughout the city for more black teachers and supervisors and for a greater student voice in establishing discipline procedures. The Board of Education responded with a "bill of rights" for students, which would permit them to dress as they wish and to distribute flyers outside of their schools. Quite rightly, the black students were furious. When they forcefully and stridently made their anger known at a public meeting, the Board of Education responded by doing absolutely nothing. It tabled the "new" rights, and it ignored the old grievances.

Frequently intellectuals will criticize organizations like United Bronx Parents for spending so much time dealing with the system. They will tell us, "You must ignore the system and develop your own issues and alternatives to the system." That is a very good philosophy on paper. But the fact is that our children are attending those schools; they are indeed "trapped" in that system. We therefore must deal with the system and its agenda, as much as we do not want to. But at the same time, we must understand what we are being pushed into doing; and we must develop techniques for forcing the system to respond to us.

Parents Who Criticize the School System Are Called Bad Names

To listen to school professionals one would think that there are only two types of parents: "responsible, cooperative, reasonable and constructive parents"—the good guys; and "irresponsible, uncooperative, unreasonable and destructive parents"—the bad guys. All of us are susceptible to flattery. Parents like to hear highly educated professionals tell them that they are behaving "intelligently." If the board officials agree with us, we are called "moderate." If they disagree, we are "militant."

In 1964, when parents were organizing a school boycott to protest segregated and inferior school conditions, those parents were labeled lawbreakers. In 1968, while the teachers broke the law and conducted a strike, those parents who tried to keep the schools operating were labeled scabs and bigots. Parents who take no role in school affairs are "apathetic" and "uninterested." Parents who take too much interest in these same affairs are "rabble rousers" and "meddlers." Name-calling, however, is merely a preliminary phase of a more powerful board tactic.

Parents Are Divided, Bought Off and Thus Conquered

The oldest strategy in the world is nevertheless the most effective weapon the school system has. Until parents learn how to deal with it, we will continue to be outmaneuvered and outwitted by its use.

For instance, a group of parents may be critical of the grouping policies in their school. They believe that the "top" classes are getting the best teachers and the hardest schoolwork, and that the rest of the children are being short-changed. They organize a campaign to change the system. The principal invites one of the most outspoken mothers into his office. "I've been looking over your daughter's records," he tells her. "She is really doing exceptionally well, and so I have decided to transfer her to the top class. If she continues to do such good work, I think she will get into the Intellectually Gifted Program." The parent is thrilled. Is it surprising that she no longer is opposing the tracking system? Her child has been placed in the best group; why should she continue to fight?

Or look at this story. Some parents are very angry about a certain teacher. She yells at the children, and several students say that she has even hit some pupils. A committee gets together to go see the principal. When they arrive in his office, he has two other parents sitting next to him: the officers of the parent association who also happen to be working in the school as paraprofessionals. The principal doesn't answer the complaints; he sits back and lets the parent officers deal with the group. "Oh, you are absolutely wrong about that teacher," they tell the others. "The children are running wild in this school; she is only trying to make them learn how to behave." A few of you might remember that last year those same two parents were angry about conditions in the school—until they were offered jobs by the principal.

It is rare that this approach does not work. School officials have learned how to weaken effective parent groups by neutralizing their leadership. They isolate one or two members, solve their problems, help their children, and often succeed in cooling the entire situation. Parents argue and fight among each other, and the school system is left alone to conduct its business as usual.

I can hear my liberal, sophisticated friends scornfully criticizing: "Those parents should know better. Don't they realize they have been bought off? Don't they see that their basic problems will never be solved if they allow themselves to be coopted that way?" But the point is, all parents are selfish—we *all* want the best for our children. Look at those sophisticated people who are analyzing and lecturing. How many of them have their children in our city's public schools? They may fervently believe in the value of urban public education, but they have removed their own children from the battle. How can we attack those parents who, not being rich enough to afford suburban or private schools, grab the best of what there is in the public schools? How can we expect parents to consider the "long-range point of view?" A child gets only one chance at second grade. How can a parent be expected to put her trust in: "If we only keep fighting we will soon be able to beat the system"? If she is offered a chance for her child *right now,* what is wrong if she grabs that chance— even if the price she must pay is not fancy tuition but simply shutting her mouth?

And remember, most Northern school officials do not resemble Bull Connor. In the South everyone recognizes the enemy. He calls you names; he won't sit down with you; he fights you openly. But in the North, things are not so clear. A friendly, kindly gray-haired professional calls a parent into his office and says, "We really need to learn how to respond to the needs of the community. You have strong connections with the other parents;

they respect you and trust you. Won't you please help our teachers understand your community? If you would come to work for us in our school you could help us do a much better job of educating the children."

How can we say to that parent, who undoubtedly needs the job very badly, "Don't take it. You are being bribed. You are selling out to the enemy." It is a rare parent who can resist this offer—such a parent must have strong will power *and* enough financial resources to be able to afford to turn down the money.

And once the parents get into the school, of course they change even more. Working inside the school each day, talking to teachers instead of neighbors, parents cannot help changing. I remember once, when I was on the local school board in Harlem, we suggested to our district superintendent that he meet regularly with the Harlem Parents Committee, in order to resolve problems before they flared into crisis. He agreed and made the offer. But the Harlem Parents Committee turned him down. Later, their chairman told me privately, "If we start meeting with him regularly, we may get to like him. If we start to like him, we will begin to see problems from his point of view. And then we will not fight him as strongly or as effectively. We will constantly be diluting our demands."

Staying aloof is an extremely hard position to maintain. It is correct—theoretically. But just as individuals seem unable to resist the offer of jobs or benefits for their children, so organizations also have been coopted by the system. Many groups that were busy exposing, criticizing and attacking the schools have slowly and imperceptibly been defused; district superintendents have identified them, and have invited them to write educational programs, participate in "advisory councils," recommend people for jobs. Again, it is far easier to denounce these organizations than it is to understand what they are up against.

If you are working in a neighborhood church or community center, and the children on your block are woefully behind in reading and math, and if the district superintendent invites you to serve on a special committee to help him decide how to spend some special federal monies, do you refuse? And if he encourages you to write a program which will meet the needs of the children, do you attack him? And after you work hard and design the program, and the Board of Education begins to alter it and revise it, do you quit? Or do you hope that by sticking with it, working hard, not antagonizing anybody, you will be able to win out and salvage some of the program the children so desperately need?

Many parents and parent organizations believe they can change the system best by working from within. They join a committee, go to work inside a school, let themselves be "co-opted," and then they become disillusioned and fed up. They have tried to work cooperatively, and they are bitterly disappointed when they fail. *They* are ready to make an all-out attack on the system. But there are always *new* parents who have not had these experiences and who still have hope. For every parent who quits a job, for every group which resigns from a Board of Education committee, there are many others willing and eager to take their place. And the result is that parents and community groups continue to argue and fight among each other, debating strategy, accusing each other either of selling out or being too militant. Thus preoccupied, tearing at each other's throat, they are distracted from battling the real enemy: the school system.

The Most Potent Weapon the System Has to Use Against Us Is that We Are Afraid

Parents are afraid, and when we stop being afraid, we will begin to win our battle against the school system.

First, we are afraid for our children. They are so vulnerable. They sit in those classrooms day after day. We protest, and then we are afraid that the teacher will find some way to get back at us through our children. We demonstrate, and then we are afraid that the principal might take out his anger at us on our children. Many parents have taken jobs as paraprofessionals in the schools not to "sell out," but to make sure they can keep an eye on what is happening, to make sure their children are protected.

It is foolhardy to ignore these fears, and it is stupid to pretend that they are unwarranted. In writing this book I purposely omitted any specific mention of my own children's schools or teachers so that my children would be shielded from vindictiveness and reprisals. Most of the outspoken critics of the system—Rev. Milton Galamison and Evelina Antonetty, to mention two—had to remove their children from the public schools in order to protect them.

Parents remain weak and divided because we are afraid of each other. Middle-class parents are afraid of poor parents; because of that fear they did not join in the fight for community control, even though it might have helped them improve the schools in their communities too. White parents are afraid of black parents. Black parents are afraid of Puerto Rican parents. Puerto Rican parents are afraid of Chinese parents. In every community, and between every community, there is a wall of fear and distrust which effectively keeps parents apart. When will we realize that we have much more to fear from the system than from each other?

It could be argued that for all these reasons parents will never become a really formidable force for reform. Perhaps. However, I think that the parents' fears are in direct proportion to what they have to lose. If their children are still able to make it in the schools, parents are afraid to "rock the boat." They don't want to jeopardize what little they have. But as the retardation and drop-out rate and drug addiction increase, more and more parents are going to realize that there is nothing good left to protect. Many of our children are saying that now.

David Spencer, perhaps the most magnificent and able parent leader in the city, has said that "Victory is not always in the winning." Parents are up against unbeatable odds. Everything rational and logical says we cannot beat this system. But time, and our children, are on our side. If we are willing to choke back our fears, we may find a way to fight the system. And as our children watch us fight for them, we may learn that we have educated our kids and beaten the system—despite the odds.

Action Checklist for Parents

HOW TO ORGANIZE PARENTS
TO BEAT THE SYSTEM

Choose specific tangible issues which are important to parents.

Don't be abstract, vague or intellectual. Select nitty-gritty demands—the more specific the better.

Go after several things at once, including a number of easily won issues. Parents will be encouraged by their success and will then gain the strength and self-confidence to tackle the more difficult problems.

Get things which parents want right now. If there are also some long-range demands (e.g., a new school), be sure you are also fighting for some immediate help at the same time (e.g., repair of the broken toilets at once).

Parents must develop their own list of grievances and demands.

No outside group, no matter how dedicated or concerned, can do this job. Don't let anyone tell you what you should be demanding. One of the main reasons parent campaigns fail is that they are not really "parent" campaigns at all. The principal or some teachers have manipulated some parents into fighting for a particular program, and this sort of ruse soon falls apart.

Different groups of parents want different things. For example, in one elementary school, the parents of the children who come by bus may want to improve the lunch facilities and the transportation schedule; the Spanish-speaking parents may want to increase the number of bilingual teachers; the parents of the children in the top class may want French taught in the third grade. All of these demands are legitimate. All of the various groups should be encouraged to meet by themselves and prepare their own list of grievances and demands.

Parents must then come together and decide *priorities*. Which issues are the most important for all parents? Which are the most important for the different types of parents? Be careful that you don't concentrate only on those issues which the most powerful members of the parent association want. Be sure that you *hear* what all the various parents are saying. Be sure you include a wide cross-section of grievances and demands on your final list. (The UFT goes into bargaining sessions with more than six hundred different demands from all the various teacher chapters.)

Your parent group must be representative, but even more important, it must include, in large numbers, those parents who have the most serious grievances.

Many parent groups fail because they are not truly representative. Usually parent associations are heavily weighted to include mainly those parents who are satisfied with the school and trust the administration. Those parents will have an extremely narrow list of grievances. In a sense they are the "company union." It is crucial that parents do not argue with each other over the validity of a particular grievance. For example, if some parents believe that some teachers are bigoted, this is a very real issue to them. Just because other parents do not share this grievance is no reason to eliminate it. All parents want qualified, unprejudiced teachers. This is a good and legitimate demand.

Many parent groups fail because some of their members feel obliged to defend the school system from all criticism. Parents should defend and protect their children and other parents; it is up to the school employees to defend the system. If the parent association has become a "company union" you may want to set up your own parent group, or you may want to challenge the parent association to run a new election. However, a split of this sort is potentially dangerous and might weaken your group. If you can pull all the parents into a common group first, try to do so. But, priority should go to those parents whose children are suffering the most in the school. Parents whose children are doing all right simply will not fight as hard, nor will they risk very much. If keeping the parents united means losing the support of your angriest parents, forget it. It would be better to split.

Do your own research—gather facts carefully to support your demands.

Fact-finding is a good organizing tool. As parents try to gather more information about their problems, they can get angrier and angrier with the system.

However, they can also get worn-out. The most important fact for you is the way the parents and students feel about your school. Document your stories and grievances, and be sure to *protect* the *anonymity* of everyone concerned.

When fact-finding, go directly to the source if you can. For example, if you want to find out about Title I regulations, go to Washington to find out how things *can* be done; don't go to board headquarters in Brooklyn, because all you will learn there is why things cannot be done your way.

Use various resources to help you gather data. Church groups, community agencies and colleges that wish to support you can be really helpful in securing the information you need. Just be sure that they only want to help you, and don't intend to take you over.

Don't believe things you read or things you are told, if your eyes tell you differently. Often the Board of Education will show parents some facts on paper which will testify that all the children are reading or that the school is not overcrowded. Our own eyes tell us that they are lying. We see that the kids can't read and we see how crowded the school is. Believe what you see, not what they tell you. And make them come and see what you see.

Publicize your grievances and demands and broaden your support.

Many parent groups take their grievances to the officials too soon. Once you develop your list of demands, you must first be sure that most of the parents agree with you. Hold meetings, distribute flyers, encourage other parents to add to the list and provide additional documentation for those grievances they support. Get some community groups to support your demands—early in the game before you run into any trouble. And remember, "support" means just that. You are not inviting them to veto your demands or modify them. You are asking their support and sponsorship. Invite community leaders to come into your school and see for themselves why you need what you are asking for. But don't let them try to supervise you, censor you, or manipulate you. You can appreciate their advice, but remember, a parent campaign must be run by parents. If your demands are good ones, undoubtedly there will be some teachers in your school who will be willing to support you.

Decide whom you will see to discuss your grievances.

Before you start running around from one agency to another, plan your campaign. If your demands are relatively simple, perhaps you only have to see your *principal.* But most likely you will need to go at least one step beyond him. Always bring your demands to your principal first, however. See which ones he will support; try to get him to do something about at least one or two of the grievances—these will be your first victories, and you should thank him and publicize them. But if he disagrees with you, that should *not* stop you if your grievances are valid.

Force your local school board to deal with your complete list of grievances. Make them help you avoid the buck-passing game. If you have fifteen different demands, for example, you could easily be sent to see fifteen different officials. One way to deal with this run-around is to force your local school board to handle everything; they should invite all the various officials who have power to one meeting with you so that you and your fellow parents are not worn out running from one to another.

Get your local board or the chancellor of schools or the mayor to tell you in *writing* who has the final authority to determine each of the problems on your list. There is no point in wasting time seeing a lot of people with no decision-making power.

Once you get a meeting to present your grievances, be sure to:

√take a good-sized group representing a cross-section of parents. Do not limit your group to only two or three members; this will antagonize too many parents. The UFT negotiating team consists of twelve or more members.

√find out how long your meeting will last. If you prepare a half-hour presentation, but the meeting is scheduled to last only a half hour, you will have let them off the hook because there won't be enough time to force them to answer you.

√find out in advance whom the board plans to have attend the meeting. If they are inviting many "experts," bring along your own experts. If they are inviting other parent groups, find out in advance and decide if you still want to go under those conditions. Or perhaps you will want to caucus with those other parent groups in advance.

√doublecheck on the morning of your meeting to make sure the person you think you are seeing will really be there. Decide in advance whether or not you will keep the appointment if he keeps you waiting or if he delegates you to an assistant.

√make sure that you do not take up the entire meeting with your presentation. You must force them to respond to you.

√have one member of your group take minutes. But insist that the school official put all promises into *writing*. You might want to stay there while he dictates the "agreement" to his secretary, or else you may be surprised that the letter you receive later in no way resembles the agreement you thought you had.

√if the school official tells you he must "study" the matter further, give him a time limit within which he must render a decision or meet with you again. Schedule a follow-up appointment then and there.

Some things to do to avoid their buck-passing.

√*Play one agency against another.* If you are on good terms with the borough president, make him bring all the different officials together to meet with you. If they don't come, he will be angry at their arrogance and support you.

√*Go over the head of the official who is stalling you.* When you waste time with an underling, unless you are getting some information you need, you are really being stalled. If an official will not see you, go over his head. For example, if the School Lunch Division won't see you, go to the Department of Agriculture, which partially subsidizes them. If the head of School Construction stalls you, pressure the mayor or city council, which supplies school construction funds.

√*If the "proper channels" are clogged, use some improper ones.* If an official will not give you an appointment in his office, go picket his home or his church, until he agrees to meet with you.

√*Disrupt their routine business-as-usual operation until they stop stalling you.* If you are given the run-around, learn to recognize it and get angry. Sit in, picket, do whatever you can to force them to meet and deal with you; don't make it easy for them to ignore you.

√*Turn the tables and do some buck-passing yourself.* If a principal asks you to help him get an additional secretary for the school, tell him you can't because the "community" is disappointed that he didn't help solve their problems. Or if your group is demonstrating and you receive a phone call from a downtown politician asking you to call off your demonstration, tell him, "It is out of my hands; I have no control over that group, because they are so angry."

√*Every time you are stalled, expose it to the rest of the parents.* If you have an appointment, role-play in advance what might happen, so the parents will recognize the brush-off. Then come back and write up a flyer and tell the rest of the neighborhood all about it. Or when you go through proper channels, and get nowhere, expose it; put your story into a

flyer and tell everyone. If you keep your fellow parents informed every step of the way, they will be with you if and
when you are forced into using more "extreme" tactics.

Never, never, never attack other parents or parent groups.

√Don't let the Board of Education divide and conquer you.

√If you walk into a meeting where other parents have been
invited to argue with you, ask to meet with them without
any professionals present, or else leave. Take on those parents
in private; don't fall into the system's trap by fighting among
each other, and letting the school officials off the hook.

√Even when you agree to disagree with the other parents, you
can fight the system for what you want without fighting the
parents.

√Never take away something from another parent group.
Always demand that you get as much as they got; but don't
be trapped into fighting another group to give up something
for your sake. There is enough to go around for everyone,
but the school system likes to make us fight among each
other for the crumbs while it controls the real pie.

**Keep your neighbors informed and keep broadening your local base
of support.**

√Don't get so wrapped up in meetings "downtown" that you
lose contact with your fellow parents and neighbors.

√During any negotiation, keep local demonstrations, rallies and
picket lines going. Distribute flyers telling everyone what is
happening.

√Don't depend on citywide media to tell your story. If you take
lots of parents to all the meetings, they will see what is going
on and they will spread the word.

√Never stop inviting other local organizations to join with you.
Go to churches, political clubs, antipoverty agencies and
everyone else to tell them about your campaign and invite
their sponsorship. This will prevent the Board of Education

from calling you extremists or other unfavorable names. Get the most legitimate groups in your community to lend their support. If you are campaigning for things parents really want, this should not be too difficult.

Don't worry too much about city-wide support.

√Local issues are best won locally. And parents can wear themselves out by going to many meetings in other parts of the city.

√It would be wonderful if we had a citywide movement of parents. But don't try to push this artificially too soon. Fight for the things you need in your own community and the rest will follow.

√On the other hand, when opportunities arise to tell your story to the rest of the city, use them. For example, at various dedication ceremonies for new schools or parks, there is usually a television crew. Use those ceremonies for demonstrations about your grievances, and you may get some citywide attention. Use special public hearings and meetings in the same way.

√If citywide groups want to support you, invite them to come to your area and see what is going on. Don't keep leaving your own community to go to meetings; this will only weaken you.

√Force decision-makers to come into your community for meetings and hearings.

Keep your sense of humor and find ways to deflate and ridicule the officials.

The struggle is hard and long. If you get too intense or uptight, you will be worn out long before you can win. There is humor in the most critical situations. Learn to seek it out, for it will keep you going.

Beware of advisory committees, dialogues, consultations, etc.

You are interested in setting up a pattern of negotiation between two equal groups: parents and school officials. You should not walk into a situation where you are asked to give advice which they can easily ignore.

√*Pick your own leadership.* This is really one of the basic problems facing parent groups. If you don't like the procedures which are in effect for selecting parent leadership, force a change. (For example, in District 5, parents in several schools have won the point that they will not have to pay dues in order to vote for parent leaders or to vote on other crucial isues.) Unless parents work out a way to choose their own leadership (without manipulation by principals, teachers or community groups) we will be faced by splinter groups and "appointed" parent groups that have been hand-picked by the school administration.

Learn to escalate your fight if you reach a bottleneck.

√Timing and pacing are crucial. Don't start off by threatening a boycott. That should be the last possible tactic and threat.

√But if you are blocked from getting what you want, start refusing to participate in anything. For example, they need parents to help write Title I proposals. If you are angry about a custodian and they won't discuss this with you, refuse to sit in on Title I discussions.

√Parents have a great deal of *negative power*. By refusing to do certain things, they can be very strong.

√Don't split up over tactics. If one group of parents wants to circulate a petition and another wants to do something more radical, let them both do their thing.

√Remember that the issue you are fighting will determine your tactics. If you want something fairly conventional (i.e., more reading teachers) you can use one set of tactics, but if you are after something which is less "acceptable" (i.e., you want to interview your own staff), then you will need to formulate a different set of tactics.

√Parents who have connections and contacts high up in the system will choose one type of tactics when escalating their fight. Parents who are more powerless will have to do some less "respectable," more sensational things to get attention. Choose those techniques that are available to your group.

√Persevere. Whatever you do, don't give up. You may win a few fights this year and a few more next year, but if there is a particular issue you can't win the first time around, go back to it. Don't let the board tell you, "It can't be done." The UFT has learned that things that "could not be done" five years ago, can be done today. Parents too must learn to stick with their demands until they win.

Appendix

Things to Read and Do

CURRICULUM

New York City Board of Education Material

All curriculum bulletins may be obtained from the Publications Office, Board of Education, 110 Livingston Street, Brooklyn, or in Curriculum Library, 131 Livington Street, Brooklyn.

1. Curriculum of the N.Y.C. public schools, Curriculum Bulletins No. 10, 1969–70 Series.
2. General Circular 13, 1968–69, dated April 9, 1969, Grade Placement and Promotional Policies Pre-kindergarten—12
3. *Board of Education Acceleration and Enrichment Programs in Junior High and Intermediate Schools for Schools Having Sixth-Year Classes,* by Trude Weil and Irving Anker, 1967–68, Form 101
4. Special Circular 13, 1968–69, Entrance Exams for Special High

Schools and Special Courses in Academic and Vocational High
Schools

5. Directory of Public High Schools, New York City

6. General Circular 17, 1965–66, April 19, 1966, Policy Statement
    on Mathematics Courses in Ninth Year

7. Elementary Schools Memo No. 3: 1968–69, March 6, 1969, Cri-
    teria for Placement in IGC Classes

8. Elementary Schools Memo No. 4, March 6, 1969, Qualifications
    for Teachers of Classes for Intellectually Gifted Children

9. *Number and Proportion of Pupils Enrolled in Academic, Com-
    mercial and General Courses in Academic High Schools during
    the 1968–69 School Year, by Ethnic Groups,* prepared by M.
    Langlois and F. E. Allen, Educational Program Research and
    Statistics, May 1969

10. Special Circular 17, 1969–1970, dated Sept. 30, 1969, Require-
    ments for Diplomas of Graduation from Senior High School effec-
    tive June 1973

11. Administration Procedures and Programs, Bureau for Children
    with Retarded Mental Development, Board of Education Cur-
    riculum Bulletin, 1962–63 (not updated as of Jan. 1970)

12. For information on number of CRMD, IGC classes and class size
    in your elementary school, ask for Elementary Grade and Class
    Organization Sheet, filed monthly by your principal with Divi-
    sion of Elementary Schools and with your local superintendent
    of schools.

13. For reading scores for your school, if the principal won't release
    them, they are on file at the Bureau of Education Research, 110
    Livingston Street, Board of Education.

14. For information on junior high graduates see forms 837 and 837A
    filed by your principal in his office, the district office and at
    central headquarters.

General Material

1. For information on pupil evaluation, New York State, contact
    Division of Educational Testing, New York State Education De-
    partment, Albany, 12224

2. *The Educationally Disadvantaged in New York State, The Scope
    of the Problem as Revealed by the 1966 Pupil Evaluation Pro-
    gram Test Results,* Regents Examination and Scholarship Center,

Division of Educational Testing, December 1967, Department of Education, Albany, New York

3. *The New York City School Fact Book*, Institute for Community Studies, Queens College, Queens, New York
4. *College Going Rate of New York State High School Graduates, 1968–1969*, University of the State of New York, State Education Department, Albany, 12224
5. *1968 Education Law, Handbook for School Boards*, New York State School Boards Association, Albany, New York 12224
6. *Pupils and Schools in New York City, A Fact Book*, by Eleanor Bernert Sheldon and Raymond A. Glazier, 1965, Russell Sage Foundation
7. *The Case for Basic Education*, edited by James D. Koerner, Little, Brown and Company, Boston, 1959
8. *36 Children*, by Herbert Kohl, The New American Library, 1967
9. *Education and Income*, by Patricia Cayo Sexton, The Viking Press, New York, 1961
10. *Revolution in Learning*, by Maya Pines, Harper and Row, New York, 1966
11. *How Children Learn*, by John Holt, Pitman Publishing Corp., New York, 1967
12. *Teach Them All to Read*, by S. Alan Cohen, Random House, New York, 1969
13. *Learning to Read, The Great Debate*, by Jeanne Chall, McGraw Hill, New York, 1967
14. *Reading and Curriculum Data and Parent Training Kits*, United Bronx Parents, 791 Prospect Avenue, Bronx, New York
15. *Academic High Schools in Brooklyn, or Why Children Fail*, Brooklyn Educational Task Force, 525 Clinton Avenue, Brooklyn, 1969
16. *Curriculum in the New York City Schools under Decentralization*, United Parents Association, 381 Park Avenue South, New York 10016, 1970
17. *Reading Scores and the New York City Board of Education*, Brooklyn Education Task Force, 525 Clinton Avenue, Brooklyn, New York, April 1970.
18. *Grouping Pupils in New York City*, by Christina Tree, a summary of a survey conducted by and reprinted in *The Urban Review*, a publication of the Center for Urban Education, 1969
19. *Down with Ability Grouping* by Verna Binkley Bjork, in *Grade Teacher*, May 1968

20. "Seeking the 'Right Track,'" by Bernard Bard, in The New York *Post*, December 9, 1967
21. U.S. Appeals Court Judge J. Skelly Wright's decision on the District of Columbia's Track System, reprinted by EQUAL, from the *Congressional Record*, June 21, 1967

COMPENSATORY EDUCATION

New York City Board of Education Material

1. *State and Federal Programs*, 1967–68, Board of Education, April 1968, prepared by Jacob Landers, Office of State and Federally Assisted Programs (As of Jan. 1970, this was not updated)
2. *Summer Programs*, 1969, New York City Board of Education
3. *Summary of Proposed Programs*, 1968–1969 and 1969–1970, Title I, ESEA, submitted to Board of Education, Aug. 26, 1968; Aug. 28, 1969
4. *Summary of Proposed Programs*, 1969–1970, New York State Urban Education Programs, submitted to the Board of Education, Aug. 28, 1969
5. *Directory of Title III Projects*, 1968–69 and 1969–70, Board of Education
6. *Final Report Submitted to the Superintendent of Schools*, June 20, 1968, by the Committee on Experimental Programs to Improve Educational Achievements in Special Service Schools (Gordon Committee)
7. *Board of Education Press Release on Community Education Centers*, Aug. 11, 1968, Office of Education Information

Data on Federal and State Programs

1. *Catalog of Federal Domestic Assistance*, Jan. 1969, compiled by the Office of Economic Opportunity, U.S. Government Printing Office
2. *Everyman's Guide to Federal Programs*, New Community Press, 3210 Grace Street, N.W., Washington, D.C. 20007

3. *Guidelines for New York State Urban Education Program,* May 1969, N.Y. State Department of Education, Albany, New York
4. All federal and state programs are supposed to be evaluated. However, it is very difficult to get complete data on where these various documents are to be found. Evaluations from 1965–1968 are listed in the back of this useful book: *A History and Description of ESEA Title I in New York City, 1965–1968,* by Barbara Heller, June 1968, Center for Urban Education, New York City
   For all other evaluations persist in requesting them at the Office of Public Information of the Board of Education.
5. *Evaluation of District Decentralized Title I ESEA Programs,* by Roscoe C. Brown, Jr., Dec., 1968, Center for Urban Education
6. *Compensatory Education for the Disadvantaged,* by Edmund W. Gordon and Doxey A. Wilkerson, College Entrance Examination Board, New York City, 1966
7. *Is it Helping Poor Children?* A Report on Title I, ESEA by the Washington Research Project of the Southern Center for Studies in Public Policy and the NAACP Legal Defense and Educational Fund, Inc., December 1969

CURRICULUM REFORM: PROGRAMS AND PLACES TO VISIT IN THE NEW YORK CITY AREA AND ELSEWHERE

New York City Public Schools

The Office of Public Information of the Board of Education, 110 Livingston Street, Brooklyn, will give you some suggestions. Some of the most interesting are:

CS 133, Harlem: Caleb Gattegno's Words in Color Reading and Math Programs

PS 137, Ocean Hill: Engelman Becker Head Start and Follow Through Program, which includes formal instruction in academic skills for the very young child

PS 84, Manhattan: A modification, in some grades, of the English Infant School System with child-directed learning centers

PS 25, Bronx: A bilingual school

PS 219, Flushing: Modified nongrading and team teaching; unusual physical facilities

New York City Parochial Schools

Department of Education, Archdiocese of New York, 32 East 51st Street, New York City 10022, 759-1400

Ask them for suggestions; in particular try to see some of the Jesuit high schools.

For Jewish parochial schools ask the rabbi in a nearby temple.

New York City Private Schools

An excellent list and description can be found in *The New York Times Guide to New York City Private Schools,* by Grace and Fred M. Hechinger, Simon and Schuster, New York, 1968

See various types of private schools. Two quite different ones are:

St. David's School, 12 East 89th St., New York 10028, where the curriculum includes science in kindergarten, French in grade 2 and Latin in grade 6

Church of the Heavenly Rest Day School, 2 East 90th St., New York 10028, where "the school tries to prepare the students for a future which is unknown."

Suburban Districts

Try to visit the Scarsdale school system in the immediate New York City area and the Newton, Mass., school system if you can travel further.

Other places where you can get lots of suggestions

Research for Better Schools Inc.
1700 Market Street
Philadelphia, Pennsylvania, 19103
215-561-4100

For information on I.P.I. (Individually Prescribed Instruction)

Yeshiva University
Ferkauf Graduate School
55 Fifth Avenue, New York 10003
212-255-5600

A good source for information on reading programs, bilingual programs and teacher training

Bank Street College of Education
216 West 14th Street
New York, N.Y.

For information on paraprofessionals and teacher training

New Careers Development Center
School of Education
New York University
239 Greene Street, New York
  10003
212-598-2695

For information on paraprofessionals

Institute for Developmental Studies
School of Education,
New York University
239 Greene Street, New York City
212-598-1212

For information on preschool programs, research, etc.

Educational Development Center
55 Chapel Street
Newton, Mass. 02160
617-969-7100

For information on curriculum reform at all levels

John Holt
308 Boylston Street
Boston, Mass.
617-261-8713

For information on flexible programing and child-directed learning (He has a list of schools to visit.)

East Harlem Block Schools
94 East 111th Street
New York 10029

This group has started its own schools in competition with the system; it is worth seeing

Nat'l Assn of Community Schools
Citizens Advocate Center
1211 Connecticut Avenue, N.W.
Washington, D.C. 20036

Their first newsletter lists and describes community-based and community-administered schools throughout the country

Children's Community Workshop
  School
55 West 88th Street
New York 10024

Same comment as above

The American Montessori Society
175 Fifth Avenue
New York 10010

For information on Montessori schools

The Parkway Program
Philadelphia School District
1801 Market Street
Philadelphia, Pa. 19103
215-448-3761

This high school has no classrooms or building; students learn
at the police department, zoo,
libraries, TV stations, etc.

Dorsett Educational Systems, Inc.
Norman, Oklahoma

For information on educational
improvement as perceived by a
private profit-making firm.

PERSONNEL

New York City Board of Education Material

1. Guide for Newly Appointed Teachers in the New York City Elementary Schools, 1965
2. Getting Started in the Elementary Schools, 1966
3. Getting Started in the Secondary Schools, 1966
4. Agreement Between the Board of Education and the United Federation of Teachers, 1969–1972
5. Agreement Between the Board of Education and the Council of Supervisory Associations, 1969–1972
6. *Towards Excellence in Teaching,* Jan. 1966
7. *How to Become a Teacher with the City of New York,* Office of Personnel (undated)
8. *A Review of the Operations of the Office of Personnel,* July 1968
9. *Corridors of Challenge—Teaching in New York City,* Office of Personnel (undated)
10. *In-Service Program Courses,* 1968–1969, Office of Personnel
11. *A Report on School Experience Index,* by Gordon Ascher, Educational Program Research and Statistics, Jan. 1968
12. *A Report on the Ethnic Composition of Professional Personnel,* Office of Personnel, March 1967. 1969 data available on IBM sheets
13. *A Report on Minimum Daily Absence of Teachers,* by Madeline M. Morrissey, Personnel Planning and Research, Sept. 1968
14. *Salary Schedules for Teachers, Supervisors, et al.,* October 1969

15. *Board of Examiners Eligibility Requirements and Examination Announcements,* Board of Examiners, 65 Court Street, Brooklyn
16. Various Forms used for Evaluating Teacher Performance (OP 98; 98A, OP11; 11A), Bureau of Teacher Records, 65 Court Street, Brooklyn
17. "Staff Responsibilities with Respect to Racial or Religious Bigotry," 1968–69, General Circular No. 7, Jan. 29, 1969
18. "The Doubtful Rating of Staff—Limitations on its Use," 1968–1969 General Circular No. 14, May 2, 1969
19. "Principal's Reports on Teacher Services, General Circular No. 17," June 24, 1969

General Material

1. "The Rivers Report" and "The Burden of Blame" in *Confrontation at Ocean Hill-Brownsville,* edited by Maurice R. Berube and Marilyn Gittell, Praeger, New York, 1969
2. *Pygmalion in the Classroom,* by Robert Rosenthal and Lenore Jackson, Holt, Rinehart and Winston, New York, 1968
3. *Merit Pay and Alternatives,* by George Weber and William H. Marmion, Council for Basic Education, Occasional Paper No. 16; May 1969 (available from the council, 725 15th Street NW, Washington, D.C. 20005)
4. *Teacher Mobility in New York City,* by Daniel Griffeths et al., School of Education, New York University, 1963
5. *Report of Recommendations on Recruitment, Selection, Appointment and Promotion of Teachers,* School of Education, New York University, 1966
6. *Reconnection for Learning,* The Bundy Report, Mayor's Advisory Panel on Decentralization, Nov. 1967
7. *New Careers and Roles in the American School,* by Garda W. Bowman and Gordon J. Klopf, Bank Street College of Education, Dec. 1968 (available from the college, 216 West 14th Street, New York 10011)
8. *The Miseducation of the American Teacher,* by James D. Koerner, Penguin Books, 1963
9. *A Study of Teacher Tenure in New York State,* Council for Administrative Leadership, March 1967 (obtainable from New York State Teachers Association, 152 Washington Ave., Albany, New York 12210)

10. *The New York City Teachers Union, 1916–1964*, by Celia Lewis Zitron, Humanities Press, New York, 1968

11. "How to Hire a High School Principal," *School Management*, Oct. 1966

12. Teachers Kit, How to Hire Teachers, How to Fire Teachers, and various related material, prepared for United Bronx Parents Leadership-Training Program, 1969 (available from United Bronx Parents, 791 Prospect Avenue, Bronx, New York)

13. For information on New York State certification requirements, contact Division of Teacher Education and Certification, 800 North Pearl Street, Albany, New York 12204 and they will send you excerpts from the State Education Law which relate to this topic.

14. "How to Improve Staff," by Donald Rappaport in *News*, Nov. 1968 (obtainable from the National Committee for the Support of the Public Schools, 1424 16th St. N.W., Washington, D.C. 20036)

15. "A Harlem Parent Speaks," by David Spencer, in *National Education Association Journal*, March 1966.

16. "A Citizens' Review Board for Teachers?" *American Teacher*, Dec. 1966

17. *High School Principals' Study Seminar*, by Arthur J. Vidich and Charles W. McReynolds, New School for Social Research, Feb. 1969

18. *Breaking the Credentials Barrier*, by S. M. Miller, reprinted from March 1969 issue of *Training in Business and Industry* (available from New Careers Information Clearinghouse, 4301 Conn. Ave. N.W., Washington, D.C. 20015

19. *Evaluating Teaching Performance*, a circular prepared by Educational Research Service, American Association of School Administrators, National Education Association, 1201 16th Street, N.W., Washington, D.C. 20036

20. "The Schools of New York in Transition—1898–1914" by Selma C. Berrol, in *Urban Review*, Dec. 1966

21. "Pressures to Modify Tenure," by Fred M. Hechinger, *New York Times*, Nov. 2, 1969

22. "The Elusive Black Educator: How to Find, Hire and Keep Him," *School Management*, March 1969

23. "Teacher Selection: How to Weed out the Duds," *School Management*, Feb. 1967

24. "Beginning Teachers Induction into the Inner City Schools," by

Elizabeth Eddy, in *Developing Programs for the Educationally Disadvantaged,* edited by Harry A. Passow, Teachers College, New York, 1968

25. "Defense of Urban Teachers," by Allan C. Ornstein, *Integrated Education,* June–July 1966

26. "Teacher in the Brown Paper Bag," by Mortimer Kreuter, in *Urban Review,* May 1966

27. "Teacher Attitudes and Student Achievement," by Preston Wilcox, in *Teachers College Record,* Vol. 68, No. 5, Feb. 1967

28. *110 Livingston Street,* by David Rogers, Random House, New York

29. *Analysis of Puerto Rican and Black Employment in New York City Public Schools,* by Richard Greenspan, May 1970, Puerto Rican Forum, 156 Fifth Avenue, New York City

30. *Selecting a Superintendent, A Handbook for Community School Boards,* Public Education Association, 20 West 40th Street, New York City

---

REPORT CARDS

New York City Board of Education Material

1. *Guide for Newly Appointed Teachers in the New York City Elementary Schools,* 1965
2. *Getting Started in the Secondary Schools,* 1966
3. *Manual of Directions for Reporting to Parents, Grades 2–6,* Office of Elementary Schools, revised, Sept. 1967
4. *A Message to Parents about Report Cards,* Grades 2–6

General Material

1. "The Grade System: A Call for Experimentation in Grading" by a Univ. of Wisconsin teachers' association, April–May 1968, *Radicals in the Profession* (newsletter)
2. "Report Cards: Who Needs Them," *Grade Teacher,* June 1969
3. *How Children Fail,* by John Holt, Dell, New York, 1964 (See chapter entitled "Fear and Failure")

HOMEWORK

New York City Board of Education Material

1. *Homework Policy for Elementary Schools,* 1963–64, Division of Elementary Schools Circular E. P. 22, Jan. 20, 1964
2. *Getting Started in the Secondary School,* 1966

General Material

1. *Guided Study and Homework,* by Ruth Strang, Assn of Classroom Teachers, National Education Assn, 1968
2. *Using Homework as a Teaching Tool,* by Robert Shockley, Teachers Practical Press, Inc., 1964

PARENT–TEACHER CONFERENCE

New York City Board of Education Material

1. *Guide for Newly Appointed Teachers in the NYC Elementary Schools,* 1965 (See Chapter 5)
2. General Circular No. 3, 1968–1969, Dec. 2, 1968, "Open School Week, 1968–69"
3. "It Starts in the Classroom," May 1966, National School Public Relations Assn, NEA; issued by the Office of Information Services and Public Relations, New York City Board of Education

General Material

1. *Manual on Pupil Records,* issued by the University of the State of New York, State Education Department, Albany, New York, April 1967 (See especially Chapters 2 and 8)

2. "Parent-Teacher Conference: There Is a Better Way," *Grade Teacher*, Oct. 1967
3. "An Introduction to Parent-Teacher Conferences," Lomond School, Shaker Hts., Ohio
4. *Parent-Teacher Relationships*, by Irving W. Stout and Grace Langdon, Sept. 1958, issued by Dept. of Classroom Teachers, NEA, 1201 16th Street, N.W., Washington, D.C. 20036

THE CUMULATIVE RECORD CARD

New York City Board of Education Material

1. *Getting Started in the Elementary School, A Manual for New Teachers*, 1966 (pp. 169–182)
2. *Getting Started in the Secondary School, A Manual for New Teachers*, 1966 (pp. 132–153)
3. *Guidance of Children in the Elementary Schools*, 1960 (pp. 157–165)
4. *Guide for Newly Appointed Teachers in the New York City Elementary Schools*, 1965
5. UFT Contract, September 1969–1972, Article IV F-20
6. Statement by Joseph Monserrat, president, on behalf of the Board of Education re George Washington High School, *New York Times*, April 22, 1970

General Material

1. *Manual on Pupil Records*, State Education Department, reprinted April 1967
2. "Eye of UFT" by Vito De Leonardis, *United Teacher*, May 23, 1967
3. "Teacher Expectation for the Disadvantaged," by Robert Rosenthal and Lenore Jackson, *Scientific American*, April 1968
4. *Training Manual on Public School Law*, School Defense Network, 1969 (See chapter entitled "Access to Pupil Records")

5. "The Scope of the Practice," by Joseph Lederer, *Urban Review*, Sept. 1968
6. "Juvenile Delinquency and Youth Crime, Delinquency and the Schools," Task Force Report, pp. 251–253
7. *Guidelines for the Collection, Maintenance and Dissemination of Pupil Records*, Russell Sage Foundation, 1970

SCHOOL SUSPENSIONS AND STUDENT RIGHTS

New York City Board of Education Material

1. Special Circular No. 36, "Pupil Suspension," 1969–1970; Nov. 12, 1969

General Material

1. *Training Manual On Public School Law*, School Defense Network, 1969
2. *Student Grievances in New York City High Schools*, Public Education Assn, Information Series No. 2, May 1969
3. Parent Guidelines for Student School Suspensions, Harlem Neighborhood Assn Inc., Dec. 1968
4. *A Student Bill of Rights*, Memo by Ira Glasser, Associate Director, New York Civil Liberties Union, July 7, 1969
5. "The Nature and Limits of Student Dissent and Participation," by Edward Kolevzon (President, High School Principals Assn), Jan. 23, 1969
6. "Judge Weinstein Orders Readmittance of 600 Illegally Dismissed from High School," in *Civil Liberties in New York*, New York Civil Liberties Union, May 1969
7. Bernard Mackler, "Children are Human Beings," Center for Urban Education (undated mimeograph)
8. "Preserving the Right to an Education for all Children," Citizens Committee for Children, April 1967 (mimeograph)

9. "Notes Regarding School Suspension Conferences Attended" Citizens Committee for Children, April 20, 1967 (mimeograph)
10. "Discipline and Suspensions" (Parent Leadership Training Kit No. 4), United Bronx Parents, Sept. 1967
11. "End Suspensions Now," by Dana Driskell, *New York High School Free Press,* Issue No. 7, March–April 1969
12. *The New York Training School System,* Citizens Committee for Children, 112 East 19th St., New York City 10003 (Dec. 1969)
13. *The Schools Belong to the Students,* the Schools Defense Network, New York City, 1970

About the Author

ELLEN LURIE was a member of the New York City People's Board of Education which was formed by a group of parents who were walked out on by the official Board of Education. Before that, Mrs. Lurie had served for five years on Local School Board 6, in Upper Manhattan, from which she resigned in protest against the powerlessness of parents against the board. She worked on the massive school boycotts called by the Reverend Milton Galamison and the Harlem Parents Committee, and was a former chairman of EQUAL, an organization that tried to develop support for school integration in white communities.

Since her resignation from Local School Board 6, Mrs. Lurie has fought for local control in public education. During the school strikes of 1967 and 1968 she worked with the parents and teachers who helped to keep the schools open. Since 1967, Ellen Lurie has been training director for United Bronx Parents. She has taught at the New School for Social Research in New York City and has written and lectured widely on community organizing. Mrs. Lurie was graduated summa cum laude from New York University. She lives in New York City with her husband and five children, all of whom are in the public schools.